WESTMAR COLLEGE

P9-CPZ-739

REASON

AND

RIGHT

By the same author

ETHICAL INTUITIONISM

LUDWIG WITTGENSTEIN

MODERN MORAL PHILOSOPHY

THE IS–OUGHT QUESTION *(editor)*

NEW STUDIES IN ETHICS *(general editor)*

NEW STUDIES IN THE PHILOSOPHY OF RELIGION *(general editor)*

NEW STUDIES IN PRACTICAL PHILOSOPHY *(general editor)*

REASON AND RIGHT

*A Critical Examination of
Richard Price's Moral Philosophy*

W. D. HUDSON

*Senior Lecturer in Philosophy
University of Exeter*

FREEMAN, COOPER & COMPANY

1736 Stockton Street, San Francisco, California 94133

BJ
604
.P7
H8
1970b

85061

© *W. D. Hudson 1970*

Copyright, © 1970 by (Ⓕ) *Freeman, Cooper & Company*

*All rights to reproduce this book in whole or in part
are reserved, with the exception of the right to use
short quotations for review of the book.*

*Printed in the United States of America
Library of Congress Catalogue Card Number 76-119372
SBN-88735-511-8*

To my children

Contents

PREFACE   xi

INTRODUCTION   xiii

CHAPTER 1   THE QUESTION STATED   1

  I.   The Discernment of Right and Wrong   1
  II. Naturalism in Ethics   4
    II.i. The Naturalistic Fallacy   5
    II.ii. Dispute about the Faculty that Perceives Rightness   8
    II.iii. Antecedent Right   9

CHAPTER 2   EPISTEMOLOGY   11

  I.   Reason 'Superior' to Sense   13
  II. The Understanding as a Source of New, Simple Ideas   18
    II.i. Kinds of Ideas   19
    II.ii. Uses of 'Idea'   21
    II.iii. Ideas of the Understanding   22
      Substance   23
      Cause   26
      Abstract Ideas   32
    II. iv. Intuitionism   37
      (a) Intuition and Learning   40
      (b) Intuition and Valid Reasoning   41
      (c) Degrees of Intuition?   43

CHAPTER 3   MORAL EPISTEMOLOGY   45

  I.   Price's Moral Intuitionism   45
    I.i. Right is a Simple Idea   46
    I.ii. Is Rightness a Relation or a Quality?   48
    I.iii. Reason and Sense in Morals   50
  II. Right and the Nature of Things   59
    II.i. Moral Ideas and Necessary Truth   60
    II.ii. Moral Fitness as *Sui Generis*   63

III.   Criticism of Price   64
       III.i The Connexion between Moral Judgements and Action   64
       III.ii. The Meaning of Moral Language   67
       III.iii. Right and Reasons Why   73

CHAPTER 4   OBLIGATION   84

  I.   Right and Ought   84
 II.   Reason and Happiness   86
III.   Good and Ill Desert   89
 IV.   Benevolence Not the Whole of Virtue   95
  V.   The Heads of Virtue   102
       V.i. Duty to God   102
           (a) Empirical Statements about Human Psychology   102
           (b) Metaphysical or Theological Statements   103
           (c) Statements about the Deliverances of the Developed
               Moral Consciousness   104
       V.ii. Duty to Self   105
       V.iii. Beneficence   109
       V.iv. Gratitude   109
       V.v. Veracity   110
       V.vi. Justice   113
 VI.   Issues Arising   116
       VI.i. How Does the Idea of Obligation Arise?   116
       VI.ii. Do All Men Intuit the Heads of Virtue?   118
       VI.iii. Can Moral Principles be Unified?   121
       VI.iv. What Do Price's Illustrations Prove?   126
       VI.v. What Is the Relation between Deontological and
               Teleological Theories?   128

CHAPTER 5   PRACTICAL VIRTUE   131

  I.   Absolute and Practical Virtue   131
 II.   The Essentials of Practical Virtue   138
       II.i. Liberty   138
           (a) The Alleged Self-evidence of Liberty   138
           (b) Motives and the Self   139
           (c) Responsibility and Freedom   140
               (i) Libertarianism or Indeterminism   141
               (ii) Self-determinism   146
           (d) Necessity and Freedom   152

II.ii. Intelligence   161
II.iii. Regard for Rectitude   162
  (a) Is Regard for Rectitude a Sufficient Principle of Action? 167
  (b) Is Regard for Rectitude the Only Principle of Actions
        which Engage our Esteem of the Agents?   171
II.iv. Essentials of Good Character   173

CHAPTER 6 MORALITY AND THE DIVINE
     NATURE   176
  I.   The Relation of Morality to the Divine Nature   176
 II.   The Teleological Argument   179
III.   The Cosmological Argument   181
IV.   Benevolence and Virtue in God   182
 V.   Rewards and Punishments   183

NOTES   187

INDEX   203

Preface

RICHARD PRICE, with whose thought I shall be mainly concerned in this book, participated in the great eighteenth-century debate about the nature and content of conscience, which was conducted among British philosophers. His *Review* brings the issues involved in that debate into clear focus and presents skilfully and persuasively the case for rational intuitionism. Many of the issues with which Price dealt are matters of lively controversy among present-day philosophers. The *Review* still provides a valuable introduction to the principal questions and difficulties in morals. Price is not so well known as some of his contemporaries but he was a better philosopher than most of them. He deserves more attention than he has received, and this book is offered as a contribution to the interest in him which seems of late to have been reviving.

My aim has been both expository and critical. I have tried to set forth Price's views as clearly as possible, to indicate their relevance in the debate about conscience to which they were a contribution, and to show how they appear in the light of contemporary analytical moral philosophy. I hope that this book will provide readers who come new to ethical theory with an introduction to the subject which has the advantages of being rooted in the thought of one moral philosopher while at the same time drawing upon the work of many others in subjecting his thought to critical examination. Scholars, I venture also to hope, will find it useful to have a full-length study of Price's *Review*.

I gladly acknowledge the debt which I owe to other writers in moral philosophy and which will be apparent throughout the following pages. In particular, I should like to record my thanks to Professor D. J. O'Connor, Head of the Department of Philosophy in this University, who supervised my early work on Price and who, in the production of this book as in so many other ways, has been unfailingly helpful and shown me many kindnesses. My thanks are also due to Mrs Pamela Huby of the University of Liverpool, with whom I discussed some of the matters dealt with in this book. I hardly need add that the persons named bear no responsibility for the opinions which I have expressed or any of the mistakes which I may have made. Two secretaries, Miss M. Gardiner and Miss P. Ffookes, assisted me in preparing the typescript and I am grateful to them for their patience and industry, as I am also to Mrs E. Ridgeon for her help in correcting the proofs.

DONALD HUDSON

University of Exeter

Introduction

RICHARD PRICE was born in 1723 at Tynton in Glamorganshire and died at Hackney in 1791. He was educated at various Dissenting Academies and entered the Nonconformist ministry at the age of twenty-one. He published work in mathematics, politics and theology as well as moral philosophy. In 1765 he was elected to a Fellowship of the Royal Society in recognition of papers 'towards solving a problem in the Doctrine of Chances'; and he earned considerable renown for work on the actuarial basis of life insurance and on national finance. An ardent advocate of civil liberties throughout his life, Price actively supported the revolutionary movements both of America and France. His *Observations on the Nature of Civil Liberty*, published in 1776, sold 60,000 copies within the year. In it Price defended the colonists and also called attention to the imperfect liberty enjoyed in this country. His sermon on *The Love of Our Country*, preached in 1789, printed and widely circulated in Britain and France, hailed the storming of the Bastille with unconfined delight. This sermon is said to have been 'the red flag that drew Burke into the arena'.

Price's moral philosophy is set down in *A Review of the Principal Questions and Difficulties in Morals*, which was first published when he was thirty-five. There was a second edition in 1769 and a third in 1787. Though he modified some of his views on the theory of knowledge, Price's ethical theory remains unchanged in the later editions. It is said that, soon after its publication, the *Review* was acknowledged to be the most able defence of rational intuitionism in the English language (see R. Thomas, *Richard Price* p. 34). More recently, Professor C. D. Broad took a similar view: 'until Ross published his book *The Right and the Good* in 1930 there existed, so far as I know, no statement and defence of what may be called the "rationalist" type of ethical theory comparable in merit to Price's' (*Proceedings of the Aristotelian Society* 1944–5).

REASON
AND
RIGHT

I

The Question Stated

I. THE DISCERNMENT OF RIGHT AND WRONG

AT the beginning of the preface to *Principia Ethica*, G. E. Moore says that many difficulties and disagreements would be eliminated in ethics, as in all branches of philosophy, if only philosophers 'would try to discover what question they were asking, before they set about to answer it . . .' . This passage might be quoted either in commendation or in criticism of Price's *Review of the Principal Questions and Difficulties in Morals*. He is to be commended for attempting to begin his inquiry with a clear statement of what he took to be the fundamental question in moral philosophy. Unfortunately, he is also to be criticised for having, in this preliminary statement, failed to draw a sufficiently clear distinction between the epistemology, ontology, and logic of morals.

Price begins, rightly enough, from the facts of moral experience, as he sees them:

> Some actions we all feel ourselves irresistibly determined to approve, and others to disapprove. Some actions we cannot but think *right*, and others *wrong*, and of all actions we are led to form some opinion, as either *fit* to be performed or *unfit*; or neither fit nor unfit to be performed; that is, indifferent. (p. 13, Raphael's edition. See *Notes*, Chap. I, n. I.)

He recognised, of course, that we do not all approve and disapprove of the same actions, and elsewhere in his *Review* (pp. 170–6) he discusses the significance of these difficulties in the moral judgements of mankind. His point here is simply that men do form moral judgements. We speak of actions as right, wrong or morally indifferent and, in doing so, we believe that we are saying something significant and distinctive about them. That is to say, we do not form these judgements by mere caprice; when we pass a moral judgement on any action, it is always because we feel 'irresistibly determined' to pass that

one and not another. This raises what is fundamentally an epistemological, rather than a psychological, question, though Price states it as
follows: 'What the power within us is, which thus determines' (p. 13),
or again, 'What is the power within us that perceives the distinctions
of *right* and *wrong*?' (p. 17).

Price intended his own answer to this question to be a refutation of
that which Francis Hutcheson had given. According to the latter, just
as we are so made that certain physical sensations give us pleasure and
certain others give us pain, we are so made that certain acts, and, more
particularly, certain of the motives and intentions from which actions
spring, arouse in us a certain kind of agreeable feeling and so we call
them right, whereas others give us a certain kind of disagreeable feeling
and so we call them wrong. In a word, we have a moral *sense*. Price
declares that he would have no quarrel with Hutcheson, if, by using
the word 'sense' in this connexion and likening our moral judgements
to pleasurable and painful sensations, he had intended only to imply
(*a*) that our moral judgements are formed immediately, apart from any
reflexion upon the consequences of actions; and (*b*) that, in the exercise
of our moral faculty, we can experience the highest forms of satisfaction. Neither of these would have conflicted with Price's point that
we are 'irresistibly determined' in forming our moral judgements.

At this point, the issue between Price and Hutcheson seems to be
nothing more than a dispute about words, as Price himself appears to
have realised. What Hutcheson said of his moral sense Price might
equally well have said of his understanding. For example, Hutcheson
said: 'We must then certainly have other perceptions of moral actions,
than those of advantage: and that power of recognising these perceptions may be called a moral sense, since the definition agrees to it,
namely a determination of the mind, to receive any idea from the
presence of an object which occurs to us, independent on our will.'[2] As
Professor D. D. Raphael has pointed out, this clearly begs the question
whether the moral faculty be sense or rational intuition.[3] Hutcheson
realised that this definition of sense takes us far beyond the five bodily
senses: 'If we may call "every determination of our minds to receive
ideas independently on our will, and to have perceptions of pleasure
and pain", a sense, we shall find many other senses besides those commonly explained.'[4] But he never considered the possibility that reason
might be a faculty of immediate intuition whereby we directly apprehend the nature of things. When he spoke of reason[5] it was always in
the sense of discursive reasoning: 'What is reason but that sagacity we

have in prosecuting any end?'[6] Hutcheson never questioned the empiricist assumption that all direct apprehension of the nature of things is by sense. Even so, the disagreement between Price and Hutcheson, at this point, seems to amount to nothing more than a difference of opinion as to the term which should be used for the moral faculty: 'moral sense' or 'understanding'. Both are treated by their exponents as faculties of immediate intuition which apprehend directly the simple ideas of moral good and evil. Epistemologically, it is difficult to see that there is any difference between them.

The real issue between Price and Hutcheson, however, lay in the ontological implications of these two terms for eighteenth-century rationalists and empiricists. The rationalist believed that knowledge of reality is provided by reason, the empiricist that it is provided by experience, i.e. feeling or sensation. The rationalists took the self-evidence of the necessary propositions of mathematics as a guarantee that the latter provides us with knowledge of the real world. Price wished to discover a similar self-evidence in moral judgements as a guarantee that moral attributes really do belong to actions. He saw Hutcheson's use of the word 'sense' as a threat to the necessity and objectivity of moral judgements. Just as God might have made us other than we are so that what tastes sweet to us now would have tasted bitter and what looks beautiful would have looked ugly; so, if the moral faculty is sense, God might conceivably have made us such that what we now judge to be right we should have judged to be wrong and vice versa. Our moral judgements, on this view, are determined by a contingent fact about the constitution of our minds and, therefore, can have no necessity. Nor can they have any objectivity. If, when we say, 'This is right', the correct analysis of our statement is 'This produces in me a certain kind of agreeable feeling' or 'This produces in all men or some class of men an agreeable feeling', then the statement 'This is right' does not refer to anything in the action of which we are speaking, but only to 'certain effects in us' (p. 15).

Price restates his question in ontological terms: 'Whether right and wrong are real characters of *actions* or only qualities of our *minds*', and this expresses his prime concern; he wished to uphold the necessity and objectivity of moral judgements and the cosmology which these implied. He believed that the only effective way to do this was by means of an epistemological argument which would show that the moral faculty is rational intuition. We shall have to consider this argument in due course, and discuss whether it justified the ontological conclusions which Price drew from it concerning moral properties. But first we must take note of an important preliminary to the argument.

II. NATURALISM IN ETHICS

At the close of his chapter 1, section 1, Price briefly discusses 'schemes which found morality on self-love, on positive laws and compacts, or the divine will'; and with regard to them he indicates two possibilities:

> they must either mean, that moral good and evil are only other words for *advantageous* and *disadvantageous, willed* and *forbidden*. Or they relate to a very different question; that is, not to the question, what is the nature and true *account* of virtue; but, what is the *subject matter* of it. (p. 16)[7]

The distinction which Price draws is the same as that which Ross (after Mill) drew: 'The correctness of a definition may be tested by two methods: (i) by asking whether the denotation of the term and that of the proposed definition are the same, whether the definition applies to all things to which the term applies, and to no others. But that is not enough. "Equilateral triangle" and "triangle having all its angles equal" have exactly the same denotation, but the one is not a correct definition of the other, since what we *mean* when we call a triangle equilateral is not that its angles are equal but that its sides are equal. We must therefore ask a second question, (ii) "does the definition express explicitly what we had implicitly in mind when we used the term?" '[8] Ross's first question is Price's second question, namely that with reference to the subject-matter of virtue. Ross's second question corresponds to Price's first question, whether the 'other words' express the nature and true account of virtue.[9]

If the theories with which Price is dealing are meant only to refer to the subject-matter of morals, i.e. to indicate what is, in fact, right or wrong, then he would regard them as meaningful, even though mistaken. If I say, 'Actions which are to my advantage (or, alternatively, in accordance with the laws of the country or the will of God) are right', I am not talking nonsense, although what I say may be untrue. On the other hand, if these theories imply that 'right' and 'wrong' are 'only other words' for 'advantageous', 'enacted', 'willed by God', i.e. if they are intended to define right and wrong, then, Price held, they must be rejected. He gives three reasons why they must be rejected.

II.i THE NATURALISTIC FALLACY

Right and wrong when applied to actions which are commanded or forbidden by the will of God, or that produce good or harm, do not signify merely that such actions are commanded or forbidden, or that they are useful or hurtful, but a *sentiment*[10] concerning them and our consequent approbation or disapprobation of the performance of them. Were not this true, it would be palpably absurd in any case to ask, whether it is *right* to obey a command, or *wrong* to disobey it; and the propositions, *obeying a command is right*, or *producing happiness is right*, would be most trifling,[11] as expressing no more than that obeying a command, is obeying a command, or producing happiness, is producing happiness. (pp. 16–17)

This passage anticipates G. E. Moore's famous discussion of what he called 'the naturalistic fallacy' at the beginning of his *Principia Ethica* (1903). Price's argument very closely parallels Moore's. The point being made is that, if 'right' is defined – call its *definiens* X – then 'What is X is right' will be an insignificant tautology, and 'Is what is X right?', a self-answering question. But there is no conceivable value which can be given to X, such that the former would be an insignificant tautology, or the latter a self-answering question. The basic appeal here is, presumably, to the lexical definition of 'right', i.e. to what ordinary users of the word mean by it. Two questions, at least, arise: (i) Is what ordinary users of the word mean by 'right' that which Price took it to be? (ii) If the answer to that question is yes, then what precisely, according to Price, is the fallacy which those who define 'right' are committing?

In reply to the former question, we must note that there have been some thinkers – ethical naturalists, as they are usually called – who would deny that the meaning of 'right' is what Price took it to be. They would say that there is, at any rate, one definition of 'right' – call this X – such that 'What is X is right' is a tautology and 'Is what is X right?' is not an open question. They vary in what they take X here to be. Some have said that 'right' means 'producing happiness'; others, 'commanded by God'; and so on. For the purposes of this argument, the difference between naturalistic (e.g. producing happiness) and supernaturalistic (e.g. commanded by God) definitions may be ignored. 'The naturalistic fallacy', so called, is the attempt to define 'right' in either way. Price does not use that expression but what Moore, who used it of attempts to define 'good', meant by it is precisely what Price was objecting to in the above passage. We have to decide, then, who is correct about the meaning of 'right', Price or ethical naturalists.

I think we may best find the answer to that question by considering possible replies to the second of the two above questions. What precisely, to Price's way of thinking, is the mistake, or fallacy, which those who define 'right' in the offending ways are committing? I will consider a few possibilities in turn.

(*a*) There is, first, the possibility that Price was objecting to propositions such as 'producing happiness is right' on the ground that they identify one property with another; they involve, that is, the 'definist fallacy'.[12] If this was his point, then two criticisms can be levelled against it, namely (i) It would invalidate, not only naturalistic definitions of right and wrong, but every other definition or analysis which amounted to more than a verbal tautology.[13] It would apply, not only to definitions which identify ethical properties with non-ethical, but also to those which identify non-ethical properties with non-ethical (e.g. redness with pleasantness) or ethical with ethical (e.g. rightness with goodness).[14] (ii) It begs the question. The naturalist can only be accused of identifying two properties, when he says 'producing happiness is right', if there are, in fact, two distinct properties, namely 'producing happiness' and 'being right', which an action can have. But whether 'being right' is a distinct property, attributable objectively to actions, is the very point at issue between Price and those whose views he is considering.

If Price was actually accusing his opponents of the 'definist fallacy', then his argument was based on two assumptions: that there is a non-natural, objective property of rightness; and that this property is discernible by all men. The latter is important as well as the former. The naturalists can only be charged with a fallacy[15] if, when they are aware of a property of rightness, they identify it with another property. The naturalists could certainly object that they are not aware of any such property, and that whether or not it is discernible is the point at issue between them and Price.

(*b*) In view of the distinction which Price draws between 'what is the nature and true *account* of virtue' and 'what is the subject-matter of it', it may be that he objected to propositions of the kind which we are considering on the ground that those who use them are confusing synthetic propositions about what is right with definitions of rightness. This has been called the fallacy of 'misconstrued proposition'.[16] But, again, the naturalist could reply that the question is begged, for the distinction drawn here between a significant ethical generalisation and a definition assumes that there is an indefinable property, rightness, distinguishable from what it is right to do, and whether there is such a property is the point at issue.

(c) Price may have been objecting to propositions of the kind 'producing happiness is right' because he thought that those who used them were guilty of the fallacy of drawing a conclusion from an inadequate premise. If one were to say 'X is right because X produces happiness', then this is a fallacious argument of the form, 'A is B because A is C'. But the naturalists could reply that their reasoning is not really of this form. It contains a suppressed premise:

> X produces happiness.
> That which produces happiness is right (by definition).
> Therefore, X is right.

In this form the argument is not logically fallacious. Whether the suppressed premise is admissible – whether, that is, right can be defined as that which produces happiness – is still, of course, open to question. But this is the question with which the discussion began and is the very point at issue between Price and the naturalists.

(d) Price's objection to definitions of 'right' such as those instanced in the above passage may have been based upon a conviction that ethical naturalists are inconsistent in their use of 'right'. Those ethical naturalists who are hedonists, for example, treat 'What produces happiness is right' as both true by definition and something more than an insignificant tautology. The objection to so doing is not simply that they confuse a definition with a synthetic proposition (cf. (b) above). It is that they try to have it both ways when it is logically impossible to do so. When they are rebutting opponents who deny their hedonism, they accuse such opponents of self-contradiction or at best of not knowing the meaning of the words which they are using. If 'right' means 'producing happiness', then anyone who says 'What produces happiness is not right' is either contradicting himself or does not know what he is saying. To be able to accuse an opponent of being in either condition is to have a knock-down argument against him. When hedonists are advocating their hedonism, however, they do not treat 'What produces happiness is right' as a proposition which is true but trivial. They deem themselves to be saying more than that what produces happiness produces happiness. For, if that is all that they were saying, none of their opponents could, or would, wish to deny it. In seeking

to convert such opponents from whatever ethical opinions they hold
to hedonism, hedonists must (logically) conceive themselves to be
uttering more than an insignificant tautology. *Mutatis mutandis* what
I have said about the inconsistency of hedonists could be said with equal
force of religious moralists or any other ethical naturalists. I think that
it was this charge of inconsistency which Price was really bringing
against ethical naturalists in the above passage and the charge, I think,
is a damning one. Moore's objection to the naturalistic fallacy ran along
the same lines.[17] In the sequel I shall have more to say about the
similarities between Price and Moore.[18]

II.ii DISPUTE ABOUT THE FACULTY THAT PERCEIVES RIGHTNESS

The second reason which Price gives for rejecting the ethical naturalism
which he is discussing is as follows:

> Besides; on the supposition, that right and wrong denote only the
> relations of actions to will and law, or to happiness and misery, there
> could be no dispute about the faculty that perceives right and wrong,
> since it must be owned by all, that these relations are objects of the
> investigations of *reason*. (p. 17)

It is plainly the case that reasoning would be involved, as Price says,
in discovering how actions are related to the will of God (e.g. by
reference to the Bible and deductions therefrom), or the law of the land
(by reference to the statute book), or the general happiness (if this could
be defined). But there are three comments to be made on this
argument.

(*a*) It is inconsistent with another argument which Price introduces
in section III of his chapter I. By 'there could be no dispute about the
faculty that perceives right and wrong' here Price clearly implies that
there *is*, in fact, such a dispute. The dispute which he had in mind was
no doubt that between himself and Hutcheson, between reason and
sense. In section III, however, Price appeals to 'the natural and universal
apprehensions of mankind, that our ideas of right and wrong belong
to the understanding' (p. 46), and seems to suggest that there *is not*, in
fact, any dispute as to the nature of the moral faculty. The two points
are plainly inconsistent with each other.[19]

(*b*) Naturalists against whom Price is contending could, on one
interpretation, have accepted his point without demur. Of course
reasoning, in the sense of discovering relations in which actions stand,

comes into ethics. If this is what is meant by saying that reason is the moral faculty, then they must agree.

(c) But, of course, the reason which, on this interpretation, Price says here 'must be owned by all' to be the moral faculty is quite distinct from the reason which he himself regarded as the moral faculty. In a footnote to his next section (p. 18), he says: 'There may be further some occasion for observing, that the two acts of the understanding, being intuition and deduction, I have in view the former.' If it is admitted that reasoning, as interpreted in the foregoing argument, comes into ethics (and every non-intuitionist would admit as much), this in no way lends support to rational intuitionism, any more than to any other form of intuitionism. It is rather difficult to see why Price brought this argument in. He seems to have at the back of his mind some idea that, in pointing out to naturalists that their own theories bring reasoning into ethics, he is scoring a point for his own view that the understanding is the moral faculty. But he is doing nothing of the kind.

II.iii ANTECEDENT RIGHT

Price's third reason is as follows:

> Happiness requires something in its own nature; or in ours, to give it influence, and to determine our desire of it and approbation of pursuing it. In like manner; all laws, will, and compacts suppose *antecedent right* to give them effect; and, instead of being *constituents* of right, they owe their whole force and obligation to it. (p. 17)[20]

Again, the point which Price is making could be so interpreted that even critics of intuitionism would not dispute it. The statement, 'X is right' cannot be analysed into 'X is an act which fulfils the law', etc., because the analysis contains no ethical word. The correct analysis of 'X is right (or obligatory)' must be 'X is an act which fulfils the law (etc.) and it is right (or obligatory) to perform acts which fulfil the law (etc.)'; where the latter part of the analysis (after the first 'and') contains the '*antecedent right*', on which 'the whole force and obligation' of 'X is right (or obligatory)' depends. But, of course, the real issue for Price lies in the question: what does this ethical word in the analysis signify, what is this antecedent right? He presents the alternatives in what he says about happiness: 'something in its own nature or in ours' – something in the act itself or in us. In modern terms, we must choose between an expressive and a descriptive theory of the nature of moral discourse. Is this 'antecedent right' the expression of a 'pro-attitude' adopted by the speaker,[21] or the description of a 'non-natural' property perceived by the speaker?[22] To substantiate his view that it is the latter, Price turned to an examination of 'the origin of our ideas in general, and the distinct provinces of the *understanding* and of *sense*' (p. 17), and this will occupy us in the next chapter.

Many issues have been raised in the present chapter – e.g. the autonomy of ethics, the notion of a non-natural property, the claim to know moral truths by intuition, the concept of having a reason for a moral judgement – and to these we shall have to return from time to time in the following pages. But enough has already been said to show that the question with which Price was concerned – namely, what are we doing when we call actions right or wrong? – is of perennial interest to philosophers; and that his approach to it has some remarkable affinities to that which contemporary analytical philosophers have taken.

2

Epistemology

IN this chapter we shall be concerned with Price's claim that rational intuition is a source of new, simple ideas. He says in the preface to his first edition of the *Review* that there is nothing to which he wishes more to engage the reader's attention than the arguments with which he tries to prove this in his chapter I, section II, which section we shall now consider. Price begins by referring to Locke's *Essay concerning Human Understanding*, and he was obviously concerned to develop an argument which would refute Locke's empiricism. In estimating the value of Price's discussion on the origin of ideas, it is only fair to relate it as closely as possible to Locke. We shall see that, though there are many defects in Price's own theory, when considered as a critique of Locke, it has some merit.

Locke maintained that ideas arise from two, and only two, 'fountains of knowledge', namely 'sensation' and 'reflection'. Price accused him of not being 'sufficiently clear or explicit' (p. 17) on this subject. The charge would be justified, if we were considering the psychology or physiology of these two mechanisms of perception. Locke felt that much of these subjects was 'incomprehensible' to him and said that he did not propose to 'meddle' with them.[1] But on the epistemological issues, he was clear and explicit enough. He wrote: 'Our observation, employed either about external sensible objects, or about the internal operations of our own minds, perceived and reflected on by ourselves, is that which supplies our understandings with all the materials of thinking. These two are the fountains of knowledge, from whence all the ideas we have, or can naturally have, do spring.'[2] Price's quarrel with him was not really that his views were not stated explicitly enough, but that the implications which Locke drew from them were mistaken. Locke drew the implication that the understanding 'has the power to repeat, compare, and unite them [simple ideas of sense or reflexion] even to an almost infinite variety, and so can make at pleasure new complex ideas. But it is not in the power of the most exalted wit or enlarged understanding, by any quickness or variety of thoughts, to invent or frame one new simple idea in the mind, not taken in by the ways before mentioned.'[3] Price, in reply, affirmed emphatically that the understanding has this power:

> The power, I assert, that *understands*; or the faculty within us that discerns *truth*, and that compares all the objects of thought, and judges of them, is a spring of new ideas. (p. 18)

In a footnote here he says that by 'ideas' he means simple ideas, i.e. 'original and uncompounded perceptions of the mind'. In Locke, complex ideas are all compounded from simple ideas by combination, comparison or abstraction,[4] but Price held that many of these so-called 'complex' ideas are, in fact, simple ideas directly apprehended by the understanding. In the footnote referred to, he distinguishes carefully between the two acts of the understanding, 'intuition' and 'deduction', and says that it is the former which he has in view.

Price was indebted to Ralph Cudworth for all the leading ideas of his epistemology. Parallels are found in the latter's *Eternal and Immutable Morality* to Price's contentions concerning the following: (i) the superiority of reason over sense, (ii) the understanding as a source of new ideas, (iii) the view that without these ideas nothing can be known, (iv) the view that the agreement and disagreement between ideas, in the perception of which knowledge consists, are new, simple ideas, acquired by the understanding, (v) the view that clearness and distinctness of apprehension are a guarantee of truth, (vi) the view that abstractionist and nominalist theories of general ideas beg the question.[5] To Cudworth he also owed (i) his contention, already discussed, that it is impossible to regard 'good' and 'evil', 'right' and 'wrong' simply as 'other words' for willed or forbidden, etc.; (ii) his belief that there is an antecedent right or obligation, prior to all laws, wills and compacts, which are, or give rise to, obligations; (iii) the view that there are 'heads of virtue' or prima facie obligations, from which particular obligations are derived.[6] Though Price acknowledges his debt to Cudworth in six places,[7] these do not make the full extent of it apparent. It has been claimed with considerable justification by a recent writer on Cudworth that 'in his epistemology . . . Price simply restates Cudworth's Eternal and Immutable Morality'.[8]

I. REASON 'SUPERIOR' TO SENSE

Price begins his case for intellectual intuition by attempting to show that reason is superior to sense. This he proceeds to attempt by means of certain 'observations', drawn from Cudworth and, through him, from Plato's 'Theaetetus'.

(i)

He speaks of reason as

> the power which judges of the perceptions of the senses, and contradicts their decisions. . . . (p. 19)

He is quite right, of course, in contending that perceptual judgement frequently needs correcting by some process of reasoning. But does this show that reason is 'superior' to sense? For instance, a car which I used to have was light blue in colour, but looked fawn by certain kinds of street lighting after dark, and people frequently mistook its colour for fawn. This mistaken perception could have been corrected, had I wished to correct it, in either of two ways, namely (a) I could have waited until daylight and then shown them my car, whereupon they would have said, 'It looked fawn, but we see now that it was really blue'; or (b) if they had seen my car before, I could have corrected their mistake on the spot simply by identifying it – 'This is my car.' Should they have thought that I had made an error, I could have pointed to the registration number, HWH 120, to confirm my statement. They would then have said, 'It looks fawn, but we realise that it must be blue.' In case (b), reasoning comes into the process of correction, but it is, if the term be allowed, inductive,[9] and certainly not intuitive, reasoning, and the ground for the conclusion 'It must be blue' is the memory of a sense impression of my car, which this induction has recalled. Empiricists would not for a moment dispute that mistaken perceptions are corrected by reasoning of this kind, but they would point out that the conclusions reached by it always need to be verified from sense impressions, and so, if we are talking of 'superiority', it must be accorded to sense, rather than reason.

(ii)

> The faculty . . . which views and compares the objects of *all* the senses, cannot be sense. When, for instance, we consider sound and colour together, we observe in them *essence, number, identity, diversity,*

etc. . . . The power which takes cognizance of all this, and gives rise
to these notions, must be a power capable of subjecting all things
alike to its inspection, and of acquainting itself with necessary truth
and existence. (p. 19)

Locke would have agreed that the understanding brings together the
simple ideas of sensation and makes new ideas of various kinds.[10] Our
idea of a number, 12 for instance, is, according to Locke, 'nothing but
the ideas of so many distinct units added together'.[11] The point at issue
between Price and the empiricists was whether these ideas of essence,
number, identity, diversity, etc., are complex or simple, i.e. whether
they can, or cannot, be analysed into simple ideas of sense. It is difficult
to see how Price thought that he was strengthening his contention that
they are simple intellectual intuitions of necessary truth by pointing out
that they apply to '*all* the senses'. If we can conceive of such ideas being
constructed out of the simple ideas of *one* sense, there is no difficulty in
conceiving of them as constructed out of simple ideas of *more than one*
sense. If we can derive the idea of 12 from twelve visual experiences, as
Locke believed, we can surely derive it equally well from six visual and
six audible experiences, for, in both cases, we are confronted by 'the
ideas of so many distinct units'. If we can perceive diversity between,
say, blue and yellow, we can as easily perceive, in the case of a red
visual sensation and a loud audible one, that one is not the other. So
what is the point of saying that these ideas (number, diversity, etc.)
apply to '*all* the senses'? Price's argument might be valid against the
most naïve form of empiricism imaginable, i.e. where it is affirmed that
we cannot have an idea of anything which is not given to us directly
and immediately in one simple idea of sensation or introspection. We
have no such single, simple sense impression of resemblance, for
instance. But this naïve empiricism has never been upheld by any
philosopher. Even Hume found room for a faculty of the imagination
which brings together the impressions of sense according to certain
principles of association.[12]

(iii)

Some of Price's arguments rest on the assumption that the idea of
substance is one with which it is impossible to dispense, e.g.

> Sense consists in the obtruding of certain impressions upon us,
> independently of our wills; but it cannot perceive what they are, or
> whence they are derived. It lies prostrate under its object, and is only

a capacity in the soul of having its own state altered by the influence of particular causes. It must therefore remain a stranger to the objects and causes affecting it.

A modern empiricist might reply that this notion of 'objects or causes affecting it' arises, not from any perception of things in the world outside us, but from the way in which we talk about our sense impressions.[13] However, Price's purpose here is to refute Locke, and Locke believed that the idea of a substratum is a necessary one. He admitted that it cannot be derived from sensation or reflexion,[14] but thought that it is self-evident that there must be a substratum in which the attributes of a thing inhere 'because we cannot conceive how they should subsist alone, nor one in another'.[15] He seemed to think that he was justified by his theory of relations in proceeding from the ideas of the attributes of a thing to the idea of the substratum[16] but, as Professor D. J. O'Connor has said, 'neither his theory of relations nor any other, however clear, consistent and satisfactory, could justify him in passing from empiricial premises to a metaphysical conclusion of this sort'.[17] Price's own arguments for a substratum are not convincing, but they do call attention to the fact that, if you believe in the idea of it as a perception of necessary truth, then you must concede that the understanding is its source.

Price proceeds now to put his finger on three other points at which Locke tried to marry his empiricism to rationalism: these concern general ideas, essence and cause.

(iv)

Sense presents *particular* forms to the mind; but cannot give rise to any *general* ideas. It is the intellect that examines and compares the presented forms, that rises above individuals to universal and abstract ideas; and thus looks downwards upon objects, takes in at one view an infinity of particulars, and is capable of discovering general truths. (pp. 19–20)

With all this Locke could have agreed, but he would have maintained that general ideas are analysable into simple ideas of sense and reflexion, from which the understanding has created or invented them by the 'way of abstraction'.[18] It is difficult to see how Locke's empiricism allowed him to retain the notion of general abstract ideas. We do not have experience of properties, qualities or attributes (nor of the complex concepts, e.g. mankind, rational animal, etc., into which they are combined; nor of the general rules of reasoning, which are another kind of general abstract idea) apart from the particular objects, or relations between objects, in which they are instantiated. It is, therefore, unnecessary, and indeed inconsistent, on empiricist principles to suppose that these general abstract ideas have independent existence. In so far as Price's argument can be interpreted to mean that, if you are going to have general abstract ideas in your epistemology, you must accept the presuppositions of rational intuitionism, it can be taken as a valid criticism of Locke.

(v)

> Sense sees only the *outside* of things, reason acquaints itself with their *natures*. (p. 20)

Here again, if there is any merit in Price's point, it must lie in his exposure of the inconsistency in Locke. Locke introduced into philosophy the idea of nominal essences. He saw the error of Aristotle's doctrine that natural objects, such as plants and animals, have 'real natures', which it is the purpose of science to discover. Confronted with a particular flower, botanists may ask, 'Is this an instance of species *A* or species *B*? What is it *really*?' But this '*really*' does not refer to some mysterious 'true nature' of the flower, but to our use of *names*. This we can see by considering how the issue would be settled in such a case. We should run the flower down and check each feature in our *Flora*. By this means we should discover what it really is, i.e. what it is called in our *Flora*. If we found it impossible to arrive at a name, we should (if other botanists found it impossible too) invent a new one for flowers of that kind. The question 'What is it really?' can be answered in a perfectly satisfactory way by inquiring into the *names* which we give to things. Locke made this very clear. But alongside this notion of nominal essence, he retained the idea of real essence: 'the real internal (but generally in substances unknown) constitution of things, whereon their discoverable qualities depend, may be called their "essence" '.[19] It seemed to him necessary to presuppose such an essence in order to give an objective basis to knowledge, but he gave no satisfactory explanation of how we come by this notion of real essence; and on his empiricist principles, of course, no such explanation can be given.

(vi)

Price next refers to causation. Sense feels pain, he says, but it is the understanding which discovers the 'causes' (p. 20) of pain. As O'Connor says, Locke's account of causation[20] is 'one of the least satisfactory features of the *Essay* . . . he nowhere tries to show how the empirical basis of our thinking about causality is related to the *a priori* element embodied in the principle that every change has to be explained by a cause'.[21] If a place is to be found for *a priori* knowledge of a *factual* proposition to the effect that '*everything that has a beginning must have a cause*',[22] and Locke took it to be factual,[23] then, since this cannot be established from experience, the empiricist must once again surrender to rational intuitionism.

(vii)

Price goes on to refer to the intellectual element in artistic appreciation. In every work of art, there are 'things which can never be represented on a sensible organ, and the ideas of which cannot be passively communicated, or stamped on the mind by the operation of external objects' (pp. 20–1). These are 'order and proportion; variety and regularity; design, connection, art, and power; aptitudes, dependencies, correspondencies, and adjustments of parts so as to subserve an end, and compose one perfect whole' (p. 20). Empiricists generally would have no quarrel with all this. They leave room for an active principle (Locke's 'understanding', Hume's 'imagination') which organises the data of sense in different ways. But from the fact that the patterns so created produce in us feelings of pleasure it does not follow that they give us new knowledge about the world.

(viii)

Sense cannot perceive any of the modes of thinking beings; these can be discovered only by the mind's survey of itself. (p. 21)

By 'the modes of thinking beings' Price must have been referring to those mental activities by which, according to Locke, the understanding forms complex ideas from simple ones: namely, 'enlarging', which gives rise to simple modes; 'comparing', to ideas of relations; 'combining', to mixed modes; and 'abstraction', to general ideas. But it is difficult to see what the point is which Price is trying to make here. According to Locke, reflexion, or inner sense, is 'that notice which the mind takes of its own operations',[24] so what is there for which he has failed to account? Professor Raphael suggests[25] that it is the need for 'some faculty beyond the senses to discern the difference between outer and inner sense' for which Price is arguing here. But he recognises that this would involve an infinite regress since, having postulated a faculty, reason, to discern that senses are senses, we should have to postulate some further faculty to discern that reason is reason. The only way out of this dilemma would be to assert that reason is self-conscious, whereas sense is not. But since the appeal on this point must be to everyman's consciousness, if it is disputed, no argument is possible.

Price sums up his own conclusion from the foregoing observations thus:

> In a word, it appears that *sense* and *understanding* are faculties of the soul totally different: the one being conversant only about *particulars*; the other about *universals*; the one not *discerning*, but *suffering*; the other not *suffering*, but *discerning*; and signifying the soul's *Power* of surveying and examining all things, in order to judge of them; which *Power*, perhaps, can hardly be better defined, than by calling it, in *Plato's* language, the power in the soul to which belongs Κατάληψις τοῦ ὄντος or the apprehension of TRUTH. (p. 21)

II. THE UNDERSTANDING AS A SOURCE OF NEW, SIMPLE IDEAS

Price now sets out his argument that if the understanding is, as Locke affirmed,[26] the source of knowledge, it must also be regarded as a source of new, simple ideas. He writes:

> The various kinds of *agreement* and *disagreement* between our ideas, which Mr Locke says, it is its office to discover and trace, are so many new simple ideas, obtained by its discernment. (p. 36)

And he illustrates his point from the equality between the two angles made by a right line standing in any direction on another and two right angles: 'Is not the idea of this *equality* a new simple idea, acquired by the understanding, wholly different from that of the two angles compared, and denoting self-evident truth?' (p. 36). It seemed to Price to possess the essential characteristics of one of Locke's simple ideas – it cannot be analysed into other simple ideas and it provides us with knowledge of an objectively real order of being.[27] The mind, Price believes, is furnished with ideas of objects from different sources and these then become the objects of the understanding, 'from whence arises a new set of ideas, which are the perceptions of this faculty' (p. 39). It is only when the understanding has supplied this new set of ideas that we can interpret our experience, that we can 'know' in any true sense of the word.

II.i KINDS OF IDEAS

These ideas of the understanding are of different kinds:

(*a*) There are mathematical ideas: 'Points, lines, and surfaces, also, as mathematicians consider them, are entirely intellectual objects' (p. 32). Confronted by a cube of matter, the understanding furnishes us with 'the ideas of *number* and *proportion*, and *lines* and *figures*; and might proceed to *arithmetic*, *geometry*, and all the different branches of *mathematics*' (p. 35).

(*b*) There are logical ideas like necessity and contingency (p. 25), identity and diversity, possibility and impossibility (pp. 36–7).

(*c*) There are conceptions in physics, such as solidity (p. 21), the inactivity of matter (p. 22), time (p. 24), space (p. 24), the infinite divisibility of matter (p. 34).

(*d*) There are metaphysical notions like substance (p. 23), causation (p. 25) and universals (p. 29).

(*e*) There are moral ideas like right and wrong (p. 37).

All these ideas, says Price, presuppose other simple ideas 'of whose natures, connexions, and qualities they are perceptions' (p. 38). He therefore suggests a general division of ideas into 'original' and 'subsequent' ones:

> The former are conveyed to us immediately by our organs of sense, and our reflexion upon ourselves. The latter presupposes other ideas, and arise from the perception of their natures and relations. (p. 38)

This distinction seems to anticipate that which W. D. Ross draws between 'constitutive' and 'consequential' attributes.[28] But consequential characteristics can be neither simple nor complex in Locke's sense. They depend on constitutive characteristics and so cannot be described as simple; and they are not wholes which can be analysed into simple ideas without remainder, and so cannot be called complex. Price retained the empiricist dichotomy of ideas into simple and complex as exhaustive; had he not done so, he might have taken further this classification of them as original and subsequent.[29] In point of fact, he immediately turns from it to another classification which he says he prefers 'on several accounts', though he does not trouble to tell us what these are.

His new classification (pp. 38–9) is as follows.

First, he divides ideas into:

(*a*) 'those implying nothing real *without* the mind', i.e. nothing real other than the mind's own affections and sensations;

(*b*) 'those which denote something distinct from sensation', i.e. objective reality, independent of the mind which has the ideas.

Both these classes are then further subdivided:

(*a*) into: (i) ideas which 'denote the immediate effects of impressions on the bodily senses without supposing any previous ideas, as all tastes, smells, colours, etc.' (ii) 'those that arise upon occasion only of other ideas', e.g. the effects produced in us by the contemplation of order, happiness or the beauty of art.

(*b*) into: (i) ideas which 'denote the real properties of external objects, and the actions and passions of the mind', e.g. figure, extension, motion; volition, consciousness, memory. (ii) ideas 'derived immediately from intelligence'.

Price, like Locke, believed that some of the qualities which objects appear to have are, in fact, the effects which they produce in us ((*a*)(i)). These qualities of smell, taste, colour, etc., are ones which can usually be attributed to objects, but not always. Furthermore, when objects do have these qualities, their determinate forms often seem to be different to different people. These ideas (Locke's secondary qualities) seemed to Price to be clearly different from the ideas in (*b*)(i). It is, of course, true that the size, shape or speed of an object may seem to be different under different conditions, e.g. when seen at a distance, or through a mist, or from a vehicle moving alongside. But there are techniques of measurement by which we can correct any false appearances in respect of these qualities and find out exactly what the size, shape or speed of an object (Locke's primary qualities) is. If it be said that we can similarly distinguish the real taste, smell or colour of an object from any false impressions by observing these under standard conditions (e.g. in normal light by a normally sighted person, etc.), it still remains true that, while we can conceive of a material object which lacks smell, taste or colour, we certainly cannot conceive of one which lacks extension, shape and either motion or rest. So Price would have persisted that his distinction is a real one. And so it is, but we need not accept his account of why it holds good: that ideas of extension, etc., denote 'real properties of external objects', whereas colour, etc., denote 'nothing real *without* the mind'. We have no reason to believe that we are apprehending the object in one case but not the other, beyond the fact that we should never speak of a thing as a material object when it lacked extension, figure and either motion or rest. This tells us something important about the term 'object', as used in our language, and cognate terms like 'material object', 'matter', etc. Shape, size, motion or rest are among the defining characteristics of these terms, whenever we use them; and from this it follows analytically that they are 'primary qualities of material substances' (p. 39) in Locke's sense of a primary quality: one that is 'utterly inseparable from the body, in what estate soever it be'.[30] If a thing lacked these characteristics, we should not call it a 'body', 'object', 'material object', etc. Much the same might be said in the case of volition, consciousness and memory. We cannot conceive of a mind which is not conscious, does not exercise volition or store memories; but this does not prove that these actions and passions, as Price calls them, must therefore inhere in some mysterious, objective reality, the mind. We have no direct evidence for the existence of this objective reality beyond consciousness, volition, memory, etc. The fact that we never speak of a mind which lacks these attributes simply tells us that they are defining characteristics of the word 'mind' as we use it. It does not 'imply real and independent existence and truth' (p. 38).

The first subdivision of (b) above must, therefore, be rejected as an analytic triviality. We must investigate more fully in the sequel whether this is also true of (b)(ii): the ideas derived immediately from intellectual intuition.

II.ii USES OF 'IDEA'

In a footnote (pp. 39–40) Price differentiates three uses of the word 'idea'. The first is to signify such sensations as tastes, sounds, colours, etc. This, he thinks, is an unwarrantable use of the word. The second is to signify 'the mind's conception or apprehension of any object'; he regards this as the correct use. The third is to signify the immediate object of the mind in thinking, a use which is derived from the representative theory of perception.[31] Price thinks that this notion of 'a *representation* or *image* of the object', intermediate between the object itself and the percipient, has led philosophers into grave errors. It led Hume, as he points out in an appendix (pp. 280–1), to regard the immediate object of perception as indistinguishable from perception itself and so to annihilate all external existence. Because it lends itself so easily to such a misinterpretation, Price says that he has tried to avoid ever speaking of ideas as though they were images.

What Prices does say about ideas in this footnote and the appendix is not very enlightening. He apparently believed that there are external objects which are not immediately present to the percipient and others which are. The former are material objects and these, if perceived at all, must be perceived by ideas of them (p. 280). But this does not give us any grounds for scepticism as to their existence, for 'all imply the *possibility* of the existence of correspondent objects; and our belief of the *actual* existence of the objects of sense, we may resolve (as Dr Reid does) into impressions on our senses *forcing* belief at the moment of the impression, in a manner we cannot explain' (p. 281). There is, to be sure, no logical or empirical impossibility in the notion of external objects, but Price's reason for believing in their actuality is far from satisfactory. It puts the ground of belief beyond explanation and so is a reason which we can have no reason to accept. Price's illustration of objects which are immediately present to the mind which perceives them is the abstract truth that every angle in a semicircle is equal to a right angle. When millions of minds contemplate this equality, Price asks, 'have they not all the same object in view' (p. 40) and 'is not the very object itself present to the mind' (p. 39)? This case is certainly different from that of material objects, but whether the 'abstract truth' here is a factual necessity concerning metaphysical semicircles and right angles, or simply an analytic necessity, is the relevant question which Price's argument has certainly not settled.

Price says, at the beginning of this footnote, that the word 'idea' should be confined 'to the mind's *conception* or *notice* of any object' and he adds, quite justly, that 'an idea would thus always imply something distinct from itself which is its object'. But this implication is, of course, simply an analytic deduction from Price's own definition. If ideas are, as he has chosen to define them, ideas of objects, then what he has said about material objects and abstract truths follows. But the definition is an arbitrary one and Price simply makes it here and draws inferences from it; he gives us no good reasons why we should accept it.

II.iii IDEAS OF THE UNDERSTANDING

As examples of Price's new, simple ideas, supplied by the understanding, we will consider briefly what he says about substance, cause and abstract ideas.

Substance

Price subscribes completely to the traditional theory of substance as *quod substat accidentibus*.[32]

He writes:

> The idea of *substance*, likewise, is an idea to which our minds are necessarily carried, beyond what mere sensation suggests to us; which can shew us nothing but accidents, sensible qualities, and the outsides of things. 'Tis the understanding that discovers the general distinction between substance and accident; nor can any perception be more unavoidable, than that motion implies *something* that moves; *extension* something *extended*; and in general, *modes* something *modified*. (p. 23)

Locke, as we have already noticed,[33] would have agreed with Price's statement of the case. In his *First Letter to Stillingfleet* he wrote:

> All the ideas of all the sensible properties of a cherry come into my mind by sensation; the ideas of perceiving, thinking, reasoning, knowing, etc., come into my mind by reflection. The ideas of these qualities and actions or powers are perceived by the mind to be of themselves inconsistent with existence. . . . Hence the mind perceives their necessary connexion with inherence or being supported; which being a relative idea superadded to the red colour in a cherry or to thinking in a man, the mind frames the correlative idea of a support. For I never denied that the mind could frame to itself ideas of relation but have showed the quite contrary in my chapters about relation.

He believed that the understanding, from a comparison of ideas, simple or complex, can derive ideas of relation between them, and once one is in possession of an idea of relation, one can call up the correlate of an idea given in experience, even if this correlative idea has not in fact been experienced. Hume also thought this[34] and gave as an illustration that, if we have been presented with different shades of blue and, by comparing them, have derived the idea of 'darker than', we can call up the idea of a blue darker than the darkest which we have in fact experienced. I do not dispute that this is possible in the case of ideas of colour or other sensible properties. But Locke's 'correlative idea of a support' is not only an idea of something which we have not hitherto experienced, but which we *never* could experience. Price no doubt realised how unsatisfactory were Locke's grounds for asserting the necessity of the idea of substance. He saw that, if it has any basis, it can only be on the ground of a thorough-going rationalism; and his defence of substance, as against Locke's, has, at least, the merit of consistency with his whole epistemological standpoint.

The fundamental difficulty about accepting it, however, is that nothing can be said about substance except that it is. If one were to say anything more than that about it, one would simply be attributing one more property, not describing the substratum itself. Hume saw the problem here. He threw out a challenge to 'philosophers, who found so much of their reasonings on the distinction of substance and accident' to say from which of the senses, or which of the ideas of reflexion, the idea of substance is derived.[35] Now Price, of course, could have replied quite cheerfully, 'None.' He made it clear that he did not regard substance as observable. And if Hume's challenge had been nothing but a demand for philosophers to say how they observe the unobservable, it could be dismissed as a piece of uncharacteristic obtuseness on his part. But Hume was not doing anything as naïve as this. He was calling attention to the fact that the word 'substance' does not describe anything of which we have actual experience, nor of which we can even imagine the possible experience. He was making the point which Mr M. Lazerowitz has expressed thus: 'The impossibility of imagining substratum is a logical impossibility, which has its source in the linguistic fact that the word "substratum" in the sense of something "in which properties inhere but which is distinct from them" has been given no application. It might, of course, be urged that "substratum" does denote something, though what it denotes eludes us; but then we should have to accept the absurd consequence that the word has an application which it has never been given and is not known to have.'[36] Because nothing can be said about substance except that it is, the statement that it is is one which it is logically impossible to verify. And even if we had to admit that substance did denote something real but completely unknowable (beyond the mere fact of its bare existence) as rationalists have believed, nevertheless it could, being unknowable, play no part in the expression of what we know and so could, for all epistemological purposes, be ignored.

Some support may seem to be lent to the unknown substratum theory by the fact that material object statements cannot logically be reduced to statements about sense-experience. Although it has been claimed that words like 'table' are definable in use[37] in terms of sense-contents, they cannot be so defined in strict logic. Any such definition of a material object statement would be incomplete because of what Dr F. Waismann called the 'open texture' of empirical concepts.[38] This open texture is evident in two ways: (i) one can never complete the empirical description of any given material object: it is always logically possible to extend the description by adding some further detail;[39] (ii) one can never be sure that some new and unforeseen experience will not cause one to modify or retract the empirical description heretofore given of a material object.[40] Waismann suggests that 'a dim awareness' of the open character of empirical concepts underlay the beliefs of Locke and Berkeley in corporeal and mental substance respectively. Much the same point can be made by saying that the truth of a statement or finite set of statements concerning sense-experience is never a necessary condition of the truth of a material object statement; and, vice versa, the existence of a material object is never a necessary condition of the occurrence of any particular sense-experience.[41] One is inclined to add that the same would also be true, if 'sufficient condition' were substituted for 'necessary condition' in the last sentence; but this is not so clearly the case. As Professor A. J. Ayer has argued, if certain sense-experiences which had, over a considerable period, been our ground for a material object statement were suddenly to cease for no apparent reason, we should not have to say, for instance, 'We have been deceived. There never was a table here'; we should rather say, 'There used to be a table here, but for some unaccountable reason it is here no longer.' We do, in practice, accept the occurrence of sense-experiences as a sufficient condition of the existence of material objects;[42] but it remains true that, in strict logic, we are not really entitled to do so.[43]

Again, some support for the substratum theory may conceivably be claimed from the objections which have been offered recently to the phenomenalist interpretation of material object statements as logical constructions out of sense-data. This interpretation implies that the act of observing a physical object is one 'within' which, so to speak, there is another act of observation which is the sensing of sense-data. Professor G. Ryle dismissed this notion as a 'logical howler' on the ground that it involves an infinite regress: 'within' the second act of observation there must be another observation and so on *ad infinitum*.[44] Ayer has pointed out that phenomenalists would be entitled to reply that sensing is an observational act of a peculiar kind and does not entail further sensing: it is a direct, immediate awareness.[45] Ryle argues that words of perceptual detection, e.g. see, hear, etc., signify not experience but achievements.[46] Ayer in reply points out that it does not necessarily follow from this that the experiences do not exist: he writes, 'whatever may be said of the ordinary use of the verb " to see", "to have something in sight" . . . does signify . . . an experience'.[47] Whether the 'something' exists or not is an open question, but we certainly do have this kind of experience, Ayer claims. This debate continues.

But it is difficult to see how anything which any modern philosopher has said about material object language really lends weight to the unknown substratum theory. We know what we know about material objects through empirical observation. Whether this observation includes an awareness of sense-data is an interesting psychological question;[48] and whether the language in which we express what we know about material objects can be usefully translated into 'lower level' sensory language[49] is an interesting linguistic question. But whatever the answers to these questions may be, we are as far as ever from being in a position to claim that we have intuitive knowledge of a mysterious and unobservable X which underlies all the sensible properties of an object. That there is that in a material object statement which may not be reducible to statements about sense-contents is not in dispute. But the conclusions we can draw from this will concern language and will come to no more than the fact that nouns are not adjectives.

Cause

Price starts from empirical observation:

> Nothing may, at first sight, seem more obvious, than that one way in which they [our ideas of cause] are conveyed to the mind is by observing the various changes that happen about us, and our constant experience of the events arising upon such and such applications of external objects to one another. . . . (p. 25)

But he is quite unable to accept the empiricist account of causation:

> And yet I am well persuaded, that this experience is alone quite incapable of furnishing us with these ideas. (p. 25)

When he spoke of one event as the cause of another, Price did not think simply of their regular sequence in experience, but of a logical necessity 'within' these events, binding them together. He concedes that this connexion between cause and effect is never observed (p. 25), but he is certain of it on the logical ground that it would be absurd to think otherwise:

> . . . nothing being more palpably absurd than the notion of a change which has been *derived* from nothing. . . . (p. 26)

This argument is reminiscent of a similar one, put forward by Locke, that anything produced without a cause must be produced by nothing.

But to Locke's argument (and also one put forward by Clarke that, in the absence of causes, things must produce themselves), Hume made the following reply: "'Tis sufficient only to observe, that when we exclude all causes we really do exclude them, and neither suppose nothing, nor the object itself to be the causes of the existence; and consequently can draw no argument from the absurdity of these suppositions to prove the absurdity of that exclusion.'⁵⁰ Hume and his modern successors do exclude altogether the notion of cause, in the sense of a logically necessary link between events, on the ground that, if the constant conjunction of events is all that we can observe, then it is all that we can know. This is not, of course, to deny causation in the sense of a regular sequence in events. We know the kind of evidence which would verify the statement, 'A causes B' (i.e. as equivalent to 'A does appear in constant conjunction with B'): it is evidence drawn from empirical observation. The statement concerns what does happen in the world of physical fact and the appropriate evidence for it is discovered by observing that world. But if we take 'A causes B' to mean 'A must appear in constant conjunction with B', and take this 'must' to refer to some fact about the world, as Price does, how are we to verify it? What conceivable evidence, drawn from the world of physical fact, would take us beyond the 'does' to the 'must'? According to Price, this 'must' is unobservable (p. 25); then how can we conceivably verify it as a statement of fact? Price, of course, would have his reply to all this. He would point out that in the foregoing paragraph we have slipped in the adjective 'physical' before fact, whereas the fact about the world which he has in mind is a metaphysical one, which is verifiable, not by empirical observation, but by an intuition of the understanding:

> The necessity of a cause of whatever events arise is an essential principle, a primary perception of the understanding. . . . (p. 26)

But when he speaks of 'the necessity of a cause of whatever events arise' he brings together two different kinds of expression. Each, in its own sort of context, has a clearly determinable meaning; but when they are brought together in one context the result is a hybrid whose meaning it is very difficult, indeed impossible, to determine. (a) 'Necessity' is a word which has a clear and precise meaning in *logical* contexts. It refers only to *statements* or *propositions*. A necessary statement or proposition is: (i) one for the verification of which we do not require evidence from empirical observation; and (ii) one which it is logically impossible to deny. (*b*) The phrase 'a cause of whatever events arise' has a clear and precise meaning in empirical contexts. It refers to *events*. And (i) The evidence for a cause of any event is drawn from empirical observation. (ii) It is logically possible to deny any particular cause which is given of events which arise. The differences are clear, and there are difficulties in even considering the second of these kinds of expression (empirical statements about events in nature) on the analogy of the first (logical statements about propositions in a system). For instance, the causal connexions which would come under (*b*) above are connexions between simple and distinct entities (events in nature); but in logic there are no necessary connexions between propositions which are simple in structure and whose truth-values are independent. Moreover, in logic the rules of the system are primary in the sense that the connexions between propositions are said to be necessary when they follow from these rules. But rationalists like Price want to find a necessity in the events of nature which is primary in the sense that the laws of nature are derived from it.[51]

Price says that the understanding perceives by intuition the absurdity of

> an existence which has *begun*, but never was *produced*; of a body, for instance, that has *ceased* to move, but has not been *stopped*; or that has *begun* to move, without being *moved*. (p. 26)

When one event, to take Price's illustration (p. 25) the melting of wax, is found in constant conjunction with another, placing it in a candle-flame, we naturally describe this connexion in some such terms as 'The flame *makes* the wax melt.' We speak of it in the same way as we should if I pushed another person down: 'I made him fall.' I should be conscious of exerting force on him and he would be conscious of receiving it and the effects of it. We are inclined to read something like this into the '*makes*' of 'The flame *makes* the wax melt.' If philosophers tell us that this sentence must be rewritten 'The melting of wax is found in constant conjunction with placing it in a candle-flame', we feel that something has been left out, namely the force which the one event exerts over the other, which one 'produces' and the other 'receives'. Price does point out that, in the first instance, such language describes the inner experience of animate beings:

> Activity and self-determination are as essential to spirit, as the contrary are to matter; and therefore inward consciousness gives us the idea of that particular sort of power which they imply. (p. 26)

But he thinks that this language may be used also of inanimate objects:

> Some active or passive powers, some *capacity* or *possibility* of *receiving* changes and *producing* them, make an essential part of our ideas of all objects. . . . (p. 27)

The fact that he italicises the words '*receiving*' and '*producing*' shows that he finds some special significance in our use of them. He fails to see that this is nothing more than an animistic survival.[52]

Price uses (pp. 28–9 n., cf. 245–7) the illustration of casting a die to support his argument that our expectation of the future occurrence of the regular sequences between events, observed in the past, occurs

> Because we see intuitively that, there being some reason or cause of this *constancy of event*, it must be derived from a cause regularly and constantly operating in given circumstances.

Suppose a die comes up six every time it is thrown. Our expectation of its happening again at the next throw is strengthened each time it happens. This is so because each time it becomes, says Price, 'the more evident' that (a) all sides of the die are sixes or (b) the thrower knows some trick or (c) the die is loaded. We feel sure that it cannot be just a run of luck. Each time it happens makes that more unlikely. We realise that there must be a cause. And it is this growing awareness that there is a reason for the six coming up which increases our expectation of the same result at the next throw. Now, the 'conviction produced by experience' that regular sequences which we have observed in the past will be repeated in the future, says Price, is built on the intuition that a cause is operative in this regular sequence, a cause which, like the three alternatives in the case of the die which comes up six, is additional to the regular sequence. Apart from one of the suggested causes the run of sixes would be mere chance. We cannot believe that in the case of the die, so how can we believe it in the case of the regular succession of other events? He thinks that we only manage to do so because it is so 'self-evident' that there must be a causal connexion operative in these sequences of nature. It is not a subject of 'deduction', but of intuition: a truth 'so plain, that there is nothing plainer from which' it 'can be inferred'; and this is the very reason why we overlook it.

But if we compare Price's case of a die which comes up six every time with that of a regular sequence in nature, e.g. water, thrown on fire, which always quenches the fire, we shall see that they are not really analogous. In the former, experience has taught us the constant conjunction of casting the die (A), and six coming up on the average one time in six (B). But we now observe a different sequence: casting the die (A), and six coming up every time (C). Experience suggests that, where this latter sequence occurs, there is some third event (or events) (D), occurring between A and C, and this D is likely to be one of the alternatives given above. The case of water quenching a fire is a sequence of the kind A–B above, not of the kind A–D–C; that is to say, it is a familiar, not an unfamiliar, sequence. We can, of course, ask for an explanation of the fact that water quenches fire and the reply 'Because it cuts off the supply of oxygen from the combustible material' may be accepted as answering the question. In such a case it has been shown that the sequence: water poured on fire (A) and the fire going out (B) is more correctly described if we introduce the explanation that the water cuts off the oxygen (E). The sequence is then A–E–B. And it may be necessary to elaborate this further by introducing other explanatory events between A and E or E and B, so that the explanation reads A–X–E–Y–B. But such an explanation, however full, is still the description of a regularly observed sequence in events. Now, what Price thinks he is showing by his illustration of the die is not that the link between A and B can be elaborated by introducing further terms as instanced here, but that between the several terms of any such explanation some further link is required to hold them together. Just as we should say, 'There must be some explanation of this', when the die comes up six every time, so, thinks Price, we ought to say, of the regular sequence A–X in the explanation of A–X–E–Y–B, 'There must be some explanation of this.' But the whole reason why we say that there must be a reason in the case of the die which comes up six every time is that this sequence is unfamiliar and we want to reduce it to the familiar. It gives us no grounds for saying that there must be a reason why the familiar sequences of nature do occur as they do.

Price is on firmer ground when he says that the goal which thought always pursues is a clearer perception of the causal connexions in which objects stand to one another:

> 'Till we can discover this [causal connexion between events], we are always conscious of somewhat further to be known. While we only see one thing constantly attending or following another, without perceiving the real dependence and connexion; ... we are necessarily dissatisfied, and feel a state of mind very different from that entire acquiescence, which we experience upon considering *Sir Isaac Newton's* laws of motion, or any other instances and facts, in which we see the necessary connexion and truth. (p. 27)

Scientists certainly assume that connexions between events in nature can be discovered and are not satisfied until they have discovered them. If they believed that in any part of the universe this was impossible, then they would lose interest in it because there scientific investigation would be impossible. Every event or group of events which takes place is regarded by the scientist within whose field it falls as belonging to a class of events or groups of events (E), which is related to a class, or classes, of relevant conditions (C), in such a way that, when an instance of C occurs, it is accompanied or followed by an instance of E and it is his aim to discover what C is in the case of each event within his particular field.[53] This principle, 'Every event must have a cause', is something more than the generalisation from experience which J. S. Mill took it to be. Bertrand Russell claimed that 'an independent logical principle, incapable of being inferred either from experience or from other logical principles'[54] is assumed, if we say that we have reason, where event A has been invariably accompanied or followed by event B, for believing that the next instance of A will be accompanied or followed by B. Professor Paul Edwards has replied that all we mean by 'having a reason' to believe this is (a) that past observation, in all or most cases, has shown us A followed or accompanied by B, that the number of such observations is fairly large, and that they come from extensively varied sets of circumstances; and (b) that we have found that large collections of exclusively positive and widely varied instances of events following or accompanying one another, such as is the case with A and B, are a reliable basis for prediction.[55] Though it may be, to some degree, derived from experience, however, the causal principle has, as Price recognised, an a priori character which cannot be ignored. 'To say that such a law is a generalisation like any other is to misrepresent its logical status; it cannot be derived from experience since it is one of the principles which determine developed experience.'[56] What, then, is its status? It does not appear to be merely analytic. But, if it is not analytic, it must be synthetic: it must say something about the world. However, the reasons which lead us to say that it is a priori cancel out those which lead us to say that it is synthetic. If it can be affirmed whatever the course of events may be, then it tells us nothing as to what the course of events in fact is.[57] Kant suggested[58] an account of this principle which is now widely accepted. He took it to be not a statement of fact, but a rule, a postulate, a proposal, a leading principle; or, since it would be, strictly speaking, inaccurate to call it any of these, something like a rule, etc. The causal principle is a priori in the sense that we *bring it to* experience. We admit no exceptions to it. If we come upon an event which appears to have no cause, we do not admit, even as a possibility, that it has none. We say that there must be a cause, and we assume, if we are scientists, that if only we search diligently enough, we shall find it. The important question, then, seems to be: how effectively does this principle enable us to deal with the natural world? The answer is: very effectively. This, of course, makes it different from any capricious postulate or rooted prejudice into which we might try to make experience fit. There seem to be excellent pragmatic grounds for accepting it. But, apart from these, there is no evidence of its truth. We can say that this world is one which the causal principle increasingly seems to fit. We cannot say that in the causal principle we have an insight into the nature of the real world which is more certain than, or independent of, experience.

In contemporary physics the notion of cause has been replaced by that of laws or uniformities. The constancy of these laws consists in the sameness of differential equations. For instance, there is nothing which can be called cause, as distinct from effect, in the motions of bodies related by the law of gravitation. 'Certain differential equations can be found, which hold at every instant for every particle of the system, and which, given the configuration and velocities at one instant, or the configurations at two instants, render the configuration at any other earlier or later instant theoretically calculable. That is to say, the configuration at any instant is a function of that instant and the configuration at two given instants.'[59] This notion of uniformity substitutes for causing the idea of determining; and this can hold between future and past, or present, events as well as between past, or present, and future events. But what has been said about the *a priori* character of the principle of causality will apply with equal force to this principle of uniformity. It is a leading principle which guides the scientist in his inquiries, a demand which he makes of the world and insists that it must satisfy.[60]

Abstract Ideas
Price now turns his attention to 'abstract ideas', that is, general ideas or universals.

Of their use by the understanding he writes:

They are, undoubtedly, essential to all its operations; every act of judgment implying some abstract or universal idea. (p. 29)

We shall see what Price means here by considering the simplest sort of judgement, e.g. when I have a certain sense experience and say, 'That is red.' In so doing I am relating my present experience to others which I have had in the past through something which is common both to this and them. If I were unable to do this, then I should be unable to think or speak at all.[61] The point at issue is: what account are we to give of this universal or general element in the knowing process? Price intended his own theory to be a restatement of Platonic realism against Locke's view that universals 'concern only signs, whether words or ideas'.[62] In defending this theory, Price expressed his main contention thus:

> Were they (abstract ideas) formed by the mind in the manner generally represented, it seems unavoidable to conceive that it *has* them at the very time that it is supposed to be employed in *forming* them. (pp. 29–30)

By 'the manner generally represented' he was, no doubt, referring to the views of Locke, Berkeley and Hume.

Locke wrote: 'Words become general by being made the signs of general ideas: and ideas become general by separating from them the circumstances of time, and place, and any other ideas that may determine them to this or that particular existence. By this way of abstraction they are made capable of representing more individuals than one; each of which, having in it a conformity to that abstract idea, is (as we call it) of that sort.'[63] Here we have: (i) the word, (ii) the general idea which it names, (iii) the particular objects comprehended within that general idea. There is some uncertainty as to what Locke meant by 'general idea'. Berkeley and Hume evidently took him to mean a general image.[64] However this may be, the important point is that Locke believed that there is some intermediary between general terms and the things which they signify. He accepted this rationalist premise without question. Berkeley and Hume did not. They entirely rejected the notion of a psychological or metaphysical intermediary and substituted for Locke's theory that the abstract idea indifferently represents the particular members of a class, the theory that it is the *name* which does so. 'A word', wrote Berkeley, 'becomes general by being made the sign, not of an *abstract* general idea, but of several particular ideas, any one of which it indifferently suggests to the mind.'[65] We have only particular ideas, but one of these may 'represent or stand for all other particular ideas of the *same sort*'.[66]

Against nominalism of this kind Price advances the following argument:

> That the universality consists in the *idea*; and not merely in the *name* as used to signify a number of particulars *resembling* that which is the immediate object of reflexion, is plain; because, was the idea to which the name answers and which it recalls into the mind, only a particular one, we could not know to what other ideas to apply it, or what particular objects had the resemblance necessary to bring them within the meaning of the name. (p. 30)

Price does not explain here how we pass from the general idea, which a general word is supposed to evoke in our minds, to particular instances of it. This seems to be just as much in need of explanation as the mystery of how we pass from the word, or particular idea, to other particular ideas, about which Price professes to be puzzled. But he does fasten on the important matter of the resemblance necessary between particular ideas to bring them within the meaning of one name. Berkeley presupposed this resemblance in his phrase 'of the *same sort*', but did not apparently think that it required any explanation or justification. Price's point is that these are certainly required. He saw that the most effective point which can be made against empiricists turns upon this matter of resemblance. He did not take the argument as far as modern writers have done, but he was on the track of the kind of objection which has been brought against all empiricist attempts to get rid of universals: that whatever else is analysed away, it seems impossible to dispense with the abstract, general idea of resemblance.[67]

The theory of universals, which rationalists like Price adopted, was intended to explain the fact that events recur. But does this need to be explained? We have a visual sensation, A, another one, B, another, C; and because they have a certain degree of likeness we can apply to them the general term 'red'. The proposed explanation of the fact that we can do this is that a universal is instantiated in A, B and C. But what does this explanation explain? It does not explain the fact of A, B and C, for they are simply sense-data and sense-data can only be experienced, not explained. 'Why A?' (in the sense that is relevant to our argument) is a question to which no conceivable answer could be given. The instantiated-universal explanation does not explain the redness of A, B and C any more than it explains the occurrence of A, B and C. 'Redness' is simply the general name for the given element in our experience of A, B and C. 'Why the redness of A?' is as inadmissible as 'Why A?' Of course, we may ask questions like 'Why does blue litmus paper turn red when it is dipped in acid?' and if it is such scientific explanations that we are seeking when we ask 'Why A?' or 'Why the redness of A?' then they can certainly be provided. But it is not questions of this sort that the theory of universals purports to answer, but questions such as 'Why is litmus paper, which has turned red when dipped in acid, red?' or since, no doubt, chemical or physical answers to this question could be found, it is the question which persists beyond the ultimate such answer – the question 'Yes, but why is what is the case the case?' which can always be put at the end of any scientific explanation. The only way of answering such a question is 'Because it is.' Does this theory of universals, then, explain the *resemblance* of A, B and C: the fact that they are '*of the same sort*'? This fact is a fact of observation, just like the redness of A, B and C. If we were asked 'What does "red" mean?' we might point to three objects, A, B and C, and say, 'That and that and that, and anything which has the same degree of similarity to these as they have to one another.'[68] But if we are now asked 'What does it mean to be similar?' we may point to three pairs of objects (e.g. two red apples, two automobile engines and the faces of a pair of identical twins) and say again, 'That and that and that, and anything which is as similar to these as they are to each other.' To the objection that the notion of similarity is left in this definition which is supposed to analyse it, we can reply that it is only the word 'similar' which is left and that has been, like 'red', ostensively defined by pointing to pairs of objects which are similar.

But even if general abstract ideas are, as Hume maintained,[69] really nothing more than the series of particular ideas which general words raise in the mind through custom, Price might still have claimed, with some justification, that an *a priori* factor is operative in this process. On Hume's view it is the fact that a general word revives a set of particular ideas, habitually associated, which enables us to avoid the inaccuracies which would arise if all that it suggested to us were one particular idea. For instance, if the word 'triangle' calls up first of all the idea of an equilateral triangle and we then assert that the angles of a triangle are equal, other ideas of scalene or isosceles triangles 'crowd in upon us', and make us realise that having all its angles equal is a property only of one particular kind of triangle and not of all triangles as such. However, we not only let custom revive ideas which test our use of words, but on occasion test by a criterion of meaning the ideas which are revived and, in some cases, reject them as not being within that meaning. Consider, for instance, the word 'castle' in the statement 'Castles are large stone buildings.' 'Castle' may suggest to me the small wooden object on which I garrisoned my toy soldiers as a child. This particular idea (i) resembles other ideas of castles in numerous ways, and (ii) is habitually associated with the word 'castle' in my mind. Yet we should not accept the objection that because the definition of castles above does not fit this particular castle it is untrue.

It is not enough that ideas have a sufficient resemblance to cause them to be habitually associated in our minds: a resemblance beyond that is required. Hume, on his principles, cannot account for this 'authoritative' resemblance,[70] but unconsciously he recognised the need for it when, in his account of general ideas, he wrote: 'When we have *found a resemblance* among several objects, that often occur to us, we apply the same name to them all'; and 'As the individuals are collected together, and placed under a general term *with a view to that resemblance*, which they bear to each other, this relation must facilitate their entrance in the imagination, and make them be suggested more readily upon occasion.' In the sense of a standard of meaning brought to experience, not derived from it, this may be called *a priori* resemblance,[71] and to talk of 'finding a resemblance' among objects or classifying them with a view to resemblance, Price would have said, is to concede his point that the mind knows the meanings of general words at the very time that it is supposed to be engaged in forming them. So Price believed that the only way of accounting for the *à priori* standard of meaning was in terms of a real world of universals over and above the particulars of experience. But Berkeley suggested an alternative explanation which has been developed by his successors. 'It is one thing for us to keep a name constantly to the same definition, and another to make it stand everywhere for the same idea: the one is necessary, the other useless and impracticable.'[72] The definition of a general word is our standard. It may be that when we consider any definition our imaginations represent to themselves some of the particulars comprehended under it (as Price says (p. 30)) but the definition itself is an intellectual construction. It is an attempt to determine precisely the limits within which the word applies and the criteria in accordance with which it may be used. This attempt is completely successful only within narrowly restricted fields of discourse, such as mathematics or the rules of games like chess. When we turn to language in general use, we find that it is much more difficult to give precise definitions to general terms. They are, as Locke said of his nominal essences, 'the workmanship of the understanding', but they have their 'foundation in the similitude of things'.[73] They are arbitrarily constructed, but they are based on observation of natural objects, and where they fail to do justice to experience, it is the definition which we reject and not, as in mathematics, the facts. It is therefore difficult to accept the view that such general terms put us in touch with ultimate reality, as Price held. According to the time-honoured theory of real definition, a definition is an account of the essence of a thing. Aristotle taught that everything, in some sense, has a determinate essence; and so there is really one, and only one, definition of a thing, the definition which states the essence. But this notion of essence, even in mathematics where Price believed it to be most obviously necessary (p. 28), can be quite satisfactorily analysed into our decision as to what we will mean by a word;[74] and if we do not retain it in that connexion, there is no reason why we should retain it in any other. It was no doubt from this theory of essence that philosophers derived the view that, when we use a general word, what we are naming is a general essence, i.e. a universal. The answer to the question: what does a name mean? must provide 'an exit from the maze of words'.[75] Realism's exit opens into a mysterious world of abstract ideas or universals, but the only evidence which we have for the existence of this world is our use of general words. The argument is circular. It starts from the fact that we use general words and justifies its explanation of this fact by the fact itself. It does not really enable us to cross the gap from words to things. This theory that a general word names some eternal essence which belongs to the nature of things is further discredited by the fact that the meanings of general words are constantly changing in use. Naming has been compared to electing a member to a club. We cannot really say to what club he is elected because it is not the same club after he has been added to it as it was before. Similarly, there is no changeless essence which is the meaning of the word. The only way out of the world of words lies in indicating particulars which are classified under the general word in question. If this is not considered enough, then it is impossible to see what more there could be.

II.iv INTUITIONISM

Price drew on Cudworth and Cudworth on Greek philosophy. According to a recent writer on Cudworth, however, the latter owed another debt which has been 'usually overlooked, often denied, by writers on Cudworth'.[76] This was to Descartes, from whom he derived, among other things, his view that 'Truth is nothing else but clear intelligibility', and 'no man ever was or can be deceived in taking that for an epistemonical truth which he clearly and distinctly apprehends . . .'.[77] It is not surprising, then, to find Cartesianism in Price. He takes a thoroughly Cartesian view of intuition and the part which it plays in the knowing process. In the final paragraph (p. 40) of section II of chapter I he reaffirms the distinction which he has earlier (p. 18 n.) drawn between reasoning and intuition. Reasoning 'consists in investigating certain relations between objects', but the ideas of these relations must be 'previously in the mind'. Reasoning cannot be concerned to find out that of which it has no idea, and so it must necessarily suppose us already to have the ideas we want to trace:

> When, from the view of objects to which they belong self-evidently, we have gained ideas of proportion, identity, connexion, etc., we employ deduction, or reasoning, to trace these amongst other objects, and in other instances, where they cannot be perceived immediately. (p. 40)

He says that Cudworth in his *Eternal and Immutable Morality* has dealt with this in a way 'not quite clear and satisfactory' (p. 91 n.). This Cartesian view of reasoning is expanded in chapter V of the *Review* and we will refer to that in a moment. But first we might notice what Price has to say in chapter V about another Cartesian question: the extent to which doubt can be sustained concerning the rectitude of our faculties (pp. 91–7). He does not attempt, as Descartes did, to follow scepticism as far as doubt can go, but launches a direct attack on its premises. The question to be answered is: do our faculties deceive us, and if not, how can we be sure that they do not? Sceptics have maintained that any answer would beg the question, since it would involve trusting the very faculties whose trustworthiness is in dispute. Price turns the edge of this argument against the sceptics and maintains that, if we are to doubt the trustworthiness of our faculties, we must have a reason, or reasons, for doing so, and this implies that we must trust the faculties with which we reason: '. . . nothing is more plainly self-destructive, than the attempt to *prove* by reason, that reason deserves no credit, or to assert that we have *reason* for thinking, that there is no such thing as *reason* . . .' (p. 92).

This argument, Price is sure, shows thorough-going scepticism to be logically impossible. He reinforces it by two further considerations: (*a*) If the sceptic answers the question: can we perceive truth? in the negative, he contradicts himself, because his answer implies 'a tacit acknowledgement that there is somewhat true', i.e. it is true that we cannot perceive truth (p. 93). Most sceptics would, of course, readily admit that scepticism implies the truth of some perceptions, but they would reply that it does not follow that those which we trust are trustworthy. We still need to find reasons which give us the right to be sure of them, and this may be impossible in any given case.[78] (b) Price, for his part, however, thought that there are some perceptions of which we can be absolutely certain and he saw in this further proof of the rectitude of our faculties. There are propositions which it is logically impossible to deny. If, he says, we have no reason to doubt these perceptions, then neither can we have any reason to doubt the reason which apprehends them (p. 95). These necessary propositions resolve themselves into the apprehension of relations of difference or similarity between our ideas. Price gives illustrations – to have the ideas of a whole and a part 'is the same with seeing' that the former is greater than the latter; to have the ideas of two figures and the idea of 'exact coincidence' between them is 'the same with seeing' that they are equal (p. 94). The sceptic could reply that these propositions do not record perceptions of the world outside us; or at least we have no reason for saying that they do. The necessity in both cases can be explained as an analytic one, which follows from the definitions of the terms used. A whole must be greater than its part because that is the definition of a whole. Two objects which exactly coincide must be equal because this is what the word 'equal' means in this sentence. Our knowledge of necessary analytic propositions gives us no ground for believing what our faculties lead us to believe concerning the external world. If we could prove that we know necessary *synthetic* propositions, the case would be vastly different. If it were shown that it is logically impossible to deny certain empirical propositions, such as 'every event has a cause', then it would be logically impossible to deny that the faculties with which we know these inform us rightly about objective reality. But analytic propositions do not give us any information, reliable or otherwise; they simply explicate our definitions.

But we must return to intuition and what Price says about it in chapter v of the *Review* (pp. 97–103). He defines it as 'the notice it [the mind] takes of what is or is not true and false' (p. 98: the first and second editions of the *Review* insert 'absolutely and necessarily' between 'what' and 'is') and differentiates it from two other 'grounds of belief', namely immediate consciousness or feeling and argumentation or deduction. Price includes induction as well as deduction in the second ground of belief. The important distinction for him was between discursive and intuitive reasoning. He argues that some truths must be self-evident 'otherwise nothing can be proved, or known'. If our right to be sure of what we claim to know is to be sustained, then the evidence for it must, in the last analysis, shine by its 'own light'; that is, it must consist of truths which it is logically impossible to deny. Intuition provides us with such truths. 'It is on this power of intuition, essential, in some degree or other, to all rational minds, that the whole possibility of all reasoning is founded' (p. 98). We proceed in any valid reasoning from step by step of the argument by perceiving self-evident relations between the ideas involved. When the relation between two ideas is not immediately apparent, an 'intermediate idea, whose relation to either is self-evident, or made out by some precedent reasoning' (p. 99) is introduced to effect the necessary connexion. Thus 'every process of reasoning is composed of intuitions, and all the several steps in it are so many distinct intuitions'. There are 'various degrees' of intuition. When 'clear and unquestionable', it produces 'demonstration and certainty'; but 'when otherwise', only 'opinion and probability'. And so it is worth taking time often 'to resolve our reasonings into their constituent intuitions; and to observe carefully, what light and evidence attend each, and in what manner, and with what degree of force, they infer the conclusion' (p. 100). This would save us from 'much error and confusion, and shew us what degree of assent is due to the conclusions we receive . . .'. So the claims which Price makes for intuition are as follows: (a) that unless we know some things by it; we can learn nothing; (b) that valid reasoning proceeds by means of it, (c) that it admits of various degrees. What is to be said for these claims?

(a) Intuition and Learning

In order to know anything we must be able to classify it. This is true even of the simplest kind of knowledge. I know, for instance, that the paper on which I am now writing is white. This means that, as I look at it, I am able to relate the present visual experience to certain other experiences which I have had in the past and to which it bears a certain degree of resemblance. This resemblance I mark by using the sign 'white'. At the same time, of course, I differentiate it from visual experiences which I classify under different signs. To know this present sense-datum I must recognise it but, in order to recognise it, I must recognise it *as something*, i.e. as white. It is by the sign 'white' that this object of knowledge is, so to say, held in my mind. My knowledge of the whiteness of this paper is certainly not intuitive in the sense that it requires, or admits of, no further testing. In calling this paper white, I am claiming that it can be classified with those objects which normally sighted people designate by the sign 'white'. This is a claim which may be questioned, and if it is, I must support it by an appeal to evidence. My knowledge of this whiteness is only correct, i.e. it is only knowledge, if I have in fact learned to use the sign 'white' correctly.[79] So the reverse of Price's contention seems to be the case: unless I have learnt something, I can know nothing.[80]

All our empirical knowledge rests on the assumption that our criteria of classification are adequate to the complexity and variety of events. This assumption is always open to doubt and our classifications to revision. So there arises the point of view which, at least, since C. S. Peirce's time, has been called fallibilism. Professor Gallie sums it up as the 'conception of knowledge as the claim that we have learnt to apply certain methods of classification and systematisation ideally well; this claim, however, being always open to possible questioning and testing'.[81] This view does not lead its exponents to believe that no piece of reasoning can be regarded as more reliable than another. The scientific explanation of a given phenomenon (e.g. the rising of the sun) rests on premises which are no more self-evident than those upon which the explanations of primitive animism rested; but the scientific explanation is more reliable, in any significant sense of that word, than the animistic. All the knowledge which science accumulates is based on assumptions; but this does not lead those who make these assumptions to doubt the value of science or to say that by it 'nothing can be proved or known'.

(b) Intuition and Valid Reasoning

Price's point may still, of course, be pressed that, if we are to know anything as 'absolutely and necessarily' true, then the reasoning by which we have learnt it must rest ultimately on premises and principles of inference which are beyond all doubt. This we must concede. Price believed, like Descartes, that the paradigm of all reasoning is mathematics and that any piece of valid mathematical reasoning can be analysed into self-evident relations or 'constituent intuitions' (p. 100). For example, the equality of two angles, made by a right line standing in any direction on another, to two right angles is, he says, 'a new simple idea acquired by the understanding, wholly different from that of the two angles compared and denoting self-evident truth' (p. 36). But while it is true that the 'constituent intuitions' of mathematics are beyond all doubt, the important question is whether they reveal the nature of things, as Price takes for granted, or are simply constituents of an axiomatic system. Price says:

> In like manner, did we know that inward fabric and constitution of the bodies surrounding us on which all their properties and powers depend, we should know beforehand what would be the result of any experiments we could make with them: just as from having a complete idea of the real essence of a circle, we can deduce the several properties of it depending on that essence, and determine what will be the proportion of lines and angles drawn, after a certain manner, in it. (p. 28)

He believed that the definition of a circle is a real definition, stating an essence, which is part of the nature of things. But this notion of essence is a very difficult one to sustain, even in mathematics. There seems to be no good reason for regarding certain of the features of a geometrical figure as constituting its essence and others as being merely properties entailed by this essence. We do indeed define figures by certain of their characteristics, but there would be nothing to prevent us from defining them by others, if we chose. The definition of a circle as a plane figure contained by one line, which is called the circumference, and is such that all straight lines drawn from a certain point within the figure to the circumference are equal to one another (Euclid, *Elements* I, def. 15) entails that it is a figure with a radius recta describing an angle of 360°. But if we chose to define a circle as a figure with a radius recta describing an angle of 360°, this would then entail that it is a plane figure contained by one line, which is called the circumference, and is such that all straight lines drawn from a certain point within the figure to the circumference are equal to one another. It seems then that 'essence is just the human choice of what to mean by a name, misinterpreted as being a metaphysical reality'.[82]

Since Price's day, mathematicians have shown that it is possible to invent new rules, axioms or definitions and, on the basis of these, to construct new arithmetics and geometries which are perfectly logical in structure and, in some cases, more useful than traditional ones for describing the external world.[83] Non-Euclidean geometries and 'queer' arithmetics can have practical uses in dealing with the external world. In describing interstellar space, for instance, astrophysicists find the

Riemannian geometry most useful; whereas, in describing 'visual space' (i.e. space as psychologically observed by people with normal sight), the Lobachevskian geometry is said to be best. The fact that various systems can all be useful for describing various aspects of the external world reinforces the conclusion that no one system of mathematical rules and axioms is to be regarded as containing an intuition of the ultimate nature of things.

(c) Degrees of Intuition?

It is very difficult to see how Price could speak significantly of different degrees of intuition, if the word is taken to mean, as he took it, the apprehension of 'self-evident truths . . . without making use of any process of reasoning' (p. 98). It is conceivable that an argument will need to be broken down into its several stages in order that each of these may be separately apprehended; but if this apprehension is an immediate awareness of truths which, as Price said, shine by their 'own light' and are 'incapable of proof', then, if we see them at all, we must surely see them whole and entire. What sense is there in saying that a thing is self-evident, but I cannot quite see it? We can only assume that Price here confused two common uses of the word 'intuition', which we may differentiate as the intuition of discovery and that of proof. An expert in any field, e.g. mathematics, natural science, statecraft, etc., can sometimes 'see' the solution of a problem in his field, or, at least, can 'see' the best way to set about finding one. He has a 'hunch'. His insight may be the mark of peculiar genius or, more commonly, the fruit of long experience. It consists in a recognition of certain relevant facts, and of probabilities in the light of them, though the expert in question may not be explicitly aware of these at the time when he forms his judgement. Later he, or his biographer, may 'extract' these several 'intuitions' on which the judgement was based. It must be noted, however, that these so-called intuitions are, in fact, hypotheses; and the expert who is guided by them does not accept them himself, nor ask others to do so, until he has discovered supporting evidence by calculation, experiment or discursive reasoning of some kind. The case is quite different with the supposed intuition of proof. This is an immediate intuition, giving us, so it is believed, knowledge of certain things as absolutely and necessarily true. It requires no supporting evidence of any kind. Price believed that three kinds of proposition are intuitive in this sense, namely (a) mathematical and logical propositions, (b) some propositions of physics, like causality, and (c) certain moral propositions, e.g. that it is right always to keep one's promises. It is impossible to conceive of the contradictories of these propositions, he thought, and so we know them to be certainly true.

Before we can accept this, however, we must consider what it involves to say 'I know X.' Three conditions must be fulfilled: (*a*) X must be true; (*b*) I must believe that X is true; (*c*) I must be able to give a satisfactory answer to the question: how do you know that X is true? i.e. I must be able to point to evidence which gives me, in Ayer's phrase, 'the right to be sure'.[84] Is 'By intuition' a satisfactory answer to this question, when intuition is regarded as neither requiring, nor admitting of, any further supporting evidence? It is open to three objections: (*a*) It assimilates the third condition of knowledge to the second. It simply reaffirms that I firmly believe a certain proposition to be true. (*b*) The feeling of certainty is indistinguishable in cases where it is ultimately shown to have been mistaken from those in which it is not refuted by later evidence. (*c*) We do not, in fact, accept this answer as a satisfactory one. If we did, then, when we claim to know something by intuition, i.e. when we feel absolutely certain of it, we should continue to believe it, however overwhelmingly contradictory the evidence subsequently brought to light before us might be. But unless we are madmen, we always do, in practice, accept the principle that beliefs of which we feel absolutely sure must be modified, if contradictory evidence, in sufficient weight, comes to light. In the sense, then, that Price gave to 'By intuition', it is never a satisfactory answer to 'How do you know?'[85]

3

Moral Epistemology

PRICE believed that his moral intuitionism is *obviously* correct. He said that it 'must appear so plain to those who have not much studied the question about the foundation of Morals, or who have not before viewed it in the light in which I have placed it, that, I fear, it will be difficult for them not to think that I have trifled in bestowing so much pains upon it' (pp. 3–4, preface to first edition). Not all moral philosophers would agree that intuitionism is the plain man's view.[1] Be that as it may, we will now test the claims which Price made for his moral epistemology and consider some of the questions which it raises.

I. PRICE'S MORAL INTUITIONISM

In the first chapter, I discussed Price's argument to the effect that 'right' cannot (logically) be defined by naturalistic or supernaturalistic descriptions, such as 'producing happiness', 'commanded by God', etc. If, for example, 'right' is defined as 'producing happiness' then 'What produces happiness is right' would be an insignificant tautology and 'Is what produces happiness right?' would not be an open question. But, in ordinary use, the former is not insignificant and the latter is not self-answering. And the same goes, whatever 'naturalistic' definition we substitute for 'producing happiness'. Ethical naturalists themselves would not regard the statement here as tautologous or the question as self-answering. So they are inconsistent. They define 'right' in such a way that 'What produces happiness (or whatever) is right' becomes an analytic proposition, true but trivial. They also call what produces happiness (or whatever) right, when they are advocating their hedonism (or whatever), and clearly take themselves to be uttering a synthetic proposition, that is to be saying something *more* than that what produces happiness (or whatever) produces happiness (or whatever).

The root defect of ethical naturalism, to Price's way of thinking, was, I suggested, this inconsistency in its exponents.

In reply to his argument, tough-minded naturalists have taken either or both of two lines. (i) They have said, in effect, 'When we say that what produces happiness (or whatever) is right, *all* we mean is that it produces happiness (or whatever), *not* that it is something else (namely right) in virtue of producing happiness (or whatever).' (ii) Or they have said, 'We realise that people talk as though actions possessed an ethical property called rightness, but, in fact, this is simply the objectification of their own feelings. There is no such property. Statements which assert that anything has it are simply false.'[2]

To rebut such counter-arguments Price contends against ethical naturalists, not merely that they are inconsistent, but: (i) Rightness is a logically ultimate and irreducible notion. No other concept can be substituted for it without change or loss of meaning. (ii) Actions can be known by moral intuition *truly* to possess this property of rightness or to lack it.

I.i RIGHT IS A SIMPLE IDEA

Just as Moore in *Principia Ethica* insists upon the logical 'simplicity' of the notion of good, so Price insisted that right is a simple idea. He wrote:

> 'Tis a very necessary previous observation, that, our ideas of *right* and *wrong* are simple ideas, and must therefore be ascribed to some power of *immediate* perception in the human mind. He that doubts this, need only try to give definitions of them, which shall amount to more than synonymous expressions. Most of the confusion in which the question concerning the foundation of morals has been involved has proceeded from inattention to this remark. There are, undoubtedly, some actions that are *ultimately* approved, and for justifying which no reason can be assigned; as there are some ends, which are *ultimately* desired, and for choosing which no reason can be given. Were not this true; there would be an infinite progression of reasons and ends, and therefore nothing could be at all approved or desired. (p. 41)

Moore, in similar vein,[3] wrote of the simplicity and indefinability of 'good': 'My point is that "good" is a simple notion, just as "yellow" is a simple notion . . . ', and again he said that 'good' has no parts and therefore is indefinable in the most important sense of definition,

namely that in which a definition describes 'the real nature of the object
or notion' which a given word denotes by stating 'what are the parts
which invariably compose' it. He wrote also of the ultimacy of 'good':
it is one of 'the ultimate terms by reference to which whatever *is*
capable of definition must be defined'.

There are difficulties about Moore's comparison of the simplicity of
ethical ideas with that of our ideas of colour. For instance, if this comparison is valid, why do we *disagree* about morals? Men do not have
different perceptions of colour in accordance with differences of cul-
tural or educational background as they do different ideas of what is
right or good. Again, how is it that we can be *mistaken* in morals? A
man cannot be mistaken about his own sense-experience as he can about
what is right or good. True, there are, in one sense, disagreements and
mistakes about colour also. But it is easy to account for these by distinguishing the 'simple ideas' of colour that any given individual has
from the 'real' colours of things as determined by agreed tests. The
former are subjective; the latter objective. In the case of ethical properties, however, there are, according to intuitionists at any rate, no objective tests. They rely solely on direct perception. Moreover, they
claim that moral ideas are not subjective as those of colour are. They
are direct perceptions of the natures of actions, ends, etc. Now, it is
easy to see how men may disagree or be mistaken about simple ideas, if
these are subjective in the way that each individual's sense-experiences
are subjective; but it is very difficult to see how disagreements or
mistakes arise about moral attributes, *if* these 'simple ideas' are immediate perceptions of the objective nature of things. Price was aware of
the difficulties which mistakes and disagreements about morality raise
and we shall see later what he had to say about them. At the moment,
I simply note that, unlike Moore on good, he did not compare the
notion of right with that of any colour. He compared moral ideas, not
with those of sense, but with intellectual intuitions like mathematical
equality. In a moment we shall see why.

If rightness were not a simple idea, Price argued, then all ethical
deliberation or argument would become logically impossible. Suppose
a utilitarian, who believes that 'right' means conformable to the principle of utility,[4] is arguing as to whether act *X* is right or not. In point
of fact, he will not be considering an ethical question, 'Is *X* right?' at
all, but a physiological, psychological or sociological one, 'Is *X* useful?'
Or, suppose that a hedonist is trying to prove an evolutionist wrong. If
he starts from a naturalistic definition, 'right' means what produces

happiness, and sticks to it, he will simply be trying to show that what conduces to higher evolution (the evolutionist's naturalistic definition) does not produce happiness. The argument could dispense with such terms as 'right' altogether; it is simply about whether certain natural causes have certain natural effects. Now Price, like Moore, was convinced that there is something wrong with such a reduction of ethical deliberation and argument to non-ethical terms. In his critique of utilitarianism (pp. 131–8), he instances certain cases upon which one might have to pronounce judgement: Would a general be doing right, if he persuaded his enemies to trust themselves to him and then destroyed them? Would it be a morally indifferent matter whether a man, recently returned from an unknown country, gave a true or false account of it? And so on. He argues that, in resolving these problems, we do not consider whether such acts will cause more or less happiness than their omission, but whether 'there is *intrinsic rectitude* in keeping faith and sincerity, and *intrinsic evil* in the contrary' (p. 133).

It was with such arguments, then, that Price purported to dispose of the first of the two possible replies which, I said, ethical naturalists might offer to his criticism. If right is a simple, i.e. a logically ultimate and irreducible, notion, then the naturalist *cannot* (logically) mean by 'right' 'producing happiness' (or whatever). To do so would not be a case of 'tough-mindedness' in a naturalist; it would be a case of talking nonsense.

We turn, then, to the naturalists' second possible line of argument: that those who say that actions are, or are not, right are making false statements. Against this Price claimed that actions can be known by moral intuition *truly* to possess rightness or to lack it. First, I shall briefly discuss a question as to how Price conceived of this rightness which we intuit. Then I will discuss his arguments to the effect that the faculty which perceives moral distinctions is reason and not sense. It was necessary for him to show this latter to be the case because, as we saw in the last chapter, he takes reason to be the faculty which discerns truth, and it is his object to show that, in intuiting an action to be right, we can (logically) be intuiting a *truth*.

I.ii. IS RIGHTNESS A RELATION OR A QUALITY?

Some intuitionists have believed that 'right' denotes a relation; others, a quality. Clarke held the former view; Cudworth the latter. It is not altogether easy to determine which view Price held. He says that 'fit' and 'unfit' are synonymous with 'right' and 'wrong' and he distinguishes their moral use from their non-moral (p. 104). The non-moral use of 'fit' and 'unfit', which Price gives as denoting 'aptitude or inaptitude of any means to accomplish an end', certainly indicates a relation; and there are some passages in which Price seems to have thought of moral fitness also as a relation. For instance:

> all actions being necessarily right, indifferent, or wrong; what determines which of these an action should be accounted is the *truth of the case*; or the relations and circumstances of the agent and the objects. In certain relations there is a certain conduct right. There are certain manners of behaviour which we unavoidably approve, as soon as these relations are known. Change the relations, and a different manner of behaviour becomes right. Nothing is clearer than that what is due or undue, proper or improper to be done, must vary according to the different natures and circumstances of beings. If a particular treatment of *one* nature is right, it is impossible that the same treatment of a *different* nature, or *all* natures, should be right. (pp. 124-5)

Similarly:

> from the various relations of beings and objects, there result different *moral* fitnesses and unfitnesses of action. . . . (p. 129)

And:

> When we compare innocence and eternal misery, the idea of *unsuitableness* between them arises in our minds. (ibid.)

Such passages led Ross to claim that his view that rightness is 'fitness, in a certain specific and unanalysable way, to a certain situation' was also Price's view; Raphael, however, doubts this.[5] The passages which seem to support Ross's view, says Raphael, are all found in places where Price is discussing the theory of other rationalists; and he thinks that Price failed to differentiate his own view clearly from their views, though in fact it was different. When Price gives his own examples of moral fitness, they do seem to be non-relational. For instance, he writes:

> reverencing the Deity is *fit*, or beneficence is fit to be practised. (p. 104)

And, in speaking of merit, he seems to use 'fitness' absolutely. Merit, he says, is an agent's

> virtue considered as implying the fitness, that good should be communicated to him preferably to others. (p. 81)

Of absolute virtue, he writes that it is

> most properly a quality of the external action or event. (p. 177)

Raphael does not believe that Price thought of rightness as a quality, however, but as 'an entailment . . . perceived immediately by the understanding to follow of necessity'. But surely this view would not be incompatible with the view that rightness is a unique kind of relation. Other intuitionists, Ross for instance, have found no difficulty in thinking of rightness in both of two ways: (i) as a property of certain actions necessarily entailed by other properties, such as being the fulfilment of a promise; and (ii) as a relation of fitness in a unique way of actions to situations. Raphael himself interprets Clarke to have held both these views.[6] We have no reason to believe that Price would have dissented from either view; on his premises there was no need to do so. And since his language lends itself to both interpretations, it would seem a fair conclusion that he subscribed to both.

It should perhaps be pointed out, however, that in either case it is odd to speak of right as a simple idea. It can be argued, of course, that relations and entailments are not complex ideas, i.e. wholes made up of simple ideas, as, for instance, the complex ideas of a table or a horse; but neither are they simple in the usual sense, since they depend for their existence upon other ideas.

I.iii REASON AND SENSE IN MORALS

In order to show that rightness can be truly attributed to actions, Price, in the light of his presupposition that the faculty which apprehends truth is reason, had to show that the faculty which apprehends moral distinctions is also reason, not sense. He advances four arguments in support of this latter view (pp. 41–50).

(i)

He says that it is 'at least possible' (p. 41) that we know right and wrong by intellectual intuition. Even if we were prepared to agree that some truths are apprehended intuitively, however, it would be difficult to follow Price's argument that, because there are some propositions which it is logically impossible to deny and some ends which it is psychologically impossible not to desire, it is 'very credible' (p. 42) that there are actions which rational beings, *qua* rational, find it impossible not to approve. He advanced this against Hutcheson's view that our ideas of right and wrong are productions of an implanted sense. But there seems to be no such analogy as that which he tries to draw here. For one thing, though it is logically impossible to deny a statement when to do so would be self-contradictory, a man would not be contradicting himself if he denied, for instance, that it is right to keep a promise. Again, so far from it being psychologically impossible to disapprove of keeping a promise, many of us manage to do so, in the case of our own promises at any rate; and we quite easily convince ourselves, often enough, when we have broken our word, that, after all, it will be the best thing in the long run.

Price believed that the absurdity of attempting to derive moral ideas from sense is evident, if we consider Locke's account of them. Locke had said that they signify 'the conformity or disagreement of our voluntary actions to some law, whereby good and evil is drawn on us from the will and power of the law-maker'.[7] The law-maker may be fashion, the government or God. Said Locke, virtue consists in 'actions conformable to God's will, or to the rule prescribed by God, which is the true and only measure of virtue, when virtue is used to signify what is in its own nature right and good'.[8] Locke realised that, on his view, all that this amounts to is that obeying God's commands is obeying his commands. Nevertheless, he also says that God has a 'right' to rule us, because 'he has goodness and wisdom to direct our actions to that which is best'.[9] But what can 'right' or 'goodness' here mean, except that God wills to rule us? As Price put it, on Locke's view 'it is an absurdity to apply *rectitude* to rules and laws themselves; to suppose the *divine* will to be directed by it; or to consider it as *itself* a rule and law' (p. 43). No doubt he was correct in adding that Locke 'would have detested these consequences' and was 'strangely embarrassed' by them. Some contemporary philosophers, who have denied '*antecedent right*' (p. 17), as Price calls it, have certainly found themselves somewhat embarrassed by their opinions. Bertrand Russell, for instance, writes: 'But what are "good" desires? Are they anything more than desires that you share? Certainly there *seems* to be something more. Suppose, for example, that some one were to advocate the introduction of bull-fighting into this country. In opposing the proposal, I should *feel*, not only that I was expressing my desires, but that my desires in the matter are *right*, whatever that may mean. As a matter of argument, I can, I think, show that I am not guilty of any logical inconsistency in holding to the above interpretation of ethics and at the same time expressing **strong ethical preferences**. But in feeling I am not satisfied. I can only say that, while my own opinions as to ethics do not satisfy me, other people's satisfy me still less.'[10] Price believed that, if our moral ideas are something more than expressions of feeling or taste, then they can only be intuitions of the understanding.

(ii)

Price refers the matter 'to every man's consciousness' (p. 44). He claims that, if we compare our ideas of right and wrong with, on the one hand, our ideas of sensation, such as pleasure and pain, and, on the other, with our mathematical ideas, such as that of equality, we shall see by introspection that they 'most resemble' the latter. It is, he admits, true that certain emotions (pleasure and pain, satisfaction or disgust) 'generally attend' our perceptions of virtue and vice, but these are simply the 'effects and concomitants' of that perception, and must not be confused with it. Such a confusion, thinks Price, has been responsible for the mistaken theory that the moral faculty is sense, but we only need to examine our ideas of right and wrong and we shall find that, just as we are sure that certain lines and figures are 'really equal', so we are sure that some actions are 'really right'. He illustrates his point: 'When we contemplate the happiness of a species, or of a world, and pronounce concerning the actions of reasonable beings which promote it, that they are right; is this judging erroneously? Or is it no determination of judgement at all, but a species of mental taste? – Are not such actions really right?' (p. 45). Assuredly, as the above quotation from Russell shows, Price was calling attention to a fact of moral experience when he pointed out that we often feel that things are right or good, not just as satisfying our desires, but in some objective way. But the fact that we feel this to be so does not prove that it is so. The explanation offered by Hutcheson and Hume, that actions are recognised as really right when they are approved by all or most men of a certain class,[11] admittedly will not do. The kind of feeling to which Price, and Russell, refers is not a feeling that all or most men agree with our moral judgement, since it has often been strongest in those who have consciously held minority opinions. Russell's feeling that his opposition to bull-fighting was right would not have been one whit less strong, if the majority of Americans (he was in America at the time) had favoured its introduction into their country. No doubt modern psycho-analysts could offer explanations of the objectivity which we feel our moral judgements to possess, and these would account for it as entirely a psychological, and not an ontological, phenomenon. Whether these explanations are adequate is, of course, debatable; but the mere existence of the feeling does not exclude them. The point is that, from the sole fact that we have a certain feeling, we cannot draw conclusions about the world outside us, and this is what Price tries to do. Appeals to introspection such as his are, of course, final; if they do not produce assent, then no further discussion is possible. The empiricists' reply to Price at this point would simply be to affirm that to them moral judgements feel like sensations[12] and after that what more can be said? Price himself recognises that there is something wrong with this argument. He admits that his opponents might easily reply that men have exactly the same sort of feeling about secondary qualities, colour, taste, etc., as they have about right, namely that they are real properties of objects; but he would not accept this as evidence that these secondary qualities are objectively real (p. 46). He therefore goes on to deal with the difference between moral ideas and our ideas of secondary qualities.

(iii)

In differentiating these he appeals to self-evidence: to that the denial of which is unintelligible (pp. 46-0). First, he considers what is self-evident about sense qualities. 'We need no experiments to prove that heat, cold, colours, tastes, &c. are not real qualities of bodies; because the ideas of matter and of these qualities, are incompatible.' In a footnote, he explains that he means by 'incompatible' two things:

(a) 'the unintelligibleness of colour and other secondary qualities, when considered as modifications of matter'. The point seems to be that the colour, for instance, which we see in objects, like the pleasure which we feel when looking at something beautiful, is obviously a sensation. It is an effect produced in our minds by the object. It is unintelligible, thinks Price, that qualities like this, which are obviously 'modes of consciousness', should be 'real qualities of bodies'. But why need we regard secondary qualities as mere modes of consciousness any more than primary qualities? Locke defined a primary quality as one which is 'utterly inseparable from the body, in what estate soever it be'.[13] If we take 'quality' to mean determinable quality, the same seems to be true of secondary qualities. When we speak loosely, we may say, 'This food has no taste'; but, if pressed, we should admit that all food has some taste. Objects have some colour, smell, temperature, etc., just as they have some shape. True, it is easier to secure agreement about the shape of objects than it is about their taste or smell, though not perhaps their colour and certainly not their temperature; but this only shows that our technique for measuring shape has been perfected much more completely than that for measuring the other qualities. It does not prove that taste or smell are modes of consciousness in some sense that shape is not.

(b) 'the repugnancy to coexistence in the same subject which we perceive between these qualities and solid extension'. What he has in mind here is, presumably, the fact that we do not speak of a 'loud, square note' or a 'square, loud box'. This fact is quite intelligible, if 'loud' and 'square' denote sensations in the mind of the person listening or looking, or if one of them does; but it would be unintelligible, if they denoted properties of matter itself, since it would necessitate our believing that a quality is a property of matter and yet a given piece of matter may not possess it. But this fact could be explained without assuming any ontological difference between primary and secondary qualities. Every material object has motion, or rest, figure and extension because these are the defining characteristics of 'material object'. There need not be any justification for saying that the shape of a red object is 'there' in some sense in which its redness is not, beyond the linguistic fact that shape is one of the determinable qualities in virtue of which we call it an 'object', whereas colour is not. It is only fair to Price to quote his own observation in the footnote already referred to: 'Most of the facts alleged in confirmation of this [that secondary qualities are not properties of matter], are in themselves no sufficient proofs of it, being equally applicable, as may be easily seen, to the real and primary qualities of matter.'

Now he turns his attention to what is self-evident about right and wrong. It seems to him just as self-evident that our ideas of them are different from the secondary qualities which we have been considering: 'Who can help seeing, that right and wrong are as absolutely unintelligible, and void of sense and meaning, when supposed to signify nothing true of actions, no essential, inherent difference between them; as the perception of external and internal senses are, when thought to be properties of the objects that produce them?' In support of this he points out: (a) That it would be absurd to maintain 'that there is no possibility of *mistaking* with respect to right and wrong'; since 'all sensations must be alike *true* sensation', he argues, then, if right and wrong were ideas of sense, every man's ideas about them would be 'alike just'. (b) That it would be equally absurd to 'suppose, that the *moral rectitude* of an action is nothing absolute and unvarying'. Sensations like pleasure and pain do rise and sink 'with the force and liveliness of our feelings'; and so, he argues, we should have to believe that the rightness and wrongness of an action could increase or decrease, in accordance with our feelings, if we held them to be ideas of sense.

(*a*) Moral judgements certainly are corrigible in a way that judgements of sense-perception are not. The point may be illustrated from the case of a colour-blind man, who, at first, says that objects *A* and *B* are both grey. It is then pointed out to him that normally sighted people see *B* as red. He may, as most colour-blind people do, admit himself mistaken and say, 'It looks grey to me, but I now know that it is really red.' But what he cannot say is 'I now *see* that it is red.' His sense-experience remains the same and, as such, is incorrigible. Suppose, however, that a man judges that acts *X* and *Y* are both right, and then, after deliberation or argument, comes to believe that *Y* is wrong. He will say, 'I thought it was right, but now I see that it is wrong.' He will *not* say, 'I still think it right, but I know it is wrong.' The difference which Price indicates here is a real one, and a strong argument against believing that a sense is the source of moral ideas. Unfortunately for him, as even his most sympathetic critics would admit,[14] it cuts the ground from under his own feet also. If moral judgements are corrigible, then they cannot be intuitions of the kind Price supposed them to be, i.e. immediate apprehensions of the nature of things, since such intuitions are by definition self-evident and carry their own guarantee of certainty. Modern intuitionists have tried to evade this difficulty by distinguishing between our knowledge of moral principles and our particular moral judgements. The former they believe to be intuitively certain, but the latter, they say, are judgements of probability. Raphael likened our particular moral judgements to the judgements of a law-court, where the respective force of legal principles is weighed in a particular case.[15] Ross likened a particular moral judgement to judging the beauty of a particular work of art which is, in some respects, beautiful and, in others, not.[16] There would be no difficulty about morally judging particular cases in the light of general principles, if the intuitionists did not claim self-evidence for the principles. But in the practical syllogism:

> Always keep promises!
> *X* is the fulfilment of a promise
> Do *X*!

if the conclusion is not self-evident, then there are only two possibilities, namely (*a*) we are mistaken in the factual minor premise, or (*b*) the major premise is not self-evident. We exclude the former *ex hypothesi*; and so can only be left with the second. Price, however, did not resort to any such device as that of the modern intuitionists just mentioned. He believed that particular moral judgements are intuitive. He realised quite clearly that the general principles clash and we are often in doubt about what it is right to do in a given instance (pp. 166–70); but he seems to have thought that this was a difficulty of deduction, due to the fact that our ideas are not sufficiently clear and distinct. He writes: 'In reality, before we can be capable of deducing demonstrably, accurately and particularly, the whole rule of *right* in every instance, we must possess universal and unerring knowledge. It must be above the power of any finite understanding to do this. He only who knows all truth is acquainted with the whole law of truth in all its importance, perfection and extent.' But this does not answer the objection that a judgement cannot be both self-evident and corrigible.

(*b*) We now turn to the second 'absurdity' mentioned by Price. We may find something pleasant at one time and not so at another. If acts were judged by a sentiment, sympathy for instance, it would be possible that they should, similarly, be right at one time and wrong at another. But the rightness or wrongness of actions does not vary in accordance with our feelings. We feel intense sympathy if we see our neighbours ill-treated, but we may not experience anything like the same intensity of feeling if we hear of the same thing happening in a distant land or former age. Nevertheless, we should judge the ill-treatment to be equally wrong in both cases. This is a very strong argument against a theory which compares the moral sense to sentiment or internal sense. Its cogency was admitted by Hume,[17] and he tried to defend his theory by claiming that, though in fact we may have no intense feelings about an action, e.g. a crime of long ago or committed in a foreign land, we imagine the feelings we should have had, if we had been present at its performance, and it is these which constitute our moral judgement. There is certainly something to be said for this view: imaginative sympathy, undoubtedly, plays a large part in determining our approvals and disapprovals.

Rather strangely, Hume described a similar argument, put forward by egoists, as a 'weak subterfuge'. He said, 'It is not conceivable, how a *real* sentiment or passion can ever arise from a known *imaginary* interest;

especially when our *real* interest is still kept in view, and is often acknowledged to be entirely distinct from the imaginary, and even sometimes opposite to it.'[18] Raphael argues that this passage can be turned against Hume himself: how can a known imaginary sentiment give rise to a real sentiment? If I in fact feel indifferent about a crime of long ago, it seems difficult to believe that I disapprove of it because 'I am so deceived by my imagination that I talk as if I felt a strong feeling of anger.[19] But in what sense am I indifferent to an ancient crime? Not surely in the sense that I feel nothing when I contemplate it. I feel revulsion. It is true that my feelings of anger are not so intense as they would be if the crime were nearer to me in time or place; but could not this be explained as due to a subconscious awareness of helplessness in the matter? Is there any need to suppose, as Raphael appears to do, that our indifference is 'opposite' to our sympathy, as are his opposite interests in the case of Hume's egoist? Our sympathy does not issue in an urge to do something – anger is usually this – for there is nothing we can do. But there is no incompatibility between imaginative sympathy with those who suffer and the awareness that there is nothing one can do about it, as there is, in some cases, between one's own interest and that of others. Whatever he thought of all this, however, Price's point that the moral character of a particular action cannot be supposed to vary with the way we happen to feel seems to be a sound one, and it would certainly exclude a theory which maintained that the moral character of an act is just what I happen to feel about it at a given moment, if such a theory has ever been held.

(iv)

Finally, Price attempts (pp. 47–50) a *reductio ad absurdum* of the theory that rightness is perceived by sense. All actions, he argues, have a nature, and therefore they must have some character which can be truly attributed to them. If acts are not '*in themselves*', but only in our feelings about them, right or wrong, they must be *essentially* indifferent. The understanding's proper province is to discern what is essentially true, and so it must perceive all actions to be morally indifferent. 'But are we not conscious, that we perceive the contrary?' The conviction that we do so, however, we shall have to regard as an illusion, which rational creatures, *qua* rational, should try to drive from their minds. But, do what we will, 'we shall find it out of our power, in earnest to persuade ourselves, that reason can have no concern in judging of and directing our conduct; or to exclude from our minds

all notions of right and wrong in actions'. He says that the particularly
objectionable consequence of this false view is that it means that our
faith that God, as all-perfect intelligence, pursues universal happiness,
because this is in itself right, is mistaken; God would know that universal happiness is really indifferent, and so we have no grounds for
believing that he pursues it, nor for believing in any of his 'moral
perfections'. Price thinks it sufficient to refute any theory that it should
imply that in all our moral judgements we are simply mistaking our
feelings for truth, and the consequences of this, that 'there is nothing
obligatory, but all beings enjoy, from the reasons of things and the
nature of actions, liberty to act as they will'.

The theological argument here had occurred to both Hutcheson and
Hume. The former believed that it was a sufficient answer to postulate
a moral sense in the divine nature.[20] Hume saw with regret that there are
no grounds for such a postulate.[21] From the fact that a given sense is
part of created human nature we cannot deduce that it is a part of the
nature of the Creator. Of course, any force that there is in Price's argument depends upon the assumption that there must be a God and that
he must possess moral perfections. If there is a God, and if our moral
faculty is sense, then we cannot be sure that he possesses the moral
perfections that we believe him to possess. On the other hand, if there
is a God, who is eternal reason, all-perfect intelligence, and if our moral
faculty is reason, then we can be sure that he will judge of right and
wrong as we do, or rather, more truly since his understanding is
infinite. It seems odd to encounter theological assumptions in an
epistemological argument but, in fairness to Price, we must remember
that he believed that his theological assumptions could be substantiated
by reason;[22] and so it seemed to him admissible to point out in an
epistemological argument what is, and what is not, consistent with
them. And as both Hutcheson and Hume professed, at least, to share
his belief in God, Price was justified in asking them how they reconciled
their moral theory with it. Their theory was not incompatible with
belief in God, but it left the moral side of the divine nature in great
mystery. Of course, to anyone who does not accept Price's assumptions the argument here is quite unconvincing.

The argument, before Price brings in theology, rests upon other
assumptions also, namely (*a*) that right, wrong and indifferent are the
only essential characteristics an act may possess, and (*b*) the moral
indifference is a positive, not a negative, character. Against the former,
it can be objected that there are other attributes besides ethical ones, and

if the ethical ones are denied, an act may still have some character, e.g. that of maximising pleasure. Against the latter, the objection can be brought that to say an act is morally indifferent means simply that it is neither right nor wrong, and, in this case, given Price's first assumption, 'actions would lose all character sooner than Price's argument requires, so that his refutation would be out of place'.[23]

II. RIGHT AND THE NATURE OF THINGS

The conclusion of the foregoing arguments is that its rightness belongs to the nature or essence of an action. Price writes:

> Right and wrong, it appears, denote what actions are. Now whatever any thing *is*, that it is, not by will, or decree, or power, but by *nature and necessity*. Whatever a triangle or circle is, that it is unchangeably and eternally. It depends upon no will or power, whether the three angles of a triangle and two right angles shall be *equal*; . . . Every object of the understanding has an indivisible and invariable essence; from whence arise its properties, and numberless truths concerning it. . . . The same is to be said of right and wrong, or moral good and evil, as far as they express *real characters* of actions. They must immutably and necessarily belong to those actions of which they are *truly* affirmed. (p. 50)

He points out that an action which is morally fitting in one set of circumstances may not be in another. For instance, an action, previously morally indifferent, may become fitting, if it is commanded by a being possessed of rightful authority (p. 51). An act which is the fulfilment of a promise is, in consequence, fitting although, apart from the promise, the same act would be morally indifferent (pp. 51–2). In each case, however, Price says emphatically that the action is not rendered fitting by any will or power, divine or human. Its moral nature depends upon the nature of things, according to which certain actions are fitting in certain situations and certain others unfitting. It is the 'principles of morality', the 'eternal rules of duty', under which particular acts fall, that determine whether they are fitting or not. Says Price:

> When an action, otherwise indifferent, becomes obligatory, by being made the subject of a *promise*; we are not to imagine, that our own will or breath alters the nature of things by making what is indifferent not so. But what was indifferent *before* the promise is still

so; and it cannot be supposed, that, *after* the promise, it becomes obligatory, without a contradiction. All that the promise does, is to alter the connexion of a particular effect; or to cause that to be an *instance* of right conduct which was not so before. There are no effects producible by us, which may not, in this manner, fall under different principles of morality; acquire connexions sometimes with happiness, and sometimes with misery; and thus stand in different relations to the eternal rules of duty. (pp. 51–2).

Two things seemed to Price to follow from this.

II.i MORAL IDEAS AND NECESSARY TRUTH

Moral judgements, Price believed, are perceptions of necessary truth when they are correct. It is the nature of things that acts which fulfil promises are right. Price thought that such a moral judgement is a synthetic *a priori* deduction from the essence of the action, just as he believed that the judgement that a triangle has its angles equal to two right angles is a synthetic *a priori* deduction from the essence of the triangle. If, as we have argued in the last chapter, there is no reason to believe that the axioms and definitions of mathematics are known by intuition of the nature of things, this removes the main support from the intuitionist's theory that moral judgements express immediate perceptions of the fundamental nature of the universe. But it does not necessarily make the comparison of morals with mathematics inappropriate. We can believe that Price was mistaken about the nature of both moral and mathematical thinking, and yet that he was on the right lines in drawing a comparison between them. We have seen that each of the steps in mathematical reasoning, which Price took to be intuitions, can be explained equally well as appeals to axioms or definitions. Moral arguments proceed by appeals of a similar kind. If a syllogistic analysis of moral judgements be allowed,[24] then the major premise would be a general principle, the minor a statement of fact and the conclusion either an action or some sort of judgement which implied a commitment to action.[25] In discussing his practical syllogism, Aristotle, though he has been variously interpreted, quite clearly regarded it as in some way inferior to the theoretical syllogism because it is the work of that part of reason which is 'calculative', not that part which is 'scientific', and because its conclusion is contingent and might not have been.[26] Rational intuitionists, however, do not accept that there is any fundamental difference between moral and mathematical thinking, so far as the major premise or general principle is concerned. They regard the latter, just as they would a mathematical axiom, as self-evident. Price believed that his 'heads of virtue' are self-evident (p. 168), and can be 'laid down and used as axioms, the truth of which appears as irresistibly as the truth of those which are the foundation of Geometry' (p. 169). The difficulty about this view is that, if it is true, it seems very odd that we should ever be in doubt about what is right. But we frequently are. Price does call attention to this fact, saying that it has 'not been sufficiently attended to' (p. 166). He thinks that the difficulty of determining what is right arises because the heads of virtue 'often ... interfere'. For instance, the duty of self-love may conflict with that of beneficence; and both with veracity, fidelity, gratitude or justice; and different foundations of property may give rise to different claims so that we are uncertain who has the title to it (p. 167).

It is, of course, as Price points out (p. 170), often difficult to know what a *single* principle of conduct requires in a particular case. Beneficence or self-love, for instance: 'Until we can in every particular know what is good or bad for ourselves and others, and discover the powers and qualities of objects, and what will result from any application of them to one another, we cannot always demonstrate what either of these principles requires, but must continue liable to frequent and unavoidable errors in our moral judgment' (p. 169). But there is no serious difficulty about this because the uncertainty is a matter of the factual minor premise: what effects or relations does a particular action have for ourselves or others? This kind of uncertainty does not affect the issue of the self-evidence of moral principles.

The case is different, however, when we find that moral principles themselves 'interfere' (p. 167). This is a serious objection to Price's view that they are self-evident. If they 'oppose each other in particular cases' and some 'cancel' others, then they cannot be self-evident in the same way as mathematical axioms. Price seems to think that he has disposed of this difficulty by pointing out that we often have difficulty in determining whether quantities are equal or unequal, identical or different (p. 168 n.). This, however, must always be either because our sight is defective (if we are trying to discern equality or identity by empirical observation) or because we lack the skill to do the appropriate mathematical or logical calculation (if it is formal equality or identity that we are trying to discern). It will *never* be because the axioms of geometry, in a given case, conflict. Now, if the comparison of mathematics and moral judgements seems to us just a useful analogy, as far as it goes, the fact that it breaks down here is not serious. But if, like Price, we want to believe that the self-evidence of moral judgements proves them to be perceptions of the nature of things, since it is the same kind of self-evidence as that which characterises the *a priori* propositions of mathematics, the fact that there is this fundamental difference between them is a very serious objection which would have to be explained. Price does not explain it.

Later intuitionists have endeavoured to get round the difficulty by inventing the notion of an attribute, '*tendency* to be right'.[27] This attribute is one which belongs to an act in virtue of some single feature of it, e.g. being the fulfilment of a promise. It is 'parti-resultant', as distinct from rightness or obligatoriness which is 'toti-resultant'. We are bound to do that act whose prima facie rightness, in those respects in which it is prima facie right, *most outweighs* its prima facie wrongness, in those respects in which it is prima facie wrong.[28] Price does not speak of tendency to be right, but he has this notion of 'weighing' moral principles against each other:

> It is not alone sufficient to satisfy us that an action is to be done, that we know it will be the means of good to others: we are also to consider how it affects ourselves, what it is in regard to justice, and all the other circumstances the case may involve must be taken in, and *weighed*, if we are to form a true judgment concerning it. (p. 170, italics mine.)

The notion of tendency to be right, to which this idea of 'weighing' principles gave rise, was subjected to rigorous criticism by Professor P. F. Strawson.[29] Intuitionists want to have necessary, universal propositions of the form 'All acts which fulfil promises tend as such to be right.' But, as Strawson points out, when we say of objects that they *tend* to have a certain attribute, we are saying that *most* of the particular objects which belong to that class of objects have the attribute; or, if it is one particular object of which we say that it tends to have a certain attribute, we are saying that it has this attribute *more often than not*. 'In all such cases, we are talking of a *class* of things or occasions or events; and saying, not that *all* members of the class have the property of *tending-to-have* a certain characteristic, but that most members of the class do in fact have that characteristic. Nobody would accept the claim that a sentence of the form "*Most As* are *Bs*" expresses a necessary proposition. Is the claim made more plausible by rewriting the proposition in the form "All *As tend* to be *Bs*"?'

II.ii MORAL FITNESS AS 'SUI GENERIS'[30]

Though it may be necessarily true that an act is right, such rightness must not be confused with the truth of necessarily true propositions. Because he believed that moral fitness is a unique kind of suitability, not to be confused with any other, Price criticised Wollaston for defining right as 'signifying truth' and wrong as 'denying truth'. His main criticism was that these expressions cannot be accepted as definitions of virtue because they 'evidently presuppose it' (p. 125). The point is one which Hume had previously made. He accused Wollaston of 'reasoning in a circle', and added: 'A man that is ungrateful to his benefactor, in a manner affirms that he never received any favours from him. But in what manner? Is it because it is his duty to be grateful? But this supposes that there is some antecedent rule of duty and morals.'[31] What does an ungrateful act deny? It denies that the agent has a duty to be grateful. This could only be true, if no favours had been conferred on him. Suppose that favours have, in fact, been conferred. Then the act denies this truth and is therefore wrong. But this way of thinking starts from the assumption that we have a duty to be grateful to benefactors. Calling an act a denial of truth presupposes the antecedent duty which is denied. 'How plain is it,' says Price (p. 126 n.), '. . . that the very thing that gives ground for the application of this language . . . is our perceiving, antecedently to this application, that such a manner of acting, in such circumstances, is *wrong*?'

But he is far from condemning Wollaston's theory out of hand. He only wishes to 'guard against making a wrong application of it'. It has, at least, two merits he thinks: (i) It does well to direct us to 'discover the whole truth with respect to its probable or possible consequences, the circumstances and qualifications of the object, and the relations of the agent' before judging an action, 'for this . . . is what determines its moral nature' (p. 128). (ii) It represents morality as an aspect of necessary truth, as '*founded* in truth and reason; . . . equally necessary and immutable, and perceived by the same power, with the natural proportions and essential differences of things' (ibid.). But morality is a peculiar species of necessary truth, thinks Price, and Wollaston's mistake was to have attempted to identify it with the entire genus. 'Truth . . . is a term of wider extent than right. . . . The man, who builds according to the principles of geometry, acts as agreeably to truth, and he who should transgress the rules of architecture, as much violates truth, as he who acts agreeably to the duty of gratitude, or contrary to it. But in the former of these instances, the conformity to truth is not virtue but skill; the deflection from it is not vice, but ignorance or folly' (p. 127 n., quoting Adams). The fitness of a right act to its appropriate situation must be clearly differentiated from the fitness of a proposition to the fact, or facts, which render it true. Two alternative conclusions are possible, namely (i) that moral judgements are judgements of an entirely different kind from statements of fact, or (ii) that moral judgements are propositions concerning facts of a peculiar, 'non-natural' kind. Price drew the latter conclusion, but we have already seen reason to reject it.

III. CRITICISM OF PRICE

The criticism of the claim to know by intuition, set out at the end of the last chapter, all applies to the particular case of claiming to know moral truths by intuition. This criticism can be levelled at Price's moral epistemology. Certain other criticisms can be brought against his intuitionism and to some of these I shall now turn.

III.i THE CONNEXION BETWEEN MORAL JUDGEMENTS AND ACTION

Price did not offer a satisfactory account of the logical connexion between moral judgement and action. Some moral judgements, at least, purport to guide action and the notion of a moral judgement cannot be understood without taking account of this fact. 'Right' is a term used in sentences which support answers to the practical question, What shall I do?

> Do X!
> Why?
> Because X is right.

So used, 'right' is, as Price says (p. 104), synonymous with 'fit', and 'fit' may be taken to mean that the action fits the situation.

It is not necessary, however, to regard this relation as simply a two-term one which we perceive by intuition, as Price did. It admits of further analysis. Careful attention to the use of 'right' shows that there are two things which the word always, in Professor P. H. Nowell-Smith's useful phrase, 'contextually implies',[32] namely (i) that the act which is called right conforms to a rule or principle, or set of rules or principles, concerning the kind of act which fits the given kind of situation; (ii) that the effects of conformity to this rule or principle will be in accordance with the purpose of the person for whom the act is said to be right. The moral and non-moral uses of 'right' or 'fit' both have the same logical features, a point which Price may be claimed to have, in some sense, realised, since he says that both are 'equally undefinable' (p. 104). Both uses imply (i) and (ii). Consider the following illustration.

A is a rich man who, while driving home from a party, has knocked down a poor man, B. A is awaiting trial. B, meanwhile, lies seriously ill; he has been injured in such a way that his best, and indeed only, hope of recovery is an operation by a certain surgeon, S, who specialises in his kind of case. But this would mean travelling to S's hospital, which is in Switzerland, and paying S's fee, which is very high. B cannot afford it and his relations have no means of raising the money. A is filled with remorse for causing B this injury. So strong is his sense of guilt that he cannot sleep or eat. He feels strongly inclined to go to B's family and offer them the money to pay for the operation by S. So he consults various advisers. We will call the action which he feels strongly inclined to perform X. He tells each of them about X and then asks, 'What shall I do?' The first is his lawyer, but he says, 'Don't do X. The right thing to do in a case like this is to leave well alone. If you go to see B's people, much more if you offer them money, prosecuting counsel will make this out to be an admission of liability on your part.' Next, A consults his doctor, telling him of his sleeplessness and loss of appetite and saying that he feels he will only be well if he does X. 'I don't think you need do that,' says the doctor. 'The right thing for you to do is to take this tonic and these pills. If you take them, you'll find that you can soon sleep and eat again.' Finally A consults his priest, a most unworldly man, who says, 'Certainly you should do X. The right thing for you to do is to obey your generous and compassionate instincts. Do all you can for B!'

In each case the course of action suggested by A's advisers and called right, implied: (i) A reference to a certain principle, or principles, of action deemed appropriate to the given situation. Those of the lawyer were principles of legal procedure; those of the doctor, principles of medical science; and those of the priest, principles of Christian ethics as he understood them. (ii) An assumption as to A's purpose. The lawyer assumed that he wanted to be acquitted at the trial; the doctor that he wanted to get well; the priest that he wanted to do what was in accordance with a Christian ideal of behaviour.

The point is that, whichever use of the predicate 'right' we were to take, we should find that there are peculiarities about its logical behaviour which purely descriptive predicates do *not* display. It would be, to borrow another useful phrase of Nowell-Smith's, 'logically odd'[33] to say 'This act is right but don't do it!' Of course, the lawyer in our illustration might have said something like this, but if he had done so, we should have to assume that he had, so to speak, stepped out of the role of lawyer half-way through the sentence and assumed the role of, say, moralist. His meaning would then be: this act will safeguard your legal interests best, but it would be morally better not to do it. But so long as he – and, of course, the same would apply to the doctor and the priest – stays within one role, it is logically odd for him to say, 'This act is right, but don't do it!' This logical oddness would not, however, be felt in the case of any purely descriptive predicate. It is logically possible for the lawyer, doctor or priest to have said 'This act is Y, but don't do it!', where Y describes some fact concerning this act, because a purely factual predicate does not imply anything about the purpose of the agent or the principles of action which would lead to the achievement of that purpose in the given situation. A doctor, for instance, could say, 'This act will cause you to live longer, but don't do it!' and, though this would strike us as a very unusual thing for a doctor to say, we can conceive of circumstances in which it would not be at all odd, e.g. if he were treating a patient with a painful, incurable disease. In such a case, some might object to this advice on moral grounds, but no one could object to it on logical: it makes perfectly good sense. The predicate 'right' differs from any such factual predicate just because it does not leave the questions of purpose and principles open in the same way.

A moral judgement is one from which something follows, at least in some cases, concerning what is to be *done*. Professor R. M. Hare has pointed out that some such definition as the following seems to be justified: a judgement of the form 'X is right' is a practical value-judgement if, and only if, the person making it realises that, if he assents to the judgement, he must also assent to the command, 'Do X!'[34] If this definition is accepted, then 'X is right' entails 'Do X!' in a strictly analytic sense. If, however, the suggested definition is rejected, as begging the question, our appeal can only be to the ordinary use of language. When a speaker says 'X is right, but don't do X!' he is not, apart from some such definition as that given, contradicting himself in a formal sense, but he is saying something which is logically odd and requires further explanation. We should want the speaker to say more; we should feel that more needed to be said, that the matter could not be left there. In this way the connexion between practical value-judgements and imperatives seems to be 'enshrined in the logic of language'.[35]

It is this connexion, however, of which no explanation is forthcoming in Price's moral philosophy. The latter purports to be an account of how we come to know what it is right to do. It says that, through intellectual intuition, we apprehend a certain property which belongs to certain actions. By this intuition, that is, we perceive a certain *fact* about an action, namely that it has the property of rightness. We perceive that something *is* the case. But from such a perception, for reasons already given, we cannot derive an imperative to action. It makes no difference if the property referred to by 'right' is called non-natural. The only escape from this dilemma for the intuitionist would be to claim that by '*X* is right' he is only saying in other words '*X* is an act which it is right to *do*.' But this is no way out really, because it takes us back to the question which intuitionism claims to have answered: how do we come to know what it is right to do?

III.ii. THE MEANING OF MORAL LANGUAGE

Price was inhibited by a theory of meaning to which most moral philosophers would no longer subscribe. This is the theory that the meaning of language is that to which it refers. Since 'right' does not refer to any natural property, and since its use in sentences like 'What produces happiness is right' is patently meaningful, it follows – given the referential theory – that there must (logically) be some non-natural property to which it refers. This is the view which Price took. But this view implies that the meaning of 'right' is fundamentally *descriptive*: that to say that *X* is right is to *state a fact* about *X*. And the difficulty which we were noting at the end of the last subsection is how it can ever follow from the fact that something *is* the case that anything *ought to be done*. Moral judgements do guide actions, at least on occasion, and cannot be understood if this logical fact about them is ignored. But how can they guide actions if their meaning is simply referential, descriptive, fact-stating? Not until they broke free from the referential theory of meaning were moral philosophers able to give a satisfactory account of the essentially prescriptive, or action-guiding, character of moral judgements.[36]

It was this 'referential' conception of meaning which Wittgenstein criticised so effectively in his *Philosophical Investigation*.[37] He argued for another conception of meaning, namely that 'the meaning of a word is its use in the language'. In order to understand a sentence, we must put it into its appropriate 'language-game', i.e. its appropriate 'whole, consisting of a language and the actions into which it is woven'. 'Look at the sentence as an instrument, and at its sense as its employment,' said Wittgenstein. I cannot here go into detailed exposition and criticism of his views.[38] I refer to them only because of the influence which they have had on moral philosophers. The latter have come to ask, not 'To what properties do moral words refer?' but 'What jobs does moral language do?' Their answers to this question are complicated, but whatever this job is said to be – commending, grading, persuading, guiding, or any other of the expressions which seem appropriate to what goes on when men judge or argue in moral terms – the point emerges that this seems to be a *different* job from describing. Hare put the point thus: 'If "*P* is a good picture" is held to mean the same as "*P* is a picture and *P* is *C*", then it will become impossible to commend pictures for being *C*; it will be possible only to say that they are *C*. It is important to realise that this difficulty has nothing to do with the particular example I have chosen. It is not because we have chosen the wrong defining characteristics; it is because, whatever defining characteristics we choose, this objection arises, that we can no longer commend an object for possessing those characteristics.'[39] And again: 'Now our attack upon naturalistic definitions of "good" was based upon the fact that if it were true that "a good *A*" meant the same as "an *A* which is *C*", then it would be impossible to use the sentence "An *A* which is *C* is good" in order to commend *A*'s which are *C*; for this sentence would be analytic and equivalent to "An *A* which is *C* is *C*". Now it seems clear that we do use sentences of the form "An *A* which is *C* is good" in order to commend *A*'s which are *C*; and that when we do so, we are not doing the same sort of thing as when we say "*A* puppy is a young dog"; that is to say, commending is not the same sort of linguistic activity as defining.' He brings out the difference between defining and commending thus: if asked the meaning of '*A* puppy is a young dog' we could give it by some such reply as: 'The English sentence "If anything is a puppy it is a young dog" is analytic.' But, if asked the meaning of 'An *A* which is *C* is good', we most certainly could not rewrite it: 'The English sentence "An *A* which is *C* is good" is analytic.' For the latter sentence could not be used for commending, whereas the former sentence – 'An *A* which is *C* is good' – is used for that purpose.[40]

The point which Hare is making in terms of *use* is substantially the same as that which Price made in terms of *referent*. Price conceived of 'right' as referring to a simple or indefinable property. If you define 'right' in naturalistic or supernaturalistic terms – if you take it as equivalent in meaning to 'producing happiness' (or whatever) – then you change or lose the meaning of the sentence concerned. The importance of Hare's way of making the point, as against Price's, lies in the fact that the former makes possible some explanation of the logical connexion between moral judgements and action as the latter did not.[41]

It should not be assumed, however, that words or sentences divide themselves neatly into those which describe and those which prescribe. If any reader doubts this, let him open a newspaper. He will find, I think, that anyone writing about human activities uses a host of words which are both descriptive and evaluative. Take, two examples: 'To Mr Heath's penetrating analysis of Government policy, Mr Wilson offered a cunning reply' and 'After Mr Heath's over-simplified account of a complicated matter, Mr Wilson offered a shrewd defence of Government policy.' Are we to classify 'penetrating', 'cunning', 'over-simplified' and 'shrewd' as descriptive or evaluative words? No doubt a neutral account of what Mr Heath and Mr Wilson in fact said, to which both commentators would agree, could be given; and then their evaluations differentiated from this factual description.

But there seem to be cases where it is impossible to differentiate in this way between the facts being described and the evaluation being placed upon them. Take, as an example, the sentence '*A* is *B*'s father'. It seems to be false to say that this means simply '*A* took part in certain biological processes which resulted in *B*'s birth.' As Mr A. I. Melden has pointed out, a locution like 'I have not been a father to my son' is not necessarily self-contradictory nor absurd. This shows that the concept of 'father' cannot (logically) be identified with the biological concept of 'male parent'. Melden goes on:

> To make such an identification is to impoverish the concept of 'father', to create a mystery concerning the connection between 'giving special consideration to one's father' and 'doing what is morally required' and, in consequence, to pave the way for the

desperate attempts to bridge a gap, created by our own misunderstanding, between these descriptions by looking for some general premise 'One ought to give special consideration to one's father'.... So to attempt to reconstruct the moral reasoning from 'Here is an opportunity to give special consideration to my father (or parent) to 'I ought to do so' by adding the premise 'One ought to give special consideration to one's father (or parent)' is to stutter. For the moral connection between giving special consideration to one's father (or parent) and doing what is morally required does not wait upon the introduction of a further premise, but already exists in the familiar moral use of the crucial term 'father' (or 'parent').... A paradigm case of a father is a male parent who plays his social and moral role with respect to his offspring in the circumstances of family life.[42]

It seems impossible, in the case of 'A is B's father', to indicate a certain fact, or facts, to which this sentence refers, the question whether or not these facts constitute a ground for the moral judgement 'B ought to help A' being left open. Consider the following conversation.

'B ought to help A.'
'Why?'
'A is B's father.'
'What has that to do with it?'

This latter reply would strike us as odd. Why? Is it simply because there is a very well-established convention in our society that children ought to help their fathers? In some sense, yes. But some philosophers would insist that this is not like saying that there is a well-established convention in our society that motorists ought to drive on the left-hand side of the road. The meaning of the expression 'driving on the left-hand side of the road' can be stated fully, quite apart from the judgement that this is what motorists ought to do. But the point is – if Melden and those who think like him are correct – that the meaning of 'father' cannot be stated apart from the judgement that children ought to help their fathers. It is 'logically odd' to say 'A is your father but you ought not to help him' in the way that, as we saw in the last subsection, it is logically odd to say 'X is right but don't do it!' The latter is odd, not because there is a convention in our society that what is right ought to be done, such that someone could speak of 'what is right' and *mean* by this what the rest of us mean by it, while dissenting from the convention that what is right ought to be done. That X ought to be done is part of what it means to say that X is right; part of what you are doing *in* saying 'X is right' is judging that X ought to be done, advising or recommending that it be done. That *X* ought to be done is part, to use an expression of J. L. Austin's, of the 'illocutionary force'[43] of '*X* is right.' Similarly, in the case of '*A* is *B*'s father', it is argued, one cannot separate out a factual, descriptive element which exhausts the meaning of this sentence (e.g. *A* took part in certain biological processes which resulted in *B*'s birth; *A* was married to *B*'s mother; *A* supported *B* when young, etc.) but which leaves open the question 'Ought *B* to help *A*?' In 'father' the descriptive and evaluative elements of meaning appear to be inextricably mixed.

Three points are relevant here:

(i) We could differentiate between: (*a*) using '*A* is *B*'s father' as what has been called an 'engaged participant' – i.e. as any normal member of our society, taking part in ordinary conversation, would use it – and (*b*) giving an account of how this sentence, or the word 'father' which occurs in it, is used in our society, as a social anthropologist might conceivably do.[44] It would then be true to say that the social anthropologist could (logically) talk about 'father' in the way supposed without committing himself personally to any moral value judgements; but, of course, an engaged participant could not use 'father' without so doing.

(ii) It must be understood, however, that thus to differentiate giving the necessary and sufficient conditions for the use of 'father' in our society from actually using the word is not the same thing as differentiating between the *fact* of fatherhood and some moral *value* judgement which is consequential upon this fact. We say '*A* is *B*'s father'; and this is a (true or false) statement of fact. The difficulty is to conceive of how we could state this fact without, in so doing, meaning among other things that *B* ought to help *A*. The distinction we drew in (i) does not solve this problem. '*A* is *B*'s father' *means the same*, whether one is using it as an engaged participant or discussing it as a social anthropologist.

(iii) It is true, of course, that the meaning of such a sentence as '*A* is *B*'s father' may change. Consider the following conversation for a moment.

'*X* ought not to argue with *Y*.'
'Why?'
'Because *Y* is *X*'s employer.'
'What has that to do with it?'

This latter reply would not, I think, strike many of us as logically odd; but it may well have seemed so to our grandparents. 'Employer' does not mean what it once did: it has lost some of its illocutionary force. It is conceivable that the meaning of 'father' should also change in time (indeed, it has done so in the past). The day may come when it no longer strikes men as odd to think that *A* being *B*'s father has nothing to do with whether *B* ought to help *A* or not. But to say this is not necessarily to say that there is a hard core of factual or descriptive meaning to the word 'father' which remains constant, and certain moral judgements consequential upon these facts which may change from age to age. There may be such a morally neutral hard core to 'male parent' but not to 'father'. What Melden called 'his moral and social role' belongs just as much to the core of meaning when we call someone a 'father' as his being a male parent.

Given these three points, there has been some controversy among modern philosophers as to how the logical characteristics, which we have been noting, of words like 'father' are to be explained. There are two schools of thought. According to one – the prescriptivists, most notably represented by Hare – we should analyse the statement 'He is your father' in the conversation:

You ought to help him.
Why?
He is your father.

– as an utterance which states certain facts but also incapsulates certain moral evaluations. According to the other school of thought – the descriptivists, of whom Miss Anscombe, Mrs Foot and Professor J. R. Searle are representative – there is no need to allow for any *non-factual*, evaluative element in the analysis of 'He is your father.' The latter simply states a fact. But it is a special kind of fact, namely an institutional one. It is a fact from which certain moral judgements necessarily follow, an 'is' which implies an 'ought'. I have discussed 'institutional facts' and the whole controversy between prescriptivists and descriptivists in my book *Modern Moral Philosophy* (1970), and some of the papers in which they present their conflicting opinions are to be found in my collection *The Is–Ought Question* (1969). All I wish to say here is that the existence of words like 'father' whose meaning in ordinary use seems to be both prescriptive and descriptive, does not immediately invalidate Price's insistence that 'right' cannot be defined in naturalistic or supernaturalistic terms. Descriptivists, by their recognition that 'institutional facts' are a special kind of fact, are taking some note of the *sui generis* character of moral judgements just as are prescriptivists by their insistence on the distinction between prescriptive and descriptive meaning.

III.iii RIGHT AND REASONS WHY

Though he placed such emphasis upon the importance of recognising reason as the moral faculty, Price's account of the relationship between moral judgements and the reasons given for them seems, at least at first blush, to be inadequate. He said that a judgement of right is 'a simple perception, and something ultimately approved for which *no justifying reason* can be assigned' (p. 127, italics mine). This remark raises at least two questions: (i) Did Price recognise the part which 'reasons why' play in moral thinking? and (ii) Did he offer an adequate account of what makes a reason a moral reason? I think the answer to both is that he did not, or not entirely. Any fair answer to either question would have to take account of his moral philosophy as a whole. Here I shall simply try to show: (*a*) that 'reasons why' play a most important part in moral argument, as such, and (*b*) that the question as to what makes a reason a moral reason is a complicated one. All this substantiates my criticism, if nothing more, that Price's account of the relationship between moral judgements and the reasons which are given for them was less than adequate.

The view that no justifying reason can be given for a moral judgement received perhaps its clearest and most uncompromising exposition in H. A. Prichard's article 'Does Moral Philosophy rest on a Mistake?'[45] Moral philosophy has, according to Prichard, attempted to answer the question which most reflective persons eventually put to themselves: is there really a reason why I should act in the ways in which hitherto I have thought that I ought to act? But Prichard believed that the attempt to answer this question had been pointless. If we do know certain acts to be what we ought to do, then what is the point of asking for a reason why we ought to do them? Such an inquiry, thought Prichard, rests on the illusion that it is possible to prove what can only be apprehended directly by an act of moral thinking. He would have compared the question 'Why ought I to keep my promises?' to the question 'Why are things which are equal to the same thing equal to one another?' and claimed that the only answer to both is 'This is so because it is so.'

Intuitionists, such as Price and Prichard, realised, of course, that, before forming a moral judgement, it may often be necessary to do a certain amount of thinking about the facts of the case. Did Jones in fact make a promise to Smith? Can Smith in fact help Jones? etc., etc. Prichard spoke of such questions as 'preliminaries' to appreciating the rightness of an action. That we may have to think about the consequences of alternative courses of action or the relations in which the agent stands to himself or others, before we can decide what it is right for him to do, is a point which most intuitionists would be perfectly prepared to take. But those, at any rate, who think like Prichard or Price would regard such reflexion upon the facts of the case as a kind of thinking which is logically quite independent of, and distinct from, the *moral* thinking by which we form judgements as to what ought or ought not to be done. Prichard called it 'merely a process of general and not of moral thinking'. This reduces moral thinking to a matter of apprehending certain truths by intuition; and any claim to know what is morally right or wrong, etc. in that way is open to all the objections which, as we saw above,[46] can be brought against any claim to know by intuition.

But even if we waived all such objections, it would still be remarkable to find Price saying, as he does, that 'no justifying reason' can be given for a moral judgement. For one characteristic which seems to differentiate moral judgements from other, not altogether dissimilar, utterances, such as expressions of taste or commands, is the fact that, in the case of moral judgements, it is natural and meaningful to ask 'Why?' as it is not in the other cases mentioned.[47] If, for instance, somebody, on tasting whisky, exclaimed 'Ugh!' it would be odd to say to him 'Why?' Of course, if we knew him to be a seasoned drinker, we might conclude from his exclamation that there was something wrong with the whisky and ask him why he did not like it. But the mere expression of a dislike for whisky is not something for which we should normally require a man to give a reason. Again, in a context where commands are uttered, such as when a platoon is going into action, if the commanding officer cried 'Forward!' it would be considered inappropriate, to say the least, for anyone in his platoon to ask 'Why?' But if somebody says that drinking whisky or going to war, or anything else for that matter, is morally wrong, it is not in the least odd to ask him why he says so. Giving justifying reasons, therefore, seems to be an essential part of moral discourse, and we must now try to see more clearly what conditions a 'reason why' needs to fulfil in order to play a part in moral discourse, and just what part it does play.

It has been said of the reasons which are given for moral judgements that they are 'practical from the start'.[48] One could revise this to read 'moral from the start'. Suppose I say 'Capital punishment is wrong' and when asked 'Why?' I reply, 'Because it requires one man to take another's life.' This is a true statement of fact concerning capital punishment. But there is a vast, perhaps an infinite, number of true statements of fact which I could make – or could have made – about capital punishment – e.g. that it is usually administered early in the morning, that it is administered to more men than women, that it is always administered before witnesses, etc., etc. Why do I give, as a reason for its wrongness, the fact that it requires one man to take another's life rather than any of these other facts concerning it? The answer, of course, is: because I consider it wrong for one man to take another's life. This latter moral judgement is implicit in the factual reason which I have given for saying that capital punishment is wrong. Justifying reasons, which are true statements of fact, can indeed be given for particular moral judgements; but we can infer from any such factual reason a moral principle to which the speaker is committed and which accounts for his belief that his reason is a good one.

Once a reason for a moral judgement has been given, as some philosophers have pointed out,[49] it is characteristic of moral discourse that this reason should be universalised. In terms of the example just given, if I say that capital punishment is wrong because it requires one man to take another's life, you, if you are in favour of capital punishment, may well reply in some such way as this: 'But in war men take the lives of others. Are you a pacifist?' Suppose that I am not. Your question puts me in a dilemma. I am opposed to capital punishment on the ground that it requires one man to take another's life, but I am not opposed to war in all circumstances, even though it also requires men to take the lives of others. If I want to avoid the charge of being inconsistent – i.e. unreasonable – in my moral judgement, I must now give some reason why, although capital punishment is wrong, war is not, or at least not always, wrong. I will probably say something like this: 'War may be necessary for national survival, but capital punishment never is.' If you wish to continue the argument, you will try to think of some activity which requires, or may require, one man to take another's life and the cessation of which would not endanger national survival, but of which you think I will approve. A sport in which people occasionally get killed, e.g. boxing, may come to your mind. If so, you ask me, 'Are you also against boxing?' If I am not, then once again I am landed in apparent inconsistency and must try to get out of it by referring to some fact about boxing which makes it different from capital punishment. And so on. What I have been doing all this time, it will be apparent, is defining more precisely the reason which I originally gave for thinking capital punishment wrong – 'because it requires one man to take another's life *and* its cessation would not endanger national survival *and* . . . '. If there comes a point at which I cannot define it any more precisely in order to escape one of your counter-instances (i.e. an activity to which you refer and which, I must admit, I do not think wrong, but which, if I were consistent in apply-ing the reason which I have spelled out for disapproving of capital punishment, I would think wrong), then I shall be forced to admit that the reason which I gave for my original moral judgement (capital punishment is wrong) was not a good reason.

'A good reason', as I have just used that expression, seems simply to mean a reason which I can consistently apply. The question which now arises is whether or not this is all that there is to being a good reason, or to being reasonable, in morals. Are these *simply* matters of consistency? No one would deny that part of what is meant by having a good reason for, or being reasonable in, moral judgement is having some ground for one's judgement to which one is prepared to adhere con-sistently in argument. But it does not necessarily follow that being consistently adhered to is *enough* to make a reason a good one in moral discourse. Suppose a man said that he thought it right to let his wife and children go short of food so that he could spend the money thereby saved on gambling, and when asked why he thought this, replied, 'Because I enjoy gambling.' In argument he may be prepared to stick unshakably to the position that, if he enjoys anything, it is right. But does that make his reason for thinking what he was doing right a good one?

It could be – and indeed is – said that just as those who disapproved of our man's gambling would have a reason which, to repeat an ex-pression used above, is 'moral from the start' (that his gambling results in the unnecessary hunger of his wife and children – which implies that those who give this reason consider it wrong to cause unnecessary hunger), so our man himself has a *moral* reason for thinking it right to do what he does (that he enjoys his gambling – which implies that he thinks whatever he enjoys to be morally permissible). The difference between him and those who disapprove of him is, on this view, simply the fact that he and they have different moral principles. And that is *all*. One cannot say that they have a good reason for their opinion, but he has not for his; much less, that theirs is a truly moral judgement, but his is not.

Against such an account of the matter, Mr G. J. Warnock for one, in his recent *Contemporary Moral Philosophy* (1967), has pointed out that it implies the view that our gambler and those who disapprove of him have not only decided what moral opinion to hold, but *also* what shall constitute a reason for holding it; and this view seems to Warnock to be clearly untenable. It leaves us, he writes, 'not only, as it were, free to decide on the evidence, but also free to decide what evidence is'. And he draws out what appear to him to be the absurd implications of this position thus:

> I do not, it seems, decide that flogging is wrong because I *am* against cruelty; rather, I decide that flogging is wrong because I *decide to be* against cruelty. And what, if I did make that decision, would be my ground for making it? That I am opposed to the deliberate infliction of pain? No – rather that I *decide to be* opposed to it. And so on. Now there are people, I think, whose moral views do seem to be formed and defended in this way – who, as one might say, not only make up their own minds, but also make up their own evidence; who pick and choose not only on the question what is right or wrong, but also on the question what are even to be admitted as relevant considerations. But such a person, surely, is not so much a model as a menace; not an exemplar of moral reasoning, but a total abstainer from any serious concern with reason.[50]

It may be argued, however, that, even by the criterion of universalisability alone, the opinion of our man that his excessive gambling is right because he enjoys it can be shown to be neither reasonable nor moral. If his reason, 'Because I enjoy it', is universalised, then he will have to concede that this implies that excessive gambling is right, even if it is his wife and children who engage in it and he who suffers the consequent neglect, given only that they enjoy what they are doing. He cannot accept this implication and so he cannot adhere any longer to the view that his gambling is right because he enjoys it. But in precisely what sense is 'cannot' being used here?

Are these 'cannot's' empirical? If so, the claim is plainly false. It would admittedly be unusual to find anybody who would think it right for someone else to waste, on such an activity as gambling, money which was essential to his own well-being, though it is not unknown for indulgence of loved ones to go even to these limits. If we take some issues such as apartheid for an example, we could certainly find people who would say that, since this is morally right, then, if they themselves were not white, it would be right for them to suffer the restrictions which non-whites suffer under apartheid.

Are the 'cannot's' logical? Surely not. 'I approve morally of X and I think X will be to my disadvantage' is not self-contradictory. 'A approves morally of X' does not mean 'A thinks that X will not be to his disadvantage.' It is manifest that people have approved morally of a host of things which have been highly uncomfortable. And whatever may be meant by calling their opinions nonsensical, it cannot be that the statement of any of these opinions constitutes a formal contradiction.

But we are concerned with *reasons for doing* actions. Is it not plausible to argue that a reason such as that given by our excessive gambler, if universalised in the way supposed – i.e. if applied in an instance where the roles of the man and his wife and children are reversed – ceases to be a reason for doing the action? As Professor K. Baier has expressed it:

> We must remember what sort of a 'game' the game of reasoning is. We ask the question 'What shall I do?' or 'What is the best course of action?' . . . The criteria of 'best course of action' are linked with what we mean by 'the good life'. In evaluating a life, one of the criteria of merit which we use is how much satisfaction and how little frustration there is in that life. Our very purpose in 'playing the reasoning game' is to maximize satisfactions and minimize frustrations. Deliberately to frustrate ourselves and to minimize satisfaction would certainly be to go counter to the very purpose for which we deliberate and weigh the pros and cons. These criteria are therefore linked with the very purpose of the activity of reasoning. Insofar as we enter on that 'game' at all, we are therefore bound to accept these criteria. . . . Our conclusion must be that there is a correct use of the word 'mad' and that people who prefer whatever they do not enjoy doing to whatever they do differ from normal people in just such fundamental and undesirable respects as would make the word 'mad' correctly applicable to them.[51]

Now, it is perfectly true that if X constitutes a reason for A's doing Y, then X must necessarily indicate how Y will serve some purpose, or satisfy some want, which A has. If X does not fulfil this condition, then we cannot see what would be meant by saying that it was a reason for A's doing Y. But A can be 'satisfied' or 'frustrated' – to use Baier's terms – in many different ways. One is by seeing certain ideals realised or unrealised respectively. Given that A approves morally of apartheid, then surely it makes sense to say that A is satisfied *in this respect* where apartheid obtains, independently of who is white and who is not. That he himself is white, if it is the case, is purely fortuitous, so far as his moral approval is concerned. The fact that X safeguards apartheid will constitute for A, as an approver of apartheid, a reason for doing X, and whether his own skin is white or black will be as far beside the point as whether his hair is white or black.

If we are to allow that there can be good reasons for a moral judgement, then, it seems that more is required than merely that such reasons should be consistently applied. But what more? The following considerations seem to be relevant to any attempt to answer this difficult question.

Moral discourse may be said to imply that those who engage in it have purposes[52] – i.e. there are ends or states of affairs which they either want to bring into being or to prevent. It does so in at least two ways: (i) if men had no purpose, i.e. if they were completely unconcerned about what is or is not the case, then they would have no use for, and see no point in, language which grades, evaluates, advises, exhorts, recommends, or does any of the other jobs for which moral terms are used; and (ii) if a man, speaking sincerely, applies a certain criterion, e.g. 'Does this cause unnecessary hunger?' in forming a moral judgement, and condemns whatever is being judged if the answer is 'Yes', then we can safely say that, in some sense, he wants to see a state of affairs which would conform to his criterion, e.g. a society in which there is no unnecessary hunger. It is true, of course, that he may not want this in the sense of *feeling* a positive desire to see such a state of affairs; he may be under persistent temptation to act in a way which is inconsistent with his moral judgements; but nevertheless, assuming his sincerity, he will be a man who, in the ways which are open to him tries to bring such a state of affairs into existence rather than any alternative. At the least, we shall be able to say that he wants it in the sense that such is his purpose.

Men have the purposes which they *do* have. It is, beyond doubt, always logically possible for them to have other purposes than those which they have; and it may be that their purposes vary from man to man, or that, in society as a whole, men's purposes undergo certain changes in the course of time. Nevertheless, allowing for variation in the case of many human purposes, and possible development in the case of all, it is not, I think, entirely meaningless to speak of 'the purpose or purposes which men have in common', or of 'what all men want'; certainly, if we are thinking of the normal members of some given society and perhaps even when we are thinking of mankind as a whole. Now, as Warnock shows us,[53] this places some limitation upon what can be *understood* in moral discourse. Suppose we met a man who said that he had decided that he ought to give up sex, or drink, or something else which he enjoyed, and when asked 'Why?' replied simply, 'Because I shall be miserable without it.' Should we understand this man? Perhaps there is some explanation for his remark – e.g. he has wronged someone and feels that he must punish himself. But in default of any such explanation, surely his answer would not seem to us to provide a reason for his moral judgement. Equally, I think, if someone said that the reason why he ought to do a certain action was that it would cause certain other people pain, without any further explanation, then we should find what he said unintelligible. Only where what is judged obligatory serves, or might serve, some purpose or purposes (such as the happiness or welfare of ourselves or others, or both) which we pursue, or at least with which we can sympathise, do we see the point of the moral judgement. There is, then, this limitation on what may be said to constitute a good reason, i.e. what is intelligible to us as argument, in morals.

It may, however, be said that a reason offered for a moral judgement is intelligible to us because we have *decided* that this is what 'having a reason for a moral judgement' shall mean. But if moral reasons are grounded in purposes, as I have suggested, then the point must be taken that, in the sense in which I have used 'purpose' – a state of affairs which we want to bring into being or prevent – we are not free, or at least not completely free, to choose which purposes we will have. What sense would it make to say that I have decided to want to be healthy, or to want to see my children well fed? These are things which I do want, but not which I *decide* to want.

Nevertheless, the view that the concept of a good reason in morals is grounded in 'common purposes' or 'what all men want' is still open to the following objection. There are two things which could be said of any given man's conception of 'happiness' or 'well-being' or any other such thing in which moral reasons are said to be grounded: (i) it may well be different from that of many other men, whom one would not therefore call unreasonable; and (ii) whether it is or not, it will necessarily represent an evaluative selection from the wants which man in fact has and the purposes which he could in fact pursue. To take examples at random, compare what happiness or well-being would mean to Aristotle's 'great-souled' man, J. S. Mill's man with 'a sense

of dignity' and Nietzsche's 'noble' man respectively. So, in the end, do
we not have to come back to the point from which we started? The
view which we set out to dispose of is that men decide, not only
whether an act is morally right or wrong, but also what shall constitute
reasons for its being so. We contended that good reasons for moral
judgements are grounded, not in our decisions, but in the fact of certain
wants or purposes which men have. But in the light of what has just
been said about happiness, well being, etc., it would seem that what
makes a reason a good one depends, not, or not simply, upon what the
facts are, but upon the evaluation of certain facts (e.g. the fact that I have
a desire to see my children well fed) as more *worthy* (that is, they are to
be taken as a basis for determining what is right or wrong) than certain
other facts (e.g. that I have a desire to spend the money which it takes
to feed them on gambling, or books or whatever). Are we not back at
the view that we decide, not only what is right or wrong, but also what
shall be a reason for anything being right or wrong?

Against what he calls 'the charge of circularity' – by which I take
him to mean an argument such as that which I have just set out –
Warnock says forthrightly:

> Nevertheless, I believe it is defensible to hazard . . . the view that
> the charge of circularity . . . is not likely to prove effective. There
> are, I believe, two grounds for saying this. First, I believe that we all
> have, and should not let ourselves be bullied out of, the conviction
> that at least some questions as to what is good or bad for people,
> what is harmful or beneficial, are not in any serious sense matters of
> opinion. That it is a bad thing to be tortured or starved, humiliated
> or hurt, is not an opinion: it is a fact. That it is better for people to be
> loved and attended to, rather than hated or neglected, is again a plain
> fact, not a matter of opinion. We find here no doubt a very wide
> penumbra of indeterminacy in which judgments must be made and
> may diverge, in which opinions and attitudes may differ irreducibly:
> but who believes, except for bad theoretical reasons, that there are no
> facts at all? But second – and this perhaps is the sort of point which it
> will be felt less disreputable for a philosopher to urge – the charge
> of circularity will stand, *not* if the supposed fundamental content of
> morality proves itself to be not independent of judgment and
> opinion, but only if it can be shown itself to involve the exercise of
> *moral* judgment. Those issues in terms of which morality is to be
> defined, if the definition is not to be merely circular, do not have to
> be, without remainder, issues of absolutely neutral determinable fact:
> no more is required for theoretical purposes than that they should

not themselves be issues of moral judgment. And surely it is reasonable to suppose that this condition is satisfied. That a certain person,
or a certain community of persons, would, if certain things were
done, be in a better or worse condition, advantaged or disadvantaged,
helped or harmed, may be partly or even wholly a matter of judgment; but it is, I submit, quite clear that it is not always, not wholly
or necessarily, a matter of *moral* judgment. But if so there is from the
point of view of moral theory, no reason to object to the project of
defining morality at least partly in such terms.[54]

I am not sure that his first 'ground' gets us far. It would certainly
seem odd to suppose that I have decided that 'it will result in one's
children being well fed' is a good reason for saying that an action is
right. But it does not seem so odd to contend that certain wants or
purposes constitute what seems to us the ground of good reasons in
morals *simply because* the prevailing convention in this matter is what
it is. Men have decided that this is what 'having a reason' shall mean
in morals and we take it for granted. We take it so much for granted
that if anyone offers a 'reason' for what he thinks right or wrong which
is not so grounded, we find his remarks unintelligible.

But on behalf of Warnock's view it might be asked: is this to concede any more than that the moral discourse is what it is? Is it to do
more than define 'moral?' In Wittgenstein's words, ,'This language-
game is played.'[55] When Warnock says that its being a bad thing to be
tortured or a good thing for people to be loved are *facts*, he need not
mean – and I doubt if he does mean – more than this. To say that a
game *could* be invented with rules *different* from those of the moral
language-game is – like saying that men are *not compelled* to think or
speak morally – nothing to the purpose. If you *are* going to think or
argue morally, then this being what it *means* to think or argue morally,
this is how you must do it. Otherwise what you say will not be
recognisable as moral discourse.

This brings us to Warnock's second 'ground'. If I understand him
correctly, what he is pointing out here could be taken to mean that
anyone's conception of happiness or well-being may depend – indeed
necessarily does depend – on opinions or beliefs which he holds on
questions of natural, or possibly supernatural, fact. For example, a
Christian's conception of what constitutes happiness or well-being will,
to some degree, be contingent upon his belief that man exists, here and
hereafter, in relationship with God. And quite apart from such metaphysical beliefs, every moralist has to come to a decision about some

issues of psychological or physical fact which have a bearing on his moral judgements. If, for instance, he thinks it to be the case that no one can, as a matter of psychological fact, have pre-marital sexual intercourse or be sexually promiscuous or whatever, without suffering consciously or subconsciously from a guilt complex, then this will to some extent determine his moral judgements upon these activities. But the point to stress is that what is subject to decision here is *not* what kind of grounding reasons must have, in order to be good reasons in moral discourse, but *given* the grounding which they *do* have, how are the relevant factual questions to be answered? There is no *moral* point in the question, 'Does this activity cause guilt-complexes?' unless it is taken for granted that men's happiness or well-being is the correct grounding for a moral judgement on the activity under consideration.

It is not, therefore, an argument against the view that moral judgements, to be reasonable and intelligible, must be grounded in 'common purposes' or 'what all men want' or some such matter of fact (difficult though this may be to define precisely) to point out, as some have done, that a moral thinker 'does not believe because he wants but wants because he believes'.[56] This is true, but only provided that we are clear as to the beliefs in question. These are not moral beliefs, as such. To take an example which others have used,[57] a strictly Roman Catholic mother and a scientific humanist will differ about the morality of birth control; and it is perfectly correct to say that this difference is rooted, not simply in wants, but in beliefs. But it is not that the Roman Catholic mother has decided to believe it right to do what will be harmful to families (if, as the scientific humanist says, having too many children is harmful) whereas he has decided not to believe this. They differ in their views about the facts of man's situation. The mother believes that part of that situation is God, who has forbidden birth control and in whose hands the destiny of every one of us rests for time and eternity; the humanist does not believe this. This difference determines, in some degree, what moral judgements they pronounce on birth control. But to admit this is not to concede the 'charge of circularity'.[58]

4

Obligation

PRICE claims, in his introduction to the *Review*, that he is going to treat many of the questions of morality and virtue 'in a manner different from that in which they have been hitherto treated' (p. 11). As Raphael points out, this claim to originality seems to be justified at least so far as his account of the objective content of the moral consciousness is concerned.[1] We will now deal with the latter and some of the questions which it raises.

I. RIGHT AND OUGHT

Price took up the challenge which Hume had thrown down to rationalist philosophers: to show that the connexion between rightness and oughtness is so necessary 'that in every well-disposed mind, it must take place and have its influence'.[2] He says that it will become apparent to anyone who tries to point out the difference between them that they are 'coincident and identical; so far so, that we cannot form a notion of the one, without taking in the other' (p. 105).

Against this, it is, of course, obvious that the two ideas are not, strictly speaking, identical.[3] For one thing, an act may be right, but not obligatory: it may be in my power to show gratitude to a benefactor by a number of alternative actions, all of which would be right, but all of them would not be obligatory. (Indeed, none would: it is not my duty to do a particular one, but any of them.) Again, a distinction may be drawn thus: 'right' may refer us to actions alone, 'ought' always refers us to agents also: I may say of some act, excessive generosity, for instance, that it is right, where I should not be prepared to say that anyone ought to do it. But such cases as these do not really constitute an objection to Price's point. In the former, each act would be right as being the fulfilment of a duty, namely gratitude; in the latter, the act of supererogatory generosity would be right as being the fulfilment of the duty of beneficence. It is still true, as Price said, that the notions of rightness and oughtness, when these words are used ethically, cannot be formed without each 'taking in' the other.

Price deals with the relationships between 'right' and 'ought' from three points of view: (*a*) The obligation to practise virtue is *antecedent* to all laws and independent of all wills. It is not even the fact that God commands it which makes virtue obligatory (pp. 105–6). (*b*) Virtue is a *law* to us, not just a rule: 'obligation, we see, is involved in the very nature of it' (p. 105). Reason perceives the necessary implication of 'ought' by 'right' and, because we are rational beings, reason is our '*natural* and *authoritative* guide' (p. 109). Therefore, when we perceive right or wrong, we know ourselves to be bound to do the former and avoid the latter. (*c*) The question, Why ought I to do right? is 'absurd' (p. 110). It would be self-contradictory to deny that one ought to do what it is right to do.[4]

We must not make the mistake of supposing that the reason-giving clause in 'You ought to do X because X is right' is any less a matter of moral decision than the preceding clause. In rejecting the view that obligation is created by God's will, Price writes: 'For why, upon this supposition, does not *all* will oblige equally? If there be anything which gives the preference to one will above another; that, by the terms, is *moral rectitude*' (p. 111). In selecting God's will as that which creates obligation, we have already made a moral choice. The mere fact that God wills X is not a logically valid reason for regarding oneself (or anyone else) as obliged to do X, unless one has *antecedently* accepted the principle that one ought to do what God wills.

Price was principally concerned to establish the magisterial authority of the moral faculty. It presents us with a *law*. But how is one to account for the overriding authority of conscience? It seemed to Price that the only way is to show that it follows as a matter of logical necessity from 'X is right' that X ought to be done. That it does follow necessarily is what he meant by saying that 'right' and 'ought' are identical and coincidental.

Miss G. E. M. Anscombe has argued that the notion of 'ought' 'only operates in a context of law' and, now that we have left behind the law conception of ethics – as, e.g., in the Stoics, Jews, Christians, Kant – this notion is 'the survival of a concept outside the framework of thought that made it a really intelligible one'.[5] But surely the idea of a law which an agent gives to himself is not unintelligible, if conceived as, in

some sense, the 'voice' of the rational element within him addressed
to the irrational.

Price conceived of 'ought' and 'right', however, not only as grounded in the nature of man as rational, but also in the nature of things. He
shared the desire of other eighteenth-century British moralists to find
a basis for morality which would establish it as a kind of knowledge.
Shaftesbury and Hutcheson, taking their cue from Locke's empiricism,
tried to represent it as a form of sense-perception, comparable to our
empirical observation of the physical world. Price and the rationalists,
under Cartesian influence, believed it to rest upon an intuition of the
nature of things, comparable to that which they believed we have in
mathematics.[6]

II. REASON AND HAPPINESS

Price says that the happiness of all mankind is the object of an 'affection', as distinct from an 'instinct' (p. 69), i.e. a desire which all rational
beings, *qua* rational, feel because it arises necessarily from the nature of
the object. He argues, first, that a 'sensible' being, as such, must desire
his *own* happiness. He writes:

> No being, who knows what happiness and misery are, can be
> supposed indifferent to them, without a plain contradiction. Pain is
> not a *possible* object of *desire*; nor happiness of *aversion*. . . . Then only
> can this happen, when pain can be *agreeable*, and pleasure *disagreeable*;
> that is, when pain can be pleasure; and pleasure, pain. (p. 70)

It would be 'a plain contradiction' to suppose 'sensible beings'
indifferent to pleasure and pain – or desirous of pain and averse to
pleasure – only if this could be shown analytically; if 'sensible' were
defined in some such terms as 'desirous of pleasure and averse to pain',
or 'pleasure' were defined as 'agreeable to sensible beings' and 'pain'
as 'disagreeable to sensible beings'. But, in fact, it is surely possible to
conceive of sensible beings who are indifferent to pleasure and pain, or
who desire painful sensations and avoid pleasant ones. The fact that we
feel pleasure and pain is one fact about us; the fact that we seek sensations of the former kind and avoid those of the latter is another. There
is no logical implication between the two. In point of fact, sensible
creatures, as we know them, frequently do desire pain. The penitent
sinner, for instance, may sincerely wish to suffer for his sins. To this the
reply may be offered that the pain in such instances is agreeable to the

sinner and therefore is really pleasure. But this ignores the distinction which Butler drew,[7] and of which Price himself makes use in criticising psychological hedonism (pp. 74–6), between the object of desire and the satisfaction which comes from achieving it.[8] While it would be obviously false to say, in any given case, that a feeling of achievement is not, as such, satisfying, it is perfectly possible for the object of desire, which is achieved, to be pain.

Price now goes on to argue that a reasonable being must desire, not only his own happiness, but also that of others. He writes:

> Let us . . . put the case of a being *purely* reasonable. . . . The nature of *happiness* also would engage him to choose and desire it for *himself*. And is it credible that, at the same time, he would be necessarily indifferent about it for *others*? Would the nature of things, upon this supposition, be consistent? Would he not be capable of seeing, that the happiness of others is to them as important as his is to him; and that it is in itself equally valuable and desirable, whoever possesses it? (pp. 70–1)

The argument appears to be that a reasonable being would desire his own happiness because he would see that the desire for it follows *necessarily* from the nature, i.e. the real definitions, of 'sensible being' and of 'pleasure' and 'pain'. Being a deduction from the natures of things and beings, the connexion here is universal. It makes no difference whether the sensible being is oneself or another; or whether the pleasure and pain are one's own or another's. What can be said for this argument? The last sentence of the foregoing quotation from Price recalls J. S. Mill's notorious deduction of 'desirable' from 'desired',[9] though Price did not commit the fallacy quite so crudely as Mill is taken to have done. He believed that reason is the moral faculty and therefore it was not inconsistent of him to believe also that moral judgement is the perception of a necessary connexion. But the mere fact (supposing we accept this) that the desire for happiness is a necessary deduction from the nature of things would not entail that the object of the desire is morally 'valuable'. As well might we say that the equality of three angles to two right angles has moral value because this is a necessary deduction from the nature of a triangle. Price has ignored the point, which he makes elsewhere,[10] that the necessary connexions of morals are a distinct species of necessary connexion.

Price, of course, could not help recognising that, whatever may be true of a being 'purely reasonable', in imperfect human nature as we know it, 'rational and dispassionate benevolence' is a very 'weak' and 'insufficient' principle (p. 74). He sees that such benevolent activity is motivated by what he calls variously 'instincts', 'appetites' or 'passions' (pp. 69 and 74); for example, by love of one's children or sympathy with one's fellow-creatures.[11] He sees it as a mark of the wisdom and goodness of God that he should have implanted these instinctive determinations in human nature (p. 77). They compensate for our defect of reason. Price cannot blind himself to the fact that their instincts often lead men to do unreasonable or wicked things. But he did not regard some instincts as on the side of reason and goodness and others not; all are 'in themselves natural, innocent and useful' (p. 214). Even those which lead men into folly or evil-doing, he believes, are '*intended* for *good*'. The wickedness or folly are '*accidental*'; they are due to 'the unnatural abuse and corruption' of our passions and 'happen entirely through our own fault, contrary to what appears to be the constitution of our nature and the will of our Maker'. He even goes so far as to claim: 'It is impossible to produce one instance in which the *original* direction of nature is to evil, or any thing not, upon the whole, best' (p. 78).

The problem of evil must have seemed a very simple matter to Price: sin and folly and their consequences exist because some men misdirect their instincts, and the responsibility for these things rests wholly with those who commit this abuse of instinct. True enough, it would appear that every instinct or appetite – acquisitiveness, self-preservation, sexual desire, and so on – could conceivably be expressed in ways which would be beneficial to an individual himself and to society. But, in practice, this is not what happens, and hence moral and theological problems arise. For instance, it is presumably his instincts which lead the sex-maniac to rape and violence. Can we say that this happens entirely through his own fault, as Price suggests? Again, there seems to be a 'bias' in human nature towards the expression of instinctive urges and appetites in ways that are evil rather than good.[12] Is it, on the one hand, an individual's own fault that he should be born with such a nature; and, on the other, does not the fact of a 'bias' to evil in human nature meet Price's challenge to produce an instance where 'the *original* direction of nature is to evil'? The traditional answer of Christian theology is, of course, that human nature is as it is because all men share in the guilt and consequences of Adam's sin,[13] and, in some sense, Price subscribed to this view.[14] But the notions of inherited corruption and guilt raise theological and moral problems of great complexity. Whatever Price thought about such matters, moral evil

and responsibility pose questions which cannot be summarily dismissed
with the easy answers which Price here proposes and which he seems
to think settle the matter.[15]

III. GOOD AND ILL DESERT

The desire for happiness which rational beings, *qua* rational, feel is,
however, subject to certain qualifications, according to Price, e.g. the
notion of merit. Rational beings, he thinks, approve of happiness when
it is proportionate to virtue:

> When we say, a man *deserves* well, we mean, that his character is
> such, that we *approve* of shewing him *favour*; or that it is *right* he
> should be happier than if he had been of a contrary character. We
> cannot but love a virtuous agent, and desire his happiness above that
> of others. Reason determines at once, that he *ought* to be the better for
> his virtue. A vicious being, on the contrary, as such, we cannot but
> hate and condemn. (p. 79)

Our approbation of rewarding virtue with happiness and punishing
vice with misery is 'an *immediate* approbation . . . abstracted from all
consequences' (p. 80). It arises necessarily from the natures of virtue and
vice. The merit of an agent is defined as 'his virtue considered as implying the fitness, that good should be communicated to him preferably to
others . . . ' (p. 81). Price is careful to say that he does not deny that the
tendency of virtue to the happiness of the world and vice to its contrary, and the utility of rewarding one and punishing the other, is one
'circumstance' on which the rightness of so doing is 'grounded'. But
he goes on: 'What I assert is, that it is not *all* that renders such a procedure right; but that, setting aside the consideration of public interest,
it would still remain right to make a distinction between the lots of the
virtuous and vicious' (p. 81).

In support of this view, Price puts forward for our consideration
three cases, namely

(i) Suppose one had a benefit to confer and the choice lay between
two possible beneficiaries, one virtuous, and the other vicious. 'Who
would not immediately determine in favour of the virtuous character?'
asks Price (p. 80). He thinks we should do so even if (*a*) there were no
other beings in the world whose happiness could be affected by our
decision, and (*b*) all memory of the fact were to be obliterated so that

there would be no possibility of anything which we did making virtue seem less attractive to others.

(ii) Imagine a community of reasonable beings which exists for a while and then dies out completely. In it virtue is not rewarded nor vice punished. Happiness and misery are distributed promiscuously; the evil prosper, the good suffer. On balance, however, the sum of happiness exceeds that of misery in this community. 'But will anyone say, that, were there no connexion between such beings and the rest of the universe, there would be nothing in the disposition of its affairs that would be wrong?' (pp. 81–2).

(iii) Price's third illustration concerns reformative punishment. We approve of this for wrongdoers, but not simply because reformation results in their happiness. If that were so, it would seem to us a morally indifferent matter whether we made an offender happy by reforming him or by conferring on him sufficient advantages to outweigh the sufferings occasioned by his vices. 'Can we equally approve these opposite methods of treating such a being?' (p. 82).

It is undoubtedly true that most reasonable beings approve, in a general way, of rewards for virtue and punishments for vice. It also seems to be the case, as Price's examples show, that this approval cannot be reduced merely to approval of the utility of rewarding virtue and punishing vice. Price believes that this can only be accounted for by regarding our ideas of good and ill desert as rational intuitions of the nature of things. Questions of three kinds seem to arise in this connexion: psychological, ethical and logical.

(i)

The *psychological* question concerns the explanation of the empirical fact that many, if not all, men feel very strongly and consistently that it is fitting to reward virtue and punish vice. Price's explanation of this as due to an intuitive perception of the nature of things stands in contrast to others offered by classical moralists and contemporary psychologists. Adam Smith, for instance, explained it in terms of sympathy. He attributed our sense of merit and demerit to (*a*) (predominantly) indirect sympathy with the gratitude (or resentment) of the person benefited (or injured) by an act; and (*b*) (in some measure also) direct sympathy with (or antipathy to) the motives of the agent.[16] Dr J. C. Flugel explains our strong feeling that vice should be punished as a projection of the conflict between the super-ego and the ego, and the need for punishment to relieve the guilt feelings which this conflict arouses.[17]

Price's objection to such explanations of the origin of moral ideas would be that they cannot account for the 'absolute and unvarying' quality of the latter. Analysing moral attributes, such as good or ill desert, in terms of sympathy or guilt feelings, he would have said, renders them 'capable, like all modifications of pleasure and pain, of being intended and remitted, of increasing and lessening, of rising and sinking with the force and liveliness of our feelings' (p. 47). Now it is certainly true, in the case of educated and mature people anyway, that, though one might feel more intensely resentful towards the murderer of one's own child than towards the murderer of a neighbour's child or of the princes in the Tower, one would judge all these crimes to be equally deserving of punishment. But this could be explained as due to the rationalisation and systematising of our moral ideas under the influence of dispassionate reflexion or social convention. Then it still might be true that our ideas of the merit of virtue and demerit of vice originate in feelings of sympathy or guilt. Whatever may be said against theories such as Smith's or Flugel's, as explanations of empirical fact, they seem much more plausible than Price's. He appears to start from the fact that we have a strong and persistent feeling of approval when virtue is rewarded or vice punished, and a strong and persistent feeling of disapproval when the reverse happens; and then to say, in effect, that, because these feelings are so strong and persistent, they cannot possibly be feelings, but must be intuitions of mysterious, metaphysical attributes, namely the essential merit of virtue and essential demerit of vice.

(ii)

The *ethical* question here is whether the deliverances of the moral consciousness concerning good and ill desert are so exclusively non-utilitarian as Price thinks. There certainly seems to be something wrong with the view that acts qualify to be called 'punishment' or 'reward' solely in virtue of their useful consequences. If, for instance, when we describe the caning of a schoolboy, who has played truant, as a punishment, all we mean is that the action has useful results, of which we approve, why is it odd to call compulsory games or castor oil punishments? (The unfortunate schoolboy may not think it at all odd, but his parents and teachers would!) It is clear that our ordinary use of the terms 'punishment' and 'reward' has some connexion with the notion of desert. Of legal punishment, Carritt has said that though we may allow its intention to be mainly preventive, 'the scrupulous demand for proof of guilt shows that the *justification* of this preventive measure is retributive'.[18] And Mr A. M. Quinton has argued that the element of truth in the retributive theory lies in the fact that the word 'punishment' always implies a reference to past guilt.[19] But the fact that legal procedure or linguistic usage recognises a connexion between punishment and guilt does not, of course, imply that the guilty have a right to be punished or anyone else an obligation to punish them. This is an ethical question and it remains.

It seems indisputable that the notion of desert cannot be analysed solely in terms of consequences. Suppose I have an acquaintance, a man of great ability and social usefulness. One morning, I phone him to express criticism of some work of his which I have seen. He is subject to moods of black despair and, on this particular morning, is in the depths of one of them. He has been expecting a phone call from a friend whom he admires greatly and to whom he always turns for encouragement in his melancholy moods. His disappointment on finding that it is I who have phoned him, and the discouragement of my criticisms, so deepen his despair that, when I have rung off, he walks over to the window of his sixth-floor apartment and jumps out to his death. My action has had this socially harmful result, but do I deserve punishment for it? The answer seems to depend upon whether I knew the effect that I should have upon him or not. If I did know, and deliberately phoned him, then I deserve to be punished, or even if I had a pretty good idea of what would happen; but if I had no idea that he was in despair, was expecting to hear from his friend, or would be depressed by my criticisms, then I do not deserve punishment. The point which emerges from this illustration is that 'desert', as used in our ordinary moral discourse, has reference to the agent rather than the act.[20] We seem to recognise that, in virtue of his acts, he has either one sort of right, which we call good desert, or another sort of right, or rather lack of right, which we call ill desert. The strength of Price's argument in this chapter lies here. If a violent murderer were hanged on the grounds that this is for the public good, I think most men would say (or would have said a short time ago) that he deserved it. But if an innocent man is left to die, e.g. by a retreating army, though we may approve of this having been done and think it was right in the circumstances for reasons of public utility, we should never say that he deserved it. Something would still be his, in our judgement, which the murderer forfeits: his right to a certain treatment.

What is this right which our notions of good and ill desert recognise?

It might, I suppose, be called the right to have one's other rights respected or, in Kantian terms, the right to be treated as an end, not a means.[21] If any man has such a right, this implies that some or all others have an obligation to him. Now, I think we should all agree that we have an obligation to ensure, so far as it is possible for us, that a man of good desert is not deprived of certain conditions or possessions which are his by right. We feel it our duty to protect the innocent, at least up to a point. In such cases as that of the innocent man left to die, the good consequences of letting the innocent suffer have to be very great indeed to make us feel that it is justified. Advocates of retributive punishment, however, sometimes say that the right to be treated as an end, not a means, entails the right to be rewarded for virtue and even punished for vice, as well as protected when innocent. There is a famous saying of Kant's to the effect that, if society were about to dissolve, others ought to see that the last murderer was first executed – this would be his due; and Hegelians have believed that when society punishes a criminal it is not taking anything from him, but giving him his due; they even called punishments rewards.[22] Now, Price does not speak in these terms exactly, but he does say that we have an obligation to *make* the virtuous happy and the vicious miserable, e.g.:

> ... the propriety which there is in making virtuous agents happy, and in discountenancing the vicious. (p. 79)

> We have an *immediate* approbation of making the virtuous happy, and discouraging the vicious abstracted from all consequences. (p. 80)

But is the ordinary moral consciousness aware of any such obligation to reward virtue and punish vice, apart from any consideration of consequences? Even intuitionists express doubts about this.[23] All Price would have us do is consult our own moral consciousness. On doing so, I find myself aware of a very strong duty to protect the innocent from undeserved suffering, in so far as this lies within my power; but, even in this case, only up to a certain point. I can conceive of the possibility that the amount of public good accruing from letting an innocent man suffer for a guilty would be so great that I should approve of it. If, on the other hand, I try to imagine a case, admittedly very hypothetical, in which a man has done something meriting punishment, but I know that no good will come to him or anyone as a result of punishing him, I do not think I should feel it my duty to punish him, supposing this to be in my power.[24] This is quite different from protecting the innocent.

Indeed, I should think the moral consciousness of any person who believed it his duty to punish where no good reformatory or deterrent effects would follow defective.[25] As for rewards, I do not feel it my duty to make a virtuous man happy, except in so far as this will have beneficial results upon others as well as the virtuous man in question. When I see a man caring for his poor relations or paying his debts, I am aware of no moral obligation to confer some reward upon him. If someone tried to reward me every time I did a kind action or spoke a true word, I should think it my duty (though one which I may well lack the will to practise) to discourage him, on the ground that he was tempting me to have an interested regard for virtue, which would take all the virtue out of my good conduct. In his three illustrations Price appeals to what 'every one would think' (p. 80). But I find that I do not have an immediate approbation of making the virtuous happy and discouraging the vicious, abstracted from all consequences; nor do many other people, some of whom (like Carritt or Ross) agree with Price's general moral theory.

(iii)

The *logical* question concerns the nature of the necessity which Price attributes to our 'perception' of the merit of virtue and the demerit of vice. As we have seen, he calls it 'a necessary perception of reason' (p. 83) and, in support of this, he asks us to try to conceive of it 'as inverted': '*virtue*, conceived as having *demerit*; and *vice*, as well-deserving and rewardable'. He asks: 'Can these things be? Is there nothing in any of them repugnant to the natures of things?' (p. 84)

The assumption here seems to be that what is inconceivable is also logically impossible. But 'inconceivable' can be used in at least two ways and in one of these the assumption would plainly be false. An animal which is unlike all the animals of which I have ever heard may be inconceivable to me in the sense that I cannot imagine what it would be like; but the proposition 'There is an animal which I cannot imagine' is not self-contradictory. Similarly, if a world in which virtue is not meritorious were unimaginable, this would not prove that the proposition 'Virtue is meritorious' is logically necessary. But a four-sided triangle is inconceivable because it is a contradiction in terms. Is 'Virtuous act X is not meritorious' also a contradiction in terms? Not in a strictly formal sense, since 'virtuous', as normally used, can be defined without reference to merit. Nevertheless, this statement, 'Virtuous act X is not meritorious', would strike us as extremely odd.

We should feel that anyone who made it was, in some sense, contradicting himself. It would strike us as odd in much the same way that 'X is right, but don't do it!' would.[26] We should feel that, in calling X 'virtuous', the speaker had already committed himself to the view that it is meritorious. This is the force of Price's definition of merit as 'his virtue considered as implying the fitness, that good should be communicated to him . . .' (p. 81). In the logic of ethical discourse there does seem to be an implication which carries us from virtue to merit in the sense that sentences which affirmed the former, but denied the latter, would require some further explanation. If anyone said, 'I think he has behaved virtuously, but I believe he should be punished', we should feel that the speaker had somehow changed his role half-way through the sentence; that he had ceased to speak as a moralist and had begun to speak as a politician, educator or some such other sort of person. But the fact that there is this implication in our normal use of the terms need not be explained as due to a metaphysical connexion. It seems to be quite adequately accounted for by the fact that both 'virtue' and 'merit' express the same sort of pro-attitude towards certain kinds of activity. If I were to say that one and not the other applied to X, I should be contradicting myself in the sense that I should be expressing moral approval and disapproval at the same time towards the same action.

IV. BENEVOLENCE NOT THE WHOLE OF VIRTUE

Price now proceeds to criticise the view, which he found in Hutcheson and others, that benevolence is the whole of virtue. He quotes Butler with approval:

> Benevolence and the want of it, singly considered, are in no sort the whole of virtue and vice; for, if this were the case, in the review of one's own character, or that of others, our moral understanding and moral sense, would be indifferent to every thing, but the degree in which benevolence prevailed, and the degree in which it was wanting: That is, we should neither approve of benevolence to some persons rather than to others, nor disapprove injustice and falsehood upon any other account, than merely as an over-balance of happiness was foreseen likely to be produced by the first, and of misery by the last. . . . (p. 131)

Price goes on to add his own 'cases and observations' (p. 132) to those of Butler. Promises and engagements, for instance, (i) are not binding upon us only so far as their observance will be productive of good upon the whole to society; and (ii) do not cease to be binding upon us simply because we believe (a) that violating them will not hurt the person to whom they have been made, or (b) that, if it does, the violating will be 'equally beneficial to ourselves, or, in any other way, will be attended with advantages equivalent to the foreseen harm'. If a man promised anything to one person and then gave it to another, we should think he had done wrong and we should not regard it as a vindication of his action if he said that 'he knew this other would reap equal profit from it'. Again, says Price, if a party of rebels surrendered on terms, and were then treated as if they had been suppressed by force, this 'would be generally disapproved', even though 'it might be hard to shew, that the consequences of not keeping faith with them would have been very detrimental to the public' (p. 133). It should be noted that, in all this, Price never says that we think promises should be kept, the truth told, etc., *whatever* the consequences may be. In his illustrations he refers to 'equally beneficial' consequences; 'equal profit'; consequences not 'very detrimental to the public'. He was realistic enough to recognise that the obligations to veracity, fidelity, gratitude, etc., may sometimes be cancelled by the obligation of promoting public, or even private, good (p. 167).

Price rejects the theory that, by custom or habit, there is established in our minds 'the idea of a plan or system of common utility' with which 'vices are apprehended to be inconsistent' and by which 'we are insensibly influenced' when we disapprove of them (pp. 134–5). 'Why must we have recourse to the influence of habits and associations in this case?' he asks. This, he says, has been the 'refuge' of egoistic hedonists, and it 'may serve to evade almost any evidence which can be derived from the experience we have of the workings of our minds and the motives of our actions'. True enough, such evidence is of no avail against a theory about that by which we are 'insensibly influenced'; nevertheless, Price proceeds to adduce it. His main argument is:

> Any person, one would imagine, who will impartially examine his own mind, may feel, in his dislike of several vices, something different from the apprehension of their diminishing happiness or producing misery, and easily observe that it is not merely under these notions that he always censures and condemns. (p. 136)

And he makes the following points:

(i)

In the case of obligations such as promise-keeping, truth-telling, etc., if we suppose (i) that no public exists to be influenced by what is done, or (ii) that all memory of the action is lost for ever as soon as done and the agent foresees this, we will still form the same judgements about these obligations. Mr J. D. Mabbott, writing in a similar vein,[27] suggests that this would be the conviction of nine-tenths of mankind. Even in cases where good might result from breaking a promise and no harm – if, for instance, instead of keeping a promise to someone to dispose of his property in a foolish way, we, after his death, disposed of it in a way that was likely to do good, and this without anyone else knowing of our promise, so that there was no question of public respect for the moral system or confidence in promises being affected – he thinks the overwhelming majority of men would still disapprove. (He does not think, any more than Price, that we should disapprove of promise-breaking in *all* such cases, but that we should in *some*.) He criticises Professor A. Flew, who seems to agree with him about the present moral conviction of the majority, for suggesting that this might be the sort of case where our moral convictions ought to be reformed:[28] 'a theory which can maintain itself only by reforming nine-tenths of the moral beliefs of men is not in a strong position'. But is this the moral belief of nine-tenths of men? Would so many think that breaking a promise in such a case as that supposed is wrong? I imagine that an increasing number would doubt whether they ought to keep the promise. And where it was felt that the promise ought to be kept, it would be interesting to consider why this was so. I think we should find that the moral issue: promise-keeping to the dead or good to the living? was complicated in some minds by metaphysical beliefs about life after death, etc., or vestigial remains of such. If we 'remove entirely the idea of a public', as Price suggests (p. 135), i.e. if we take conduct out of its context of personal relationships, then surely to talk of it in terms of right, ought, morally good, is meaningless. Price himself says later, in a discussion of the character of God, that, in the case of a 'solitary being', 'the exercise of gratitude, benevolence, justice, and veracity, would be impossible to him; and every duty would vanish, except that of prudence, or a wise and steady pursuit of his own highest good (p. 249)

(ii)

If we considered regard for the truth to be virtuous just because of its influence on society, then we should not think apostasy wrong, if it were (i) done secretly, and so (ii) did no harm to anyone. Price cannot believe that we should think that a Christian who secretly betrayed his faith for the sake of a quiet life had done no wrong 'provided he judged the deceit would not be known, that he could do no good by a different conduct, or that his hypocrisy had no tendency to establish and perpetuate idolatry' (p. 135). I think such a case would be judged differently by one who believes in the Christian God and one who does not. By the former, the Christian in question would be judged to have done wrong. The ground of this judgement would be that the apostasy was a breach of the covenant relationship which exists between God and those who believe in him. One term of this covenant is the loyalty of the believer, in matters of faith and practice, to God's self-revelation in Christ. This obligation, like all others, exists within a personal context: the relationship between God and believer. It would not be thought of apart from the consequences which a believer's apostasy would have for another personal being, namely God, to whom a breach of it would cause grief and pain.[29] It would not be judged to arise from the bindingness of some *thing* called Truth. In the Christian scriptures, Truth is conceived of as a person: e.g. 'I am . . . the truth' (St John xiv. 6). Most unbelievers, on the other hand, would judge, I think, that in a case where no one is in any way affected by apostasy, it has no moral significance, or at least no *objective* wrongness or rightness. Price says that the Christian merely 'judged', as against being certain, that there would be no evil consequences from his apostasy and that no other course would do any good. Unbelievers might hesitate to regard his action as subjectively right on two counts: (i) because such a judgement can so easily be the rationalisation of selfish or craven motives, and so indicate a defect of character, if not of mind; and (ii) because a Christian, *qua* Christian, is under an obligation to act not only from a regard for his relationship to other human persons, but also from a regard for his obligations to the God in whom he believes.

(iii)

'Children, particularly,' says Price, 'cannot be supposed to consider consequences, or to have any fixed ideas of a public or a community;

and yet, we observe in them the same aversion to falsehood and relish for truth, as in the rest of mankind' (p. 136). This point is sound enough in so far as it is a denial of the idea that children form their moral judgements by calculating consequences in terms of public utility. But the mere fact that they do not do this does not prove that they are not 'insensibly influenced' by regard for the public good. Their moral principles, if taken over from their society or their parents, might well have been formed originally in the light of utilitarian considerations. Price is contending, not only that they themselves do not calculate consequences, but that they have an immediate 'aversion for falsehood and relish for truth' which owes nothing to the influence of society or parents. This is a very debatable theory. Children frequently lie, or at least romance, without showing any signs of aversion to their own action. On the contrary, they seem to derive positive satisfaction from it, and their parents have to discourage such conduct by impressing upon them the unfortunate consequences of telling tall stories. Raphael thinks that Price's point could have been sustained if he had instanced the strong sense of fairness which children have 'irrespective of (and often contrary to) what their elders tell them is right'.[30] If the actual use which children make of this word 'fair' were investigated, I think it would be found that: (i) They frequently use it to express fierce resentment at having to do what they dislike, without any sense of a moral principle being involved. 'It's not fair!' says the child compelled to eat food he does not want. Asked 'Why?' he is unable to appeal to any principle. Why he uses 'fair' when it is simply a case of what he wants to do is a psychological question the answer to which probably has something to do with the prestige value of the word. It is a word which he has observed to have some force in argument and so he uses it when he wants to win an argument. (ii) Often, of course, when children say, 'It isn't fair', they can answer the question 'Why?' with an appeal to a moral principle, e.g. 'Because you promised', 'Because if you give him one, you should give me one', etc. The moral principles appealed to may be any of those acknowledged in the child's society or home. The one of which the child seems to be earliest aware is the principle of equity (every one to count as one and no one as more than one). But it is difficult to distinguish clearly, in children, between what is insistence upon this principle and what is the expression of self-assertive instincts. The child insists upon having something for himself from the first. But he seems only gradually to learn that what he is allowed to have is usually limited to a certain amount, a fair share. At the same time as he

85061

is learning that this is all he can have, he is also learning that this much
he can claim with success.

(iv)

'Falsehood, ingratitude, and injustice undermine the foundations of all
social intercourse and happiness, and the consequences of them, were
they to become universal, would be terrible.' When we realise this, it
always 'heightens our disapprobation' of them (p. 136). This is certainly true in the case of most people. We learn moral rules from our
parents or teachers. Later we may question them and seek some justification for them. The terrible social consequences which follow from a
universal disregard for them seem to most men to constitute a very
strong sanction.

(v)

If our judgement concerning vices had been determined only by what
we thought their consequences likely to be, this would have 'the worst
effects'; for our capacity to assess effects, i.e. what they will in fact be,
and how far this is good or bad, is very defective. Many men are incapable of 'enlarged reflexions' on this subject, fail to foresee 'remote
events', and hold 'the wrongest opinions' of the tendencies of their
actions, and the good or ill to the world which they may occasion.
Price goes so far as to say that if our moral judgements depended only
upon the calculation of consequences, it would not 'be sufficient to
secure tolerably the order of human society' (pp. 136–7). This would
be a strong argument against the theory that individuals judge lying,
for instance, only by assessing its consequences. If this were so, it is
more than likely that (i) very many would be able to persuade themselves that lying, in any particular instance, was justified, and (ii) very
many would feel so uncertain of the consequences of lying that they
would not know whether to approve or condemn it. And if this were
the case, then the general disapproval of lying, which is one of the
foundations of social order, would not exist. But the argument is very
much weaker if we suppose that, though particular judgements are
formed by invoking a moral principle, e.g. to the effect that lying is
wrong, this principle represents the accumulated wisdom and experience of many generations concerning what the effects of lying are and
how far these are good or ill. True, individuals err in their judgements
about many things but, by debate and experience, a cumulative
knowledge or wisdom emerges on most subjects. Why not on morals?

(vi)

'There is indeed no less evidence, that in the cases specified, we approve and disapprove *immediately*, than there is that we do so, when we consider benevolence or cruelty' (p. 136). Here we should make a distinction between 'immediately' in the psychological sense and in the logical. If we bring before our minds two cases, one of lying and one of cruelty, introspection will not discover any psychological immediacy in our judgement of the latter which is lacking in that of the former. Neither does the logical appeal to the principle 'Do not be cruel!' seem to be any more immediate than that to 'Do not lie!' Both are moral rules, and our moral judgement, 'Cruel act X is wrong' or 'You ought not to do cruel act X' logically implies a reference to the rule 'Do not be cruel!' in exactly the same way that 'Lie Y is wrong' or 'You ought not to tell lie Y' logically implies an appeal to the rule 'Do not lie!' But neither of these judgements is immediate in the sense that no reference to consequences can logically be implied. We have already seen that deontological words imply a reference, not only to rules, but also to purposes. As we shall see below, it can be argued with some force that the purposes are logically antecedent to the rules; that, if there were no ends which men desired, there could be no rules which they recognised, since they would then have no logical ground for preferring one course of action to another.[31] Neither our approval of benevolence nor of veracity is immediate in the sense that it implies no reference to ends.

(vii)

Price asks: 'Why must there be in the human mind approbation only of one sort of actions?' (p. 137). He sees no reason to reduce virtue to one all-embracing principle, benevolence or any other. He condemns 'that love of uniformity and simplicity which inclines men thus to seek them where it is so difficult to find them' (p. 138). He does not say that the philosophic craving for unity can never be satisfied, but thinks we should not be precipitate in believing that we have satisfied it with any particular principle. We must 'learn to wait' and submit all our 'general causes and principles' to the test of experience. There is no doubt much to be said for this advice. Other intuitionists have professed themselves equally undismayed by the difficulty of discovering some single rule of right conduct.[32] But where you have diverse and sometimes conflicting obligations there is the problem of weighing these against each other and the question of the scale by which their weight is to be measured. We shall return to this matter below.[33]

V. THE HEADS OF VIRTUE

Price now gives his list of the principal obligations or '*heads*' of virtue (pp. 138–64). His appeal, in each case, is to the moral consciousness of men of 'plain sense' (p. 139). In criticising his opinions we must, if we are to keep the argument on this ground, refer frequently to the deliverances of our own moral consciousness and to what we think the moral judgements of all or most men are. We should, of course, be as honest as possible in searching our own consciences, and as comprehensive as possible in our survey of other men's moral opinions. Neither of these things is easy to do, but, having done them as carefully as we can, there is nothing more we can do, and we are justified in replying to Price simply in terms of what we think as against what he thinks. It may seem an inconclusive reply to another's argument to say simply, 'I do not think that', but, where the other's contention is that all or most men think X, it is a perfectly sound reply to say, 'I do not think X and I have found that many other men do not think X either.' We will consider the heads of virtue, mentioned by Price, in turn.

V.i DUTY TO GOD

That is, the 'whole of that regard, subjection and homage we owe him' (p. 139). What Price has to say about this really falls under three distinct headings, namely

(a) Empirical Statements about Human Psychology

Some of his observations concern, for instance, the motive of religious devotion. He describes as a 'prodigious absurdity' the view that its 'secret spring' is 'some desire of contributing to his [God's] satisfaction and delight'; but he admits that 'some writers of great worth' have expressed themselves as though they thought it were (p. 139). Now, unless we give a completely behaviourist account of religious devotion, it is difficult to see how the testimony of religious men as to their own motives can be flatly denied; and some of them certainly have professed themselves actuated by a desire to do that which was well pleasing in God's sight. Some of Price's observations concern the

motives of irreligious men. When they do behave well, it is 'more from
the influence of instinct and natural temper, or from the love of distinction, credit, and private advantages, than from a sincere regard to what
is *reasonable* and *fit as such*' (p. 144). This is really something of an im-
pertinence. It would not be difficult to give instances where the conduct
of agnostics or atheists has been, to all appearance, as disinterested as
that of any Christian. While they commend religion for the moral
fruits it bears in men's lives, most Christians would dissociate themselves from Price's wholesale condemnation of unbelievers as incapable
of practising virtue for its own sake. One is only too conscious that this
argument can be turned against the Christian who expects his virtue to
be rewarded in the hereafter.

Price also makes certain claims about the effects of an awareness of
divine disapproval. If, when a man is tempted to do wrong, he would
stop 'till he has duly attended to the *sense* and felt the *weight* of this
truth: "the Deity disapproves and forbids my compliance"', he would
'lose all inclination to it' (p. 146). He would presumably say that we
have not 'duly' attended to it until we have lost all inclination; and, in
that case, the statement is analytic and indisputable. But, in fact, be-
lievers, while not denying for one moment that what they are about to
do is against God's law, frequently go on and do it, even after some
reflexion; and even more frequently retain the 'inclination' to do it.
Price argues that 'the most effectual means of forming a good temper
and establishing good dispositions, is the contemplation of the divine
administration and goodness' (p. 147). The psychology of this is sound
enough. Attention produces its own 'motor effects':[34] 'we may find
that . . . a certain motive or group of motives has not the strength and
prominence which it ought to have. We may then attempt to give it
this strength and prominence by voluntarily turning our attention in
a certain direction. . . . The voluntary determination to act issues out of
the voluntary determination to attend. . . .'[35] Like the slave girl in the
legend whose appearance improved as a result of looking daily at a
beautiful statue, we grow into the likeness of that to which we give our
attention. 'Moral education is impossible without the habitual vision of
greatness.'[36]

(b) Metaphysical or Theological Statements

Price denies 'that it is on his own account, and to advance his own
good, he [God] expects their [men's] gratitude and prayers' (p. 139).
He asserts that 'the state and happiness of the Deity, cannot be affected

by anything we, or any other beings, can do' (p. 140). He thinks these
are opinions which no one 'upon mature consideration' will see any
reason to deny. If God is omnipotent, as Price believes, then, by definition, it cannot be in the power of any other being to make him happy
or miserable, unless he wills it. But there is nothing logically impossible
in the view that he has voluntarily limited his own omnipotence by the
creation of beings, about whom he cares, to the extent that they can
please or displease him. The Christian scriptures seem to incorporate
this view. In the Old Testament, Hosea likens God's experience with
Israel to that of a husband with his unfaithful wife. In the New Testament, God incarnate suffers crucifixion. Many Christians 'on mature
consideration' have arrived at a conclusion different from Price's.[37]

(c) *Statements about the Deliverances of the Developed Moral Consciousness*
Price thinks that if a man 'of plain sense' were to be asked 'whether he
approves of piety to God as proceeding from a view to his [God's]
felicity', he would say 'No' (p. 139). If then asked why he did approve
of it, he would say 'because it was *right* – because he apprehended it his
duty'. Asked why he thought it his duty, he would reply 'because God
was the creator, governor, and benefactor of the whole world, and
particularly was *his* creator, governor, and benefactor'. But if asked
why this made it his duty, 'he would (as well he might) wonder at the
question, as much as if he had been asked, why twenty was greater than
two'. The 'grounds of duty' appealed to here seem to be:

(i) Piety to God is an act of submission to a superior being.
(ii) Piety to God is an act of gratitude to a benefactor.
The moral principles appealed to are:
(i) Submit to any being superior to you in nature, character or
ability.
(ii) Show gratitude[38] to any being who has conferred benefits upon
you.

I think men of plain sense today would not quarrel with the latter of
these principles, but I doubt if they would so readily assent to the
former. Particularly when Price argues that 'The higher the rank of
any being is . . . the greater our obligations to him' (p. 141). I do not
think a private soldier, if he reflected on it, would take his obligation to
obey an officer to arise from the nature of the officer's rank, as such, but
from his own agreement, upon enlisting, to obey orders. He would
recognise his duty to obey only so far as it was covered by the terms

of that agreement, e.g. for the period of his service. Price says that, in obeying the will of God, 'it is the *voice of eternal wisdom* we obey' (p. 148). The superiority of God which Price has in mind is clearly superiority in terms of reason. This, he thinks, the moral faculty, which is reason, must recognise.

But on the general obligation to submit to superiors, I think the moral consciousness of most men now would not support him. Suppose we worked under the authority of a very wise or very good man, who gave us an order which we disobeyed; and suppose afterwards we felt guilty or remorseful. I think our pangs of conscience would not arise from the thought that we had disobeyed a man who was, by nature, wiser or better than ourselves, but from one of two other causes, namely (i) either from the thought that we had broken the terms of our contract with the firm in which we worked under his authority, or (ii) from the thought that the wise or good man had helped us (if such were the case) and our disobedience was an ungrateful act. Where neither of these applied, I do not think we should feel guilty or remorseful.

There is also, of course, a logical point here; recognition of superior reason in another being would be recognition of a fact. We have already discussed the logical difficulties of deriving moral judgements from statements of fact.[39]

V.ii DUTY TO SELF

Price thinks our awareness of this is an incontestable proof that benevolence is not the whole of virtue (p. 149). He is very sure that prudence is a 'matter of *duty*.' Any other opinion he thinks is 'too absurd' (p. 148). He supports his contention by the following arguments:

(i)

'It is contradictory to suppose, that the same necessity which makes an end to us, and determines us to the choice and desire of it, should be unaccompanied with an approbation of using the means of attaining it' (p. 148). We have already seen the unsatisfactoriness of this line of argument.[40] There is no logical impossibility in the assertion 'A necessarily desires his own happiness, but he disapproves of acts which secure it.' What Price seems to have believed is that our reason, as the faculty of perception, could not give its assent to an end, private happiness, as a necessary deduction from the natures of things and beings, and, at the same time, as the moral faculty, refuse to approve acts which are the means of attaining it. But, even on Price's own arguments, this is open to at least two objections:

(i) It is from the nature of man as a *sensible* being, not as rational, that he deduces the necessity of the desire for private happiness.

(ii) He differentiates as *sui generis* the necessity of moral judgements from the necessity of other intellectual judgements.[41]

(ii)

'If it is my duty to promote the good of *another*, and to abstain from hurting him; the same, most certainly, must be my duty with regard to *myself*. It would be contrary to all reason to deny this . . .' (p. 149). If X is intrinsically good, then it is good whether it belongs to me or someone else. This is the argument, but it is only valid if the question, To whom does X belong? has no bearing upon X's goodness or degree of goodness. Price assumes that it has none, but the assumption, at least so far as one thing which is deemed good is concerned, has been denied even by Price's closest followers. If something is good, then we have a duty to maximise it. This seems to be the judgement of the developed moral consciousness. So far as virtue or knowledge are concerned, I think most of us would judge it to be our duty to maximise these for ourselves as well as others. Indeed, our awareness of the duty in our own case is, if anything, more clear and undivided than in that of others. We have a duty of non-interference[42] to others, which may conflict with our duty to maximise their virtue and knowledge; but this conflict cannot arise in our own case. Happiness, at any rate in the sense of experiencing pleasure and avoiding pain, is also deemed good, but here the case is different. I think that, while most of us would judge that we have a prima facie duty to maximise happiness for others,[43] we should not think that we have an obligation to do so for ourselves.[44] Does anyone think that a man who tries hard to increase his own happiness is a better man for doing so, or accumulates merit thereby, or deserves reward or praise in consequence? We do not blame a man for seeking pleasure, unless in so doing he neglects some other duty, but neither do we praise him. His act seems to be morally neutral. It appears, then, that virtue and knowledge on the one hand, and happiness on the other, are good in different senses of 'good'; and, in the case of the latter, whether the good is my own or another's does make a difference to what we think our duty to be in this connexion.

(iii)

Price makes this claim: 'it will be strange, if any one can avoid acknowledging that it is right and fit that a being should, when all circumstances on both sides are equal, *prefer* himself to another; reserve, for example, to *himself*, a certain means of enjoyment he possesses rather than part with it to a *stranger*, to whom it will not be *more* beneficial' (p. 149). We must assume that Price intends us to understand the expression 'right and fit' here in its fully moral sense, implying virtue and merit. If we take it in this sense, however, would not his view give a positive moral value to the unheroic which it does not possess? Consider the following case, quoted by Lord Inman when he was chairman of Charing Cross Hospital, as an example: 'One day there was brought into my hospital a lad of fifteen who had been badly injured in a street accident. He was a van boy and his job was to accompany the driver of a railway lorry. A smaller lad had clambered on the tail-board of that van and when discovered he had jumped off in front of an oncoming motor bus. That van boy saw the danger and his mangled body bore witness to the desperate attempt he had made to save the life of that younger lad.'[45] Here, I think, all the relevant conditions laid down by Price are fulfilled. Life and soundness of limb are 'means of enjoyment', and the van boy's dilemma (in so far as we can take him to have been conscious of it) can be presented as having to decide whether he would reserve these to himself by doing nothing, or risk parting with them in order to save the other boy's life or limbs. Again, the boys were 'strangers'. And the van boy had no reason to believe that the safety of the other boy would be 'more beneficial' to him than his own safety would be to himself. I think Price would have to concede that this is a case in point. (Something might be made, on his side, of the fact that the 'circumstances on both sides' were not strictly 'equal' because the van boy was older and bigger than the other one. But I do not think this is relevant. There is no suggestion that the other boy was so young as to be helpless or to lack the sense to leap out of the way of an oncoming bus, nor that he was too little to do so.)

Now, on Price's view, it would have been perfectly 'right and fit' for the van boy to have sat still and watched the other boy being run over. And so indeed it would, if 'right' is taken in a solely permissive sense. No one could have blamed the boy, if he had not done what he did. But surely all men must feel that what he did was virtuous and praiseworthy. And, if we are to judge by what he says elsewhere, Price would have agreed with this. He himself raises the question: 'Are there not many actions, of which it cannot be said, that we are *bound* to perform them, which yet are *right* to be performed?' and he instances 'acts of generosity and kindness' as a case in point (p. 119). Price thinks that the rightness of such supererogatory actions consists in the 'regard for goodness and right' which they evince (p. 123); and he even goes so far as to say that 'even when there is *over*doing, and a person is led to visible extremes and an undue neglect of his private concerns, we always approve, except we suspect the influence of some indirect motives' (p. 124).

So I think that we are justified in claiming that the kind of prudence which Price has in mind is morally neutral; and, furthermore, that some actions which, by his test, would be imprudent are 'right' in a sense of 'right' which he himself uses. Price concedes something to our line of criticism. He has to recognise that 'acting with a view to private advantage does not so generally and certainly prove a virtuous intention, as acting with a view to public good' (p. 150); and he says that the virtuous effort and design involved are often small 'and consequently the degree of virtue in the agent, can be but small' (p. 151). I find it difficult, where prudence such as that which he here commends is concerned, to see any virtue in either the act or the agent. I admit that there is a problem for my view in the fact that men sometimes say of one whose imprudence has had unhappy results for himself, 'He deserves it';[46] but I think in such cases they are blaming him, not for failing to act virtuously, but for being so stupid as not to foresee that unhappy results would follow. We would ordinarily say in such cases, I think, 'He should have *known* better', rather than 'He should have *done* better.' Behind the condemnation of imprudence, as deserving of punishment, lies, I think, the view that it is right that men should suffer in the degree of their stupidity and be rewarded in the degree of their intelligence. But while we tend to assume this in making many of our judgements, I think it is an opinion which the developed moral consciousness does not support on reflexion.[47]

(iv)

'Private interest affords us, indeed, the fullest scope for virtue; . . . when a person is tempted to forego his own happiness by an importunate appetite, it is as really praiseworthy to overcome the temptation, and preserve a steady regard for his own interest, as it is to perform any acts of justice, or to overcome temptations to be dishonest or cruel . . . the uniform and steadfast pursuit of our own true perfection in opposition to whatever difficulties may come in our way: This is high and true virtue' (pp. 149–50). Price thought prudence a virtue, it would appear, because he believed: (i) that we have a duty to improve ourselves, to pursue 'our own perfection', and (ii) that through virtue man finds his real happiness (he speaks of its pursuit as 'true self-love') in both this world, where it leads to 'fortune', 'health' and 'self-enjoyment' (pp. 149–50), and in the world to come, where virtue will be rewarded with eternal bliss (pp. 253–5). This line of argument, however, is surely self-stultifying. The motive of charity, in the New Testament sense, for example, is intrinsically good and we have a prima facie duty to maximise it in ourselves. We will do this by thinking and acting in charitable ways as often and as completely as possible. But if we attempt to do this *because*[48] we believe that it will be in our own best interest, then the motive of what we are doing becomes self-interest, not charity.

V.iii BENEFICENCE

There is no part of virtue 'of which we have more undeniably an intuitive perception' (p. 151) than this. As rational beings, we 'must necessarily prefer and desire' public happiness. He says that what will be productive of most public good is 'the most general and leading consideration in all our enquiries concerning *right*' (p. 153); and if the public good in question is 'very considerable', then, in any conflict of duties, this 'may set aside every obligation which would otherwise arise from the common rules of justice, from promises, private interest, friendship, gratitude . . .'. Before offering any comment on this, we will summarise what he says about the next head of virtue.

V.iv GRATITUDE

'The consideration that we have received benefits, lays us under *peculiar* obligations to the persons who have conferred them . . .' (p. 152). For evidence that this does not arise simply from considerations of utility he refers to the Butler quotation: ' suppose two men competitors for any thing whatever, which would be of equal advantage to either of them. Though nothing indeed would be more impertinent, than for a stranger to busy himself to get one of them preferred to the other, yet such endeavour would be virtue in behalf of a friend, or benefactor, abstracted from all consideration of distant consequences' (pp. 131–2).

Gratitude to a benefactor, says Price, is 'but one out of a great variety of instances, wherein particular facts and circumstances constitute a fitness of a different behaviour to different persons, independently of its consequences' (p. 152). Examples of this variety would be, to fellow-countrymen, members of one's own profession or club, members of one's family, friends, etc. He thinks we have an intuitive perception of this 'fitness' and it gives us 'just reason' for treating different persons differently. Some of these obligations, however, are 'of such little moment in themselves' that, in a conflict of obligations, 'almost any appearance or possibility of greater good may suspend their influence'.

I think most men would agree that we have obligations of beneficence and gratitude (and the others to which Price refers in a general way under 'gratitude'). It is true, as he says, that some of the latter are such slight obligations that we set them aside with a good conscience, if we have any reason to believe that any good will result from so doing. For example, suppose I know *A* very casually and, hearing that he has been unwell, feel I ought to call on him. If, as I set out, it begins to rain, I may decide quite justifiably that, to avoid the possibility of catching cold and causing inconvenience thereby to certain other people at home or work, I ought to turn back. But I think Price's contention that, where the public interest involved is 'very considerable', it cancels every other obligation, a difficult one to accept. It is a matter of very considerable public interest that murderers should be apprehended by the police; but if a close friend, having committed murder, threw himself on one's mercy, would not the claim of friendship override that of citizenship? If called upon to choose between loyalty to our country or to our friend, do not most of us hope that we should have the courage to choose the latter? And what degree of public interest would be required to oblige one to betray one's child? I suppose, if the fate of all mankind were balanced against that of one's child, this would seem to justify such a betrayal. But, even then, would not a good man hesitate?

V.v VERACITY

Our awareness of this obligation, says Price, 'has some dependence upon *different sentiments* and *affections* with respect to *truth* and *falsehood*' and he begins with 'an account of the foundation of these' (p. 153). His argument appears to rest on two premises which seem to him self-evident, namely (i) that it is the nature of reason to apprehend truth

(p. 21), and (ii) that it is the nature of mind to be rational.[49] He says: 'The difference between truth and falsehood is the same with the difference between something and nothing . . .' (p. 153). Truth denotes what is, falsehood what is not. Dealing first with the cognitive element in human nature, he goes on: 'Now, it cannot be conceived, that what is *real*, and what is not so, should be alike regarded by the mind.' His point appears to be that failure to recognise the difference between what is and what is not would be, in effect, to assert, '*A* is and *A* is not.' This would be a failure to observe the law of non-contradiction; but the observance of this law is implicit in the very notion of apprehending truth, i.e. apprehending what is in contradistinction to what is not (i.e. to falsehood). It is inconceivable that reason, which is, by definition, the faculty that apprehends truth, should fail to distinguish between what is and what is not. If we accept Price's definitions of 'reason' and 'truth', this is analytic. He goes on: 'Truth must be pleasing and desirable to an intelligent nature; nor can it be otherwise than disagreeable to it, to find itself in a state of deception, and mocked with error.' Because human nature is rational, our conation must be towards the apprehension of truth, and truth must be an object of desire and satisfaction to us. To the possible objection that we sometimes appear to take delight in falsehood, Price replies that it is not mistakes, villainy or errors, as such, that delight us, but their consequences, when they are advantageous. But: 'As soon as we discover in any instance that we err, so far in that instance we no longer err; and this discovery is always in itself grateful to us, for the same reason that truth is so' (p. 154). Of the moral consciousness Price says: 'Truth then, necessarily recommends itself to our preference. And the essence of *lying* consisting in using established signs in order to *deceive*, it must be disapproved by all rational beings upon the same grounds with those on which truth and knowledge are desired by them, and right judgment preferred to mistake and ignorance.' A lie, that is to say, aims to persuade someone that what is not is. Reason, the power which apprehends what is, must reject this contradiction. Reason being not only the cognitive, but also the moral, faculty, according to Price, it is therefore as necessary that we should reject the lie in moral judgement as it is in cognition.

Price believes it 'impossible' to deny any part of his argument. In so far as his use of 'must' or 'necessarily', when he speaks of what our cognitions, desires or moral judgements must be, or necessarily are, is logical, I think we have to agree that, given his premises, it is logically impossible to deny his conclusions. We have already seen, however, that to draw conclusions concerning matters of fact from definitions of the natures of things is an unsatisfactory epistemological method. In so far as his use of 'must' or 'necessarily' is taken to be factual, I think what he says can be disputed. To take the moral point only, I think that many men would feel no duty to tell the truth 'consequences apart' (p. 154). This judgement may be mistaken, but if any can form it with a good conscience, this refutes the argument that all men *must* approve of veracity, consequences apart.

Price regards promise-keeping as a particular 'branch or instance of *veracity*' (p. 155). If I say, 'I promise to do X', I place myself under an obligation which does not arise if I merely say, 'I intend to do X.' Therefore, Price thinks a promise 'must mean more' than an intention or resolution: 'the whole difference is, that the one relates to the *present*, the other to *future* time'. This difference is real enough. For 'I promise to do X' we could substitute without hesitation, in any context, 'I will do X'; but we should – sometimes, at any rate – feel hesitant about substituting this for 'I intend to do X.' Price argues that if, having said, 'I promise to do X', a man fails to do X, then he has lied, and this falsehood is 'known and wilful' (p. 156). He rejects any contractual theory of promise-making: when we make a promise, we simply provide the ground for another instance of veracity. As confirmation that the same obligation is involved, he points out that both obligations 'admit of the same extenuations' (p. 157); just as telling a lie on oath would be worse than telling it when not, so breaking promises made before God would be worse than breaking promises not so made.

This theory, that promise-keeping is just a particular instance of telling the truth, does not, however, seem to be at all adequate to the facts of moral experience. My obligation to answer a question truthfully may depend upon who is asking it. For instance, if a casual acquaintance asks me what I think of an article which he has recently published, I may reply, even though in fact I consider it confused or turgid, with some such answer as 'I read it with interest' or 'I admire your ability to deal with such a wide subject in such a narrow compass', etc. I feel no obligation to tell him the truth – or at any rate, the whole truth. But if the questioner is a pupil who submits a piece of work to me for criticism, or a junior colleague who asks me whether I think that his manuscript is ready for publication, I shall consider myself obliged to say what I really think. The difference lies in the nature of the relationship between me and my questioner. There is a 'tacit understanding'[50] – in effect, a promise – between me and a pupil or junior colleague, that I will say what I really think in reply to his questions, which does not obtain in the case of the casual acquaintance.

Of course, there are instances where I am under an obligation to keep promises to casual acquaintances. But even in such cases, this obligation does not seem to be reducible to the obligation to tell the truth.[51] Suppose, for example, when I have beaten a casual acquaintance at a game, I promise him a return match. Then I have to ring him up to say that I cannot manage the date fixed for this, but I ask him to select another date. He replies, 'Look, you don't have to bother. I shan't mind in the least. So let's call it quits.' I reply, 'Very well, if that's all right to you'; and I feel no compunction. But, in other circumstances, should I feel no compunction in telling a lie simply because some casual acquaintance said that it would not trouble him if I did? That the obligations to keep a promise and to tell the truth are distinct from one another may be seen from the fact that what Price called men of 'plain sense' take the circumstances which release us to be different in the case of each of these obligations.[52]

V.vi JUSTICE

Price confines his attention almost exclusively to that part of justice which concerns property. Property, he says, 'denotes such a relation of a particular object to a particular person as infers or implies that it is fit he should have the disposal of it rather than others, and wrong to deprive him of it' (p. 157). He proposes to answer two questions: (i) 'How an object obtains this relation to a person'. To this his answer is: 'in consequence of first possession; in consequence of its being the fruit of his labour; by donation, succession, and many other ways not necessary to be here enumerated'. (ii) 'Into what we are to resolve, and how we are to account for, the right and wrong we perceive in these instances.' In reply to this second question he makes the following points:

(i)

The right of property and the obligation to respect it, in the case of each of the relations mentioned, is known by rational intuition. Price seems to think that we have a separate intuition concerning each of the grounds of property (p. 158). But some, if not all, can surely be taken as instances of other heads of virtue: the obligation to allow a man the fruit of his labour, for instance, could be a case of good desert or promise-keeping.

(ii)

He believes, like Locke and Paine,[53] that the right to property is as original and inalienable as that to life or liberty. We have it 'antecedently to society, and conventions entered into for common convenience . . .' (p. 158). Proof of this, he thinks, lies in the fact that 'independent societies of men, who are looked upon as in a state of nature' are as aware of the obligation to respect each other's property 'almost as much as . . . private persons' (p. 159). I doubt if most men today would agree with Price on either of these counts. We do not judge property to be as sacred as life, liberty or security of persons.[54] It must have taken some believing, in the eighteenth century, that nations, in their military and diplomatic activities, respect in each other a natural right to possessions, as Price says; and events since then have made it even harder to believe. Such respect as they do show for each other's possessions seems to be motivated entirely by the fear of retaliation.

(iii)

Price rejects the utilitarian account of justice. Suppose two men, he says, unconnected with, and unknown by, the rest of the world, have all things common. If the sum of happiness is the only test, there would be nothing wrong in one of them seizing everything for himself, if he 'knew he should gain as much by it as the other would lose' in terms of happiness (p. 159). It was to meet this kind of objection that Bentham introduced a principle of equity into the measurement of happiness: everyone counts for one and no one for more than one.[55] Price, however, would not have been satisfied with this concession. Even counting everybody as one, if 'the greatest happiness of the greatest number' is the standard, then 'any number of innocent beings might be placed in a state of absolute and eternal misery, provided amends is made for their misery by producing at the same time a greater number of beings in a greater degree happy' (pp. 159–60); and this seems to Price 'plainly shocking' to our moral consciousness. I think it would be, even if the misery were not eternal. I think, for instance, that most men would feel that it was wrong to deprive the top income group of *all* property so that their possessions could be redistributed to a much greater number of people, even if the resultant happiness in sum were thought likely to exceed the misery of those deprived. Price allows, however, that regard for public good 'is *one* important ground' (pp. 163–4) of justice. He thinks it reinforces what he has said about property. 'Nothing is more evident than that, in order to the happiness of the world and the being of society, possessions should be stable, and property sacred, and not liable, except upon very extraordinary occasions, to be violated.' He does not say what these extraordinary occasions would be, but says what they would not: 'If under the pretence of greater indigence, superfluity to the owner, or intention to give to a worthier person, I may take away a man's property, or adjudge it from him in a court of justice; another or all, in the same circumstances, may do so; and thus the boundaries of property would be overthrown, and general anarchy, distrust and savageness be introduced.' Presumably, if Price thought it a violation of a *natural right* for one individual to take property from another on the ground of greater indigence or superfluity of possessions, he would have been hard pressed to find a reason why the state should do so. But to men unhampered by considerations of natural right the argument from public good seems a convincing reason for redistribution of property in circumstances of indigence or superfluity.

Price has argued that it is just to reward and punish men according to their good or ill deserts (pp. 79–84). Like Aristotle, he believed in equality 'according to merit',[36] and with him the merit is not natural ability or social capacity but moral worth. But even this equity is limited by the right to property. It may be that Price would have agreed that it is right to take a man's property, or some of it, away if he does wrong; at any rate, he does not explicitly exclude this, as Locke did.[57] Price does, however, expressly repudiate the idea that being a worthier person is a ground for giving one man any other man's property (p. 164). Rather oddly Price had nothing at all to say about the justice of treating men in accordance with their needs. This is, of course, much more widely recognised now than it was in Price's day, but good men then felt an obligation to help the needy. Yet neither under beneficence nor justice does Price refer specifically to the just claim which we feel the unfortunate to have upon us. Most men in modern society would agree that it is just to give the physically or mentally handicapped special training or treatment so as to make their opportunities more nearly equal to those of normal people. And, in some cases at least, we feel that it is just to compensate them for their handicap by pensions, special conditions of employment, etc., so that their standard of living does not fall below a certain level of comfort and security. In overlooking the obligation to help the needy Price missed a good argument against utilitarianism. Much that is done to help the unfortunate is no doubt less costly in the long run than it would be to neglect them; none the less, the care which we feel it just to bestow upon the completely disabled or the incurably diseased goes beyond what would be absolutely essential to prevent them from causing misery or disease to others. It is arguable that public utility would be served by the compulsory extermination of some persons, but most men find the proposal shocking.

VI. ISSUES ARISING

VI.i HOW DOES THE IDEA OF OBLIGATION ARISE?

Price believed that the idea of obligation originates through rational intuition of the nature of things. To this view certain objections suggest themselves: (*a*) We are often very uncertain what our duty is. Price defended himself against this objection by his theory that intuition admits of various degrees; but we have already seen[58] the difficulties of this theory that an idea can be self-evident and, at the same time, not quite clear. (*b*) Price hoped, by his rational intuitionism, to establish morality on a foundation, not of will or desire, but of objective fact. But morality does sometimes appear to depend upon will or feeling. If, for instance, a promise is a thing which, from its nature, ought to be kept, how is it that, if the promisee wills to cancel it, it ceases to be obligatory? If happiness is a thing which, from its nature, ought to be desired, then why are we so much less aware of this obligation in our own case than that of others? I think Price's reply, in the first of these cases, would be that the will of the promisee changes the nature of the action. In the second, if he chose, for the purpose of the argument to concede our rejection of duty to self, he could say that whose happiness it is alters the nature of the happiness. There is no way of countering such replies. The intuitionist can absorb all such objections as those above into his own theory of the nature of the act. (*c*) The question: how do you know *X*? may be taken in two senses, namely (i) how does the idea of *X* originate in your mind? and (ii) how can you be sure of *X*? Price's intuitionism purports to answer both. It was, of course, the latter (i.e. epistemological) question in which he was principally interested, and intuitionism seemed to provide him with a certain and absolute answer in both general and moral epistemology. But he did not distinguish the two questions clearly from one another. As an

answer to this latter question, intuitionism, as we have seen, will not do;
it merely disguises the fact that no answer has been given. Exactly the
same objection may be levelled against it as an answer to the former
(i.e. psychological) question. To say that the idea of obligation arises
by intuition is simply to say that it arises; it tells us nothing as to how it
arises, nor even as to the conditions which it presupposes.

It may be helpful to consider a concrete example at this point. Suppose my father is too old and feeble to work. He has always treated me
with generosity and fatherly care. He is now a widower, cannot attend
to his own needs in the house, and is too poor to afford domestic help.
I, let us imagine, live in a large house and have a substantial income.
Most men would agree that, in these circumstances, I ought to help my
father. We can see from this case some of the conditions essential to the
emergence of the idea of obligation:[59]

(a) My obligation is *to* a conscious being. If a rose tree had lived in
my garden for many years and given me pleasure, I should not have
duties to it. I could cut it down or let it die without compunction. On
the other hand, if I had a faithful dog, which was growing old, I should
feel some obligation either to care for it or, if life became a burden to
it, to have it painlessly destroyed. Obligation need not be *to* persons,
but it is always to *conscious beings*.

(b) I am obliged because I am a person. If a young dog did nothing
to assist its ageing parent, we should not say that it had failed in its
duty. Obligation is always *from a person*.

(c) I must be *aware* of my father's need. If he had gone to Australia
years ago and failed to correspond with me, so that I knew nothing of
his whereabouts or circumstances, then I should not be said to have any
obligation to relieve his poverty, though I might be said to have had
an unfulfilled obligation to find out if all was well with him.

(d) I must *care* about my father's need. There is more to obligation
than the mere cognition of natural facts. The idea of it arises within
contexts of sympathy. I may be aware of my father's condition and
say 'So what?' In that case, others may point out my duty to me – but
then it would be in their minds that the idea of obligation arose because
they had identified themselves with my father's needs sufficiently to care
what happened to him.

(e) I must think that I can *do* something to help my father. If I knew
that I could do nothing, I could not be said to have an obligation to
help. If I sincerely believed that I could do nothing, e.g. if I honestly
felt that my wife and children would suffer great hardship as a result of

my helping my father, then I should be considered by most people not
to have obligations which would have these results. If, in fact, I could
do nothing, but believed that I could, e.g. if I thought that my father
was staying away from home for a while, when in fact he had committed suicide, this would not cancel my duty to start making arrange-
ments for his care. Notice that my duty is to *do* something. I may detest
my father and the thought of having him to live with me, should that
be necessary, may appal me. In such case, I could not be said to have
a duty to feel differently towards him, but I could be said, nevertheless,
to have a duty to act towards him in a grateful or kindly manner.[60]
'Ought' implies 'can'.

(*f*) When I say 'I ought to help my father' or others tell me that I
ought, these sentences have a magisterial character. Primarily, they
neither refer to natural facts of need, nor express feelings of sympathy.
They invoke rules. The idea of obligation is of that which binds, as
Price so clearly saw. When we speak of obligation, we refer matters to
the rules by which we consider ourselves bound. These rules are not
formed without regard to natural facts, but they are rules, none the less,
and their function is to prescribe ways of action. 'Ought' contextually
implies a pro-attitude to these rules and the purposes they serve, but, if
accepted at all, they must be accepted as rules and not as advice which
we can as legitimately take as leave. This is why to speak of obligation
is to give, as Price says, 'such a direction as implies *authority*' (p. 109).
Sometimes 'ought' is in fact used where no sympathy (cf. (*d*)) is felt·
I may know the rule and act from it, or instruct another in his duty by
reference to it, without in fact caring for the conscious being (or beings)
whose claim is acknowledged by my 'ought'. But the background of
the rule itself is one of imaginative sympathy with conscious beings in
such situations. Similarly, my obligations as a citizen of a welfare state
extend to strangers for whom I feel no active sympathy; but, here
again, the principles of obligatory action are laid down on the foundations of awareness of, and care for, the needy.

VI.ii DO ALL MEN INTUIT THE HEADS OF VIRTUE?

'The foregoing general principles all men at all times have agreed in',
says Price (p. 170). He does not claim finality or completeness for his
list; he has simply enumerated 'some of the most important' heads of
virtue (p. 138). But he does claim that these principles, which he has
enumerated, are 'self-evident' (p. 168): they are 'principles of truth in

themselves certain and invariable, and forcing universal assent' (pp. 172–3). By its own terms, Price's theory is one which it is logically impossible to deny because it is analytic. All rational beings must assent to these principles because this is his definition of a rational being (p. 165). Considered as a factual statement, not a definition of human nature, however, the remark quoted at the beginning of this paragraph could only be tested by an anthropological investigation embracing the entire human race, past and present, and it is certainly not inconceivable that evidence should come to light of men who lacked, or lack, some of the principles enumerated above.

Price does not, of course, deny that there have been, and are, very great differences in the moral ideas of different countries and ages; but concerning these he makes the following points: (a) Some arise because men make mistakes about facts and cases (pp. 171–2). He illustrates his point from such cases as non-resistance, which, in a given instance, some would regard as required by divine command and regard for public good, and others not. (b) Custom, education and example are responsible for a great deal of moral 'blindness' (p. 172). They do not give us new ideas, but they may 'alter the direction' of our ideas of virtue and vice, and 'connect them with wrong objects' (p. 173). (c) He says that 'that part of our moral constitution which depends on instinct' is chiefly liable to corruption (p. 173). An obvious example would be parental fondness which led a man to tell lies about the rightful heir to a fortune in order to gain it for his own child. (d) Even the most depraved men know what is right and wrong. This is evident when they judge others, when they complain of injustices to themselves, and in the remorse which they cannot help feeling. Here Price adds the psychologically penetrating comment: 'All the satisfaction and peace within themselves, which they are capable of enjoying, proceeds, in a great measure, from a studied neglect of reflexion, and from their having learned to disguise their vices under the appearance of some virtuous or innocent qualities; which shews, that still vice is an object so foul and frightful, that they cannot bear the direct view of it in themselves, or embrace it in its naked form' (p. 174). (e) The 'interference' of moral principles with one another is responsible for 'the impossibility of a complete and scientific deduction of what we ought to do' in many particular situations; and this is a 'further ground of much greater and more unavoidable disagreements' (p. 174). (f) Even if all men judged correctly concerning right and wrong, there would still be differences in the moral practices of different ages and countries. Circumstances differ in different times and places, and the same action may not have the same 'connexions, tendencies and effects' (p. 175) and, therefore, not the same relation to the general principles of morality in one case as in another. Price illustrates: Spartans countenanced theft, but 'the little value they had for wealth, and many circumstances in the state of their affairs, might justly relax their ideas of property, and render every instance of taking from another what he possessed, not the same that it is now amongst us.'

To what extent do these six points dispose of the difficulty? Opponents of ethical intuitionism make much of the diversity of moral codes; sometimes, one feels, too much. Locke, in referring to this diversity, excepted those principles which are 'absolutely necessary to hold society together'; and more recently, Professor J. Mackie, making this same criticism of intuitionism, says: 'though perhaps there are a few feelings so natural to man that they are found everywhere'.[61] But these exceptions, if they exist, are not without significance. It is true that obligations always seem to apply only within a restricted moral community, the tribe, profession, etc., and only in the greatest men is this society co-extensive with mankind; nevertheless, granted that, there *is* a remarkable similarity in the general moral principles of different ages and races. Furthermore, many of the apparently glaring differences, with which anti-intuitionists make such play, can quite easily be explained away, not as differences of principle, but simply differences of application. It is certainly possible to deride the theory of natural law, for instance, by pointing out that in the Middle Ages it was held to condemn usury, but when capitalism arose, to sanction it. Russell attributes this change to the fact that the exponents of natural law in the Middle Ages (ecclesiastical philosophers) were landowners, or at least the Church was; whereas in the capitalist era exponents of natural law drew their income from investments (their own or those of the universities they served). 'At every stage, there has been a wealth of theoretical argument to support the economically convenient opinion.'[62] But, though the altered opinion was economically convenient, this does not prove that it was ethically invalid. Usury in one context may be a very different sort of act from usury in another, with different 'connexions, tendencies and effects'. It makes a difference whether loans are for consumption or production. If for the latter, then the demand for interest on the loan is not an exploitation of necessity or passion, as it would be on loans for consumption only. It is a demand for some share in the increase in virtue of having provided part of the means to it. We have here not really two different ethical valuations of usury, but two different meanings of money-lending, each of which receives its own ethical valuation.[63] But differences of moral opinion, where they exist, cannot be attributed to 'blindness' in any intelligible sense of that word. It is true, of course, that colour-blind and normally sighted people may see the same physical object differently, but this has nothing to do with custom, education or example, to which Price attributes moral differences. Moreover, colour-blind people would accept that their visual images are incorrect and those of normally sighted people correct. But in morals all men think that they 'see' and there are no agreed criteria for deciding who does and who does not.

It is true that wrong-doers frequently appeal to the very standards which they themselves violate when they are judging others; and that they often rationalise their own misdeeds. But I do not think this helps Price's argument for a universal recognition of certain moral principles. The standards by which wrong-doers judge others are the standards of their own society's morality; and, in the case of rationalisation, it is only their inconsistency with our accepted moral standards which makes us feel that our actions need rationalising. We must concede to Price that the more morally sensitive or intelligent members of a community may need to find a rationalisation of its standards because they are aware of themselves as members of a wider community also. Hence have arisen such 'scientific' doctrines as that of the natural superiority of the Aryan race, or the Malthusian justification of *laissez-faire*. Moral differences may sometimes arise, as Price says, because we feel ourselves involved in different obligations and cannot decide which is most binding in the circumstances. But again the point does not really help Price. It helps him with the immediate problem of why there are differences but, as we have seen in an earlier chapter, it militates against his theory that moral principles are as self-evident and axiomatic as those of geometry.

VI.iii CAN MORAL PRINCIPLES BE UNIFIED?

Price says that 'the universal law of rectitude . . . in the abstract idea of it . . . ', is 'always invariably the same' (p. 165). All the heads of virtue, he says, 'run up to one general idea'; they are all 'modifications and views of one original, all-governing law' – 'eternal reason'. 'Virtue thus considered, is necessarily *one* thing.' This appears to mean (*a*) that each head of virtue is a principle which it is logically impossible to deny: to do so would make one 'a rebel against reason'; and (*b*) that the several principles logically imply one another: they cannot be 'separated', the law which requires one requires all. The heads of virtue, he goes on, all agree very often in requiring the same actions (p. 166). An act of justice may also be one of gratitude, beneficence, etc. Price adds: 'No one of the several virtues can be annihilated without the most pernicious consequences to all the rest'; but one would have thought that if they all require the same actions, it would not matter if all but one disappeared. Price claims that 'the harmony between them' is 'in a good measure' apparent here and now; it will be 'more strict' in the hereafter. Then we shall find that love to God, to man and to self have, in fact, all the time, harmonised perfectly. This is Butler's 'cool hour' argument.[64] It reduces all morality to self-love. Moral principles = what God commands = our ultimate interest. But Price realised that duty and interest do not coincide anything like so completely in this life as some moralists had said (p. 255).

All this is of little help, however, in the practical matter of deciding, when obligations conflict, where our duty lies. Price must be given full credit for having seen so clearly that this problem arises: as he says, it had 'not been enough attended to' (p. 166). A conflict of obligations creates the need for some criterion by which to resolve it. Price says that obligations must be 'weighed' (p. 170) against each other, as they are, or appear to be, instantiated in any particular act. This metaphor of weighing is a common one: it underlies the popular and ancient representation of justice as the bearer of scales; and it is common in ethical and political philosophy. But the question is: what will serve as scales? What is the criterion which can be applied and by means of which obligations can be compared? Price specifically excluded that of results; and there certainly seem to be some cases, e.g. the punishment of the innocent, which a balance of good results would not justify. What other criteria could there be?

(i) The criterion might conceivably be: which of all possible actions would fulfil *most* obligations? Suppose I have promised *A* that I will meet him in London at a certain time and that the result of this meeting may well be of advantage to a number of people (e.g. by clinching a business deal). But *B*, to whom I owe a great debt of gratitude, wishes me to stay in Manchester at that time. If I decide by counting, I shall go to London, for thereby I shall fulfil two obligations (promise-keeping and beneficence) as against one (gratitude), if I stay in Manchester. But suppose *B*'s reason for wanting me to stay is the fact that he is about to pass through some great ordeal and needs my moral support; and suppose that the reason for my gratitude to him is that he stood by me once in similar circumstances. In that case, I may well feel it my duty to stay in Manchester. 'One' (singular) obligation may, as Price realises, cancel 'others' (plural) (p. 167).

(ii) Is the criterion then: what would the majority of men do in this situation? F. H. Bradley said that the wisest men of antiquity have given judgement that 'wisdom and virtue consist in living agreeably to the Ethos of one's people'. He even went so far as to suggest that to try to go beyond it is immoral.[65] But a man who solved his moral problems simply by finding out the majority view could be accused of evading the issue: he would be substituting for an ethical question: what ought I to do? a factual one: what do most men think that I ought to do? In Price's own theory, though he appeals so much to what anyone would think, there is a clear recognition that, in resolving moral problems, the majority may be wrong. Right judgement, on Price's view, would rest with the man who was in a position to say, 'I think X and all reasonable men must think X. If any man does not think X, that man is not reasonable.' Whatever the defects of this view, Price cannot be accused of having suggested that the majority of men were in this position. Indeed, he says explicitly that we must try to be better than men in general are (p. 231).

(iii) The criterion could conceivably be the degree of consistency with some final principle of eternal reason. Other rationalists have tried to embody reason in one ultimate principle – Kant, for instance, in consistency, Hegel in self-consistency – by the light of which duty could be discerned. But Price firmly closes this way out. All his heads of virtue are equally 'modifications' of eternal reason. Each embodies it perfectly and there is nothing to choose between them: 'All these rest on the same foundation, and are alike our indispensable duty' (p. 165).

(iv) Can the criterion, then, be the 'feel' of obligations? When full credit is given to Price for the wise things he says about rationalisation and about how easily moral conflicts would resolve themselves sometimes, if we got at the facts, it must be said that he leaves us with no better criterion than this. When a man finds himself under more than one obligation, he must simply weigh them against each other and do that which feels most obligatory. Here 'feels' *may* conceivably be taken to refer to past decisions. If, for instance, in the case we supposed a moment ago where I am torn between going to London and staying in Manchester, the claim of gratitude to persons related to me (as we supposed B to be) had on previous occasions seemed to me to outweigh the obligations of promise-keeping and beneficence, then I might have

resolved my conflict concerning *A* and *B* by recalling this to mind. The
obligation of gratitude to *B* would then have come before my mind
with a weight given to it by my past decisions. But in such case, I would
really be solving the present problem by reference to a moral rule or
principle which I had laid down in my own mind.

For a moral conflict to be settled by the 'feel' of obligations, either
of two conditions must be fulfilled: (i) the obligations concerned must
have each a fairly specific weight, in one's judgement, enabling one to
compare them in abstraction from a particular situation, or kind of
situation; or (ii) one must have previously encountered situations (at
least one) which one judges to be sufficiently like the present one to
serve as precedents. Surely there are many cases where neither of these
conditions is fulfilled. Recall the London-or-Manchester illustration
above. (i) If *A* were my child and if a great deal seemed to depend upon
my keeping my word and meeting him in London, then I should have
to choose between the obligation of promise-keeping to my child and
the obligation of gratitude to *B* who had stood by me so faithfully in
the past. Could I say what the weight of such promise-keeping is, as
compared with the weight of such gratitude, in my moral judgement?
(ii) Again, is it not conceivable that, in the case of such a situation as that
supposed in our illustration, there should have been nothing at all like
it in my previous experience, so that I had no precedents to judge by?
In cases where neither of the above conditions is fulfilled, how do I
know which obligation *feels* most obligatory? The only answer seems
to be, I know by what I *do*. I know which *feels* the most obligatory
course of action *when I have decided* which to *take*. What is this *feeling*, if
not a *decision to do* an act? (Or a decision that I ought to do an act, which
entails the imperative, Do it!) So I cannot, having decided, turn back
and say that the feeling was the reason for the decision.[66] Giving the
answer 'By feeling' to the question 'How are we to decide between
conflicting obligations?' is really just refusing to give an answer at all.
Intuitionism's answer here, as elsewhere, is just a disguised way of
repeating the question.

Its failure to answer the question has led some philosophers, while
admitting that Price's kind of intuitionism does justice to our ordinary
moral experience by recognising a number of different obligations, to
abandon it in favour of some form of utilitarianism. But utilitarianism
has not yet given us a single principle by which to decide between conflicting obligations. Bentham had to introduce a principle of equity
(that everyone should count for one and no one for more than one) and

this is obviously not deducible from his other principle of maximising pleasure. J. S. Mill introduced the notion of kind, or quality, of pleasure,[67] thereby raising in an acute form the question whether even the notion of pleasure itself could be considered as one idea and not many. Sidgwick found,[68] by a 'profound and discriminating examination of our common moral thought', that there are three 'real ethical axioms', namely justice or equity, rational self-love or prudence, and benevolence. Add to these another principle: that the sole ultimate good is pleasure or happiness, and, according to Sidgwick, you have utilitarianism. But he does not establish any logical connexion between this theory of ultimate good and his three axioms. Rashdall came up with the suggestion that equity is a form of goodness because the state of mind of those who distribute justly is good.[69] But against this latter, we can hardly believe that it is right that everyone should count for one solely because those who do the counting are better men in consequence; an equitable state of affairs, if it happened purely by chance, would be adjudged better than an inequitable. The rightness has to do with the claim of the recipients, not the motives of the distributors. H. W. B. Joseph takes up the problem and resolves rightness into three sorts of goodness: of results, of motives, of a system of life, but he does not explain how we are to measure one sort of goodness in terms of another.[70] The quest for a single principle by which to weigh duties seems doomed to end either in failure or in the enunciation of a principle so vague and all-embracing as to be of little or no practical use. Ernest Barker, for instance, wrote: 'That final and ultimate value (in the light of which conflicting claims must be balanced against each other) . . . is the highest possible development of the capacities of personality in the greatest possible number of persons.'[71] But what is personality? And how far would it be developed by the claims of promise-keeping and beneficence as against those of gratitude in a case like that which we supposed above?

Conflicts of obligation within the moral consciousness of an individual are resolved in much the same way as conflicts between two individuals. Before an individual can begin to settle the conflict, however, he will have to decide upon some ultimate principle by which the relevancy of arguments could be determined. Beneficence is, no doubt, the principle by which we most commonly resolve moral conflicts; but there are many cases where one finds it difficult, if not impossible, to judge which of possible actions will do most good. And there are cases where no moral principle, not even beneficence, seems to offer us any

guidance. J.-P. Sartre quotes what he claims was such a case.[72] A
student of his could not decide whether to go to England and join the
Free French forces or stay near his mother who needed him. Sartre
writes: 'He had to choose between those two. What could help him
to choose? Could the Christian doctrine? No. Christian doctrine says:
Act with charity, love your neighbour, deny yourself for others, choose
the way which is hardest, and so forth. But which is the harder road? To
whom does one owe the more brotherly love, the patriot or the mother?
Which is the more useful aim, the general one of fighting in and for the
whole community, or the precise aim of helping one particular person
to live? Who can give an answer to that *a priori*? No one. Nor is it given
in any ethical scripture. The Kantian ethic says, Never regard another as
a means, but always as an end. Very well; if I remain with my mother, I
shall be regarding her as the end and not as a means: but by the same
token I am in danger of treating as means those who are fighting on my
behalf; and the converse is also true, that if I go to the aid of the com-
batants I shall be treating them as the end at the risk of treating my
mother as a means.' The only advice possible in such a case does seem
to be the advice which Sartre gave: 'You are free, therefore choose –
that is to say, invent. No rule of general morality can show you what
you ought to do. . . .' Whatever may be said against the existentialist
principle that 'every man, without any support or help whatever, is
condemned at every instant to invent man',[73] there certainly seem to be
some instants when this is so. But even in such cases the individual is not
acting apart from any principle at all. He asks 'What ought I to do?'
and if he accepts the answer 'Choose!' then he affirms the principle 'In
such cases as this one ought to invent man.' Unless the principle of
his action is universalisable to this extent, it is difficult to see how his
decision can be regarded as a moral judgement.[74]

VI.iv what do price's illustrations prove?

Price uses a type of argument to which intuitionists are much addicted.
He imagines a highly artificial situation and then asks the reader to
judge what, in such a case, ought to be done. For instance, after
mentioning certain cases of ingratitude, promise-breaking and lying, he
makes the following comment:

> In the cases which have been mentioned, we may remove entirely
> the idea of a public, and suppose no persons existing whose state they

can at all influence; or, we may suppose all memory of the action to be for ever lost as soon as done, and the agent to foresee this; and yet, the same ideas of the ingratitude, injustice, or violation of truth will remain. (p. 135)

And he proceeds to give illustrations of such situations, asking us whether we should judge apostacy, etc., wrong in these circumstances.

Let us, for the purpose of argument, grant Price's contention that the same ideas of obligation would remain in these suppositional no-public-and-no-memory situations. What would this prove? It would prove that we are *psychologically* bound to make certain judgements. But this may be due merely to the triumph of irrational elements, in the super-ego. We are taught in childhood not to break promises, tell lies, etc., and these prohibitions may become the focus of such powerful emotional forces in the super-ego that no amount of reasoning can free us from their veto.[75]

Price, however, believed that such propositions as 'I ought to keep promises' are self-evident, and that this is why we cannot dispute them even in 'desert-island' situations.[76] But in what sense are they indisputable? 'I ought to keep promises' may be broken down into two indisputable propositions, namely

(a) I ought to do what is right.
(b) Promise-keeping is right.

It seems to follow that, given these indisputable premises, the conclusion 'I ought to keep promises' is indisputable also. But though (a) and (b) are indisputable, 'right' may be used in a different sense in each. It may be that in (a) 'right' is used evaluatively or prescriptively, and so 'I ought to do what is right' is virtually tautological; whereas in (b) 'right' is used descriptively – in the sense that promise-keeping is one of the items in our moral code. Whereas (a) is indisputable because tautological, (b) is indisputable because reference to the moral code should show that it is a correct statement of fact. It does not follow that 'I ought to keep promises' is indisputable. This is a value-judgement, and I can deny it without self-contradiction.

Price's suppositional cases are so artificial that no conclusions about ethics can really be drawn from them. To use 'ought', or any other ethical term, concerning situations in which there are no persons who can be influenced by, and no memories of, what is done is to use them beyond the limits of the context for which they were made and to which their logic applies.

VI.v WHAT IS THE RELATION BETWEEN DEONTOLOGICAL AND TELEOLOGICAL THEORIES?

The demand for a reason why an action should be done may be made on either of two levels. Suppose A and B are friends of C, whose child has recently been killed. 'You ought to go and see C,' says A to B. B, understandably, shrinks from such a harrowing duty. 'I don't really see why I should go,' he says. 'Well, dash it man, it's the right thing,' says A. 'You're his friend, aren't you? Surely that's reason enough.' Here A refers the particular action to a general rule of friendship, which both he and B accept as binding, and which they use in their moral judgements. This answer may be sufficient for B, who will, in that case, press the matter no further. And, so far as the obligation to do that particular action is concerned, the matter can be pressed no further. But suppose B still wants to get out of going to see C. He may then turn his attack upon the rule itself. 'But why', he asks, 'should I do what friendship requires?' The sort of answer A gives to this will be different from his answer to B's first question. He will try to show that friendship serves purposes or realises ends: 'Well, the world would be a poor place without friendship, wouldn't it?' or 'Well, you'd be miserable without any friends, wouldn't you?' etc. (Of course, he might first appeal to some other rule, e.g. beneficence, but then this would have to be justified.) A's first reply to B is deontological; his second is teleological. It is important to notice that the inquiry may lead to both these types of answer when the demand for reasons which justify obligation is made. There has been endless debate as to which type of ethical theory, deontological or teleological, accords with the logic of moral discourse. In point of fact, the answer is both.

In support of deontological theories we have seen that there are at least two obvious points to be made:

(i) The fact that something *is* the case can never, in itself, constitute a good reason why something *ought* to be the case. The fact that B is C's friend is not a logically adequate reason why B ought to visit C, *apart from B's* commitment to the general rule that one ought to do certain things for one's friends when they are in trouble.

(ii) But, even if he questions the obligatoriness of this principle, as we have supposed, the answer that it serves certain purposes, P, is not logically adequate, *apart from B's* commitment to P. Professor H. J. N. Horsburgh thinks that this shows the deontological aspect of ethics to be the more fundamental. He says that ends stand 'on the same zero

level of ethical significance' until the moral agent 'has committed himself' and thereby 'created an imperative which is categorical in the
sense that it issues from an absolute authority and that it is entitled to
take precedence over all other imperatives (save some imperatives of
the same sort)'.[77] Moral imperatives are not hypothetical, or at least are
not like other hypothetical imperatives: they do not leave open the
question whether the speaker or addressee has a pro-attitude towards
the ends for the sake of which the action ought to be done. If I say to
the next man in, as I meet him on my way back to the pavilion, 'You
ought to watch that tall chap's leg-break', I mean 'You ought to watch
that tall chap's leg-break, *if* you want to avoid being out as I was.' But
if I say to someone 'You ought to tell the truth', there is something
absolute about this which was lacking in the other case. I do not so
obviously imply that this 'ought' is relative to certain purposes of which
I, or the person I am addressing, may or may not approve; and that the
'ought' only applies if these purposes happen to be in favour at the
time. When I use 'ought' of conduct in general, not such special activities as batting, etc., then unless I make it clear that I am using it in a
secondary sense, it is assumed that, when I say 'You ought to do X', I
am not saying simply that X is a particular application of a general rule,
but that I approve of the rule and the purposes which it serves, and I
believe that the person to whom I am speaking does also, or would, if
he understood them.

However, we must not ignore all that can be said for the logical
priority of teleological propositions in moral discourse. Sentences containing 'ought' (and this applies to other deontological words also) are
used to guide choices, but their existence presupposes that certain
choices have already been made. We appeal to certain rules when we
use such words, but it is not taken to be a matter of indifference what
rules we appeal to. The very fact that certain rules get established as
obligatory implies that some are preferred to others. Why? The only
conceivable answer is teleological. These rules fulfil some purpose which
we favour. Nowell-Smith points out that, while it is possible to imagine
a world in which we had pro-words (e.g. 'good', 'desire', 'purpose',
'choose', etc.) but no deontological words ('right', 'ought', 'obligation', 'duty', etc.), 'it is impossible to imagine a world in which people
used the words obligation, duty, right and ought but did not use any
pro-words at all . . . .'[78] He goes on: 'Deontological words belong to
the language of advising, exhorting and commanding rather than
to that of choosing; but pro-words still form part of their logical

background. For we should have no use for the language of advising, exhorting, and commanding if we were indifferent to everything that everybody (including ourselves) did.'

So we have logical priority claimed for both deontological (by Horsburgh) and teleological (by Nowell-Smith) theories. But it is not necessary to choose between them. It would seem that we play two roles in morals. They are like the two roles which a member of a football team plays in the dressing-room and on the field. In the former, he confers with the manager and his team-mates about their overall plan for any game or games. On the field, he does with the ball, each time it comes to his feet, what he thinks will best fit the plan. In the dressing-room his job is to say what plan he thinks will best serve their purpose. On the field it is his job to play his particular part in the plan. I think the analogy here with morals holds in a number of ways. For instance, moral principles are social products, as is the team's plan; whereas particular moral judgements, like the separate kicks on the field of play, are matters of individual decision. Again, if an individual player decides that he has a better idea than the plan and plays accordingly, he may win his team the match or lose it for them. He does not conform to the ethos, and is on the brink of either transfer or fame. If, though an individualist, he scores goals, his club may be wise enough to exempt him from future plans, allowing him a roving commission. Similarly, society sometimes owes most to men who have refused to conform to its moral code. It would, of course, be disastrous if all members of a team claimed exemption from the plan; just as it would be disastrous if all men started to behave like Simon Stylites or even Mahatma Gandhi. But the point of comparison upon which we are insisting here is the double role. The player helps to form the plan and helps to put it into practice. In the dressing-room he is a teleologist and on the field a deontologist. There is a binding quality about the plan on the field which it does not have in the dressing-room. Similarly, there is a 'self-evident' authority about the fundamental moral principles on which we act in any particular situation. Apart from them we should have no duty (or, at least, apart from *some* such principles). But this does not mean that our moral principles cannot (logically) be changed, if we can think of others which will more effectively fulfil the ends that we pursue. Of course, the fundamental moral principles which we acknowledge are products of moral thinking through many generations and we should treat them with appropriate respect. If any individual or group does want to change them, it is more than likely that they are mistaken or ill-advised.

5

Practical Virtue

In this chapter I shall consider the difference between absolute and practical virtue, and the essentials of the latter, as Price understands them. The first of these essentials is liberty; I shall consider the notion that liberty is self-evident and the relations between the following: motives and the self, responsibility and freedom, and necessity and freedom. The next essential is intelligence and with this I shall deal very briefly. Then I shall discuss a third essential, regard for rectitude, as a principle of action, and note some of the things which Price says about good character.

I. ABSOLUTE AND PRACTICAL VIRTUE

Price draws a distinction between two different views of the rightness and wrongness of actions. The first is 'abstract' or 'absolute' virtue, which he defines as follows:

> ABSTRACT virtue is, most properly, a quality of the external action or event. It denotes what an action is, considered independently of the *sense* of the agent; or what, *in itself* and *absolutely*, it is right, *such* an agent, in *such* circumstances, should do; and what, if he judged truly, he would judge he ought to do. (p. 177)

The second is 'practical' or 'relative' virtue, which he defines as follows:

> PRACTICAL *virtue*, on the contrary, has a necessary relation to, and dependence upon, the opinion of the agent concerning his actions. It signifies what he ought to do, *upon supposition* of his having such and such sentiments. – In a sense, not entirely different from this, good actions have been by some divided into such as are *materially* good, and such as are *formally* so. – Moral agents are liable

to mistake the circumstances they are in, and, consequently, to form erroneous judgments concerning their own obligations. This supposes, that these obligations have a real existence, independent of their judgments. But, when they are in any manner mistaken, it is not to be imagined, that then nothing remains obligatory; for there is a sense in which it may be said, that what any being, in the sincerity of his heart, *thinks* he ought to do, he *indeed* ought to do. . . . (pp. 177–8)

Carritt thought that Price was perhaps the first to raise the question whether duty consists in doing the objectively right action or the subjectively right.[1] But, as Price himself points out, his distinction between absolute and practical virtue had been anticipated. He was probably thinking of the use Hutcheson had made of the scholastic distinction between material and formal goodness: 'An action is *materially* good when in fact it tends to the interest of the system, so far as we can judge of its tendency, or to the good of some part consistent with that of the system, whatever were the affections of the agent. An action is *formally* good when it flowed from good affection in a just proportion.' Sidgwick says[2] that it was on the pivot of this distinction that Hutcheson turned from the view of Shaftesbury to that of later utilitarianism; from the view that the morality of actions is to be judged by their motives to the view that it is to be judged by their effects. But this contention has been questioned:[3] it has been pointed out that Hutcheson spoke of expected or intended, rather than actual, effects[4] and that he may have thought the numbers affected and the amount of happiness produced by an action important as indications of the degree of purity of the benevolent affection from which it flowed.[5]

Price holds that in any situation where the question, What ought to be done? arises, there is one act which is the correct answer: 'what *in itself* and *absolutely* it is right such an agent in such circumstances, should do' (p. 177). This act, according to him, has, in some metaphysical sense, a 'real existence' and possesses the non-natural 'quality' of absolute virtue.[6] There is a logical difficulty about this notion that there is an act having the quality of absolute virtue, which is what we really ought to do. If an act has the quality of absolute virtue, then it must be an act which is *done*. That which does not exist cannot possess a quality, and an act does not exist until it is done. But if an act is obligatory, then it is *not yet done*. We cannot be obliged to do what has already been done. It is, therefore, logically impossible to speak of an act both as possessed of absolute virtue and as obligatory.[7]

It is, of course, true that, in our ordinary ways of thinking and talking, we frequently draw some such distinction as that which Price here draws between what we think we ought to do in any given situation and what we 'really' ought to do. We draw it, for instance, when we reflect on our own past actions and decide that we were mistaken about our duty at some point. The mistake which we now detect may have been one of fact. Suppose some philanthropist entrusted me with £100 to give away where I thought there was most need, and I gave it to *A* rather than *B*. Subsequent discoveries have shown me that *B*'s need was in fact greater than *A*'s. In such a case I should say, 'I thought at the time that I ought to give it to *A*, but I see now that I ought to have given it to *B*.' On the other hand, the mistake which we detect may concern, not the facts of the case, but the relative weight of conflicting obligations. Suppose I knew that *A* was dying and he asked if this were the case. I weighed my obligation to tell him the truth against that to spare him pain, and decided for the former. Now, let us suppose, I think differently. In such a case I should say, 'I thought at the time that I ought to tell him the truth, but I see now that I ought to have lied.' We draw this distinction between what we think ought to be done and what 'really' ought to be done when we are deliberating or debating on a moral issue with ourselves or others. Suppose a family conference is called to decide the family's duty to a member who has suffered misfortune. Assuming that all who attend sincerely wish to solve the problem in terms of duty, they will all be concerned to do 'the right thing'. This 'right thing' they will think and speak of as something which it is the purpose of their discussion to discover. They will differentiate it from what each individual member of the family may at any particular point in the discussion think ought to be done.

But it is important to avoid certain mistakes to which this distinction of common thought and speech may seem to lend support: (i) It is important, for instance, to recognise that it does not prove that there are such metaphysical entities as essentially right actions. All it proves is that we sometimes form different moral judgements on reflexion from those which we formed at the time of action; or that we sometimes have difficulty in making up our minds as to what ought to be done. (ii) We cannot draw this distinction, between what is thought to be obligatory and what really is obligatory, at the point of action, but only, so to speak, from a distance (e.g. when we are reflecting upon a past act or deliberating about a future one). We can use it of our own acts as well as those of others, but only when we are thinking as moral assessors and not as moral agents. At the point of action an agent cannot say, 'X is what I think I ought to do, but Y is what I really ought to do.' To his mind the two must coincide; and this 'must' is logical, for 'X is what I think I think I ought to do, but it is not what I think I ought to do' is surely self-contradictory.

If absolute virtue is excluded, we are left with the view that it is our duty to do what we sincerely think we ought. Price considers it happy for us that this is our duty, for if it were not, we should be in a state of endless and inextricable perplexity concerning our duty (pp. 179–80). To know the absolutely virtuous act in any situation we should need to know the 'capacities' and 'relations' of the agent and the 'consequences' of his actions in full, and this much, as Price says, we never can know unerringly. In order to know that X is the absolutely virtuous (or objectively right) act I should need to know (a) that in the situation there is a thing of the kind T capable of having a state of the kind S effected in it, and (b) that the situation is such that my act X will cause this T to assume a state of the kind S. But how much of this do I know? I *may* not know (a): I may not, for example, know that in a given situation there is a person in need whose need I could relieve. As for (b), I may believe it to be the case, but I *never* know with absolute certainty that an act of mine will have a certain result.[8] Since we never know what the absolutely virtuous act is, then, if it were our duty to do this act, some very odd consequences would follow, as recent intuitionists have pointed out: (a) we could never do our duty *because* it is our duty, if this is taken to mean because we know, not simply believe, that it is our duty; (b) we may have done our duty on some past occasion when we believed that we were doing what we ought *not* to do; (c) we may do our duty and *not know* that it is our duty.[9] From the proposition that objective rectitude is the test of obligation it would also appear to follow that there is no reason against the view that things and animals have obligations.[10]

When, however, we accept the theory that it is our duty to do what we sincerely *think* we ought to do, a question arises as to the extent of the subjectivity which is here introduced into the notion of duty. There are two possibilities concerning practical virtue, which we will distinguish as PV–1 and PV–2. It is either *PV–1*: what is *in fact* obligatory in such circumstances as the agent *thinks* these present ones to be; or *PV–2*: what the agent *thinks* obligatory in such circumstances as he *thinks* these to be.

Now to which of these interpretations did Price hold? He says that moral agents are 'liable to mistake the *circumstances* they are in, and, consequently, to form erroneous judgments concerning their own obligations' (p. 177, italics mine), and this would suggest PV-1. But his words 'what any being, in the sincerity of his heart, *thinks* he ought to do, he *indeed* ought to do' (p. 178) would suit PV-2, though they do not necessarily imply this interpretation. However, it seems clear from what Price says earlier (pp. 166–70) about conflicts of obligation that he did hold PV-2. He recognises there that we may be mistaken, where a situation appears to give grounds for more than one principle, as to which of these should cancel the others. He would have agreed, none the less, with a point which Carritt made: 'If all we could ever say were that, supposing the situation to be as we believed, we think it would involve some obligation or other (i.e. we have a putative obligation) it is hard to see what knowledge about the reality of obligations could be derived from this or presupposed by it.'[11] Price believed that there are moral axioms of the form 'A situation of kind S-1 entails an obligation of kind O-1'; and that such propositions are certainly known. The need for PV-2 arises for him because, though we have infallible knowledge of these principles, when it comes to their application in particular situations we are fallible in our judgements both as to the facts of the case and as to the relative weight of conflicting obligations.

Price took account of a false notion which may be thought to be implied by the theory that it is our duty to do acts of the kind PV-2. This is, in his own words, 'that whatever we *think* things to be, that they *are*', or, in moral terms, that 'all the fancies of men concerning their duty would be alike just, and the most ignorant as well acquainted with the subject-matter of virtue, as the most knowing' (p. 178). If this implication were entailed by Price's theory, it would be fatal to it. It is an epistemological impossibility that an act should *be* obligatory simply because it is *thought to be*: there must be a distinction between what is the case and what is thought to be the case or knowledge is indistinguishable from false opinion. If correct moral judgements are taken to be statements of fact, as they were by Price, then this epistemological impossibility must be recognised. Price had to find room in his moral theory for the distinction between what *is* virtuous and what is only *thought to be*, and this is why he was led to the conception of absolute virtue. He says here, in rejecting the false notion referred to, that all our inquiries concerning duty 'imply *objective rectitude*' (p. 179); and so they do, if they are inquiries as to what *is* the case. But Price did not, of course, think that the practically virtuous, as distinct from the absolutely virtuous, act is our duty simply because it is thought to be. He says that it is, 'in a different sense' from absolute virtue, '*real* virtue'. 'It is truly and absolutely right, that a being should do what the reason of his mind, though perhaps unhappily misinformed, requires of him; or what, according to his best judgment, he is persuaded to be the will of God' (p. 180). Price no doubt intended an appeal to theological presuppositions in his use of '*real*' here. What he probably means is that this is our duty, not because we choose to think that it is, but because it is what God demands of us. There is another line which he might have taken, as more recent moralists have done,[12] to counter the objection that if we say that it is an agent's duty to do what he thinks right, we are saying in effect that something is his duty because he thinks it is. If a willed or intended act, X, is one which the person willing or intending it thinks right, then it is a willed or intended act of a certain sort. It is, for example, different from a willed or intended act which the person willing or intending thinks wrong. The fact that it is thought right is a characteristic of the willed or intended act or, more accurately, of the agent who wills or intends, thinking this right. This is a different sort of willing or intending from if he were thinking what he willed or intended wrong. Now to say 'It is our duty to will or intend acts, thinking these right' is not equivalent to saying 'It is our duty to will or intend acts because we think these right.' I do not suggest with any confidence that Price means this, when he says that it is 'truly and absolutely right' that a being should do what he thinks right, though I suppose it is just conceivable that he did.

Summing up then: 'Our rule is to follow our consciences steadily and faithfully, after we have taken care to inform them in the best manner we can', according to Price (p. 179). This rule, or the first part of it at any rate, we can always fulfil. We can follow conscience: that is, we can do acts of the type PV–2. Most of us, I think, would agree that this is our duty in the overwhelming majority of cases, and we should praise an agent for doing it, and blame him if he did not. Suppose, to recall a former illustration, that I believe A is dying and he asks me if he is. I sincerely believe that I ought to tell him the truth rather than spare him possible pain, and so I answer 'Yes'. Suppose he is vastly distressed by this information. Suppose further that it turns out that (*a*) I was misinformed about his state of health and he was not in fact dying when I thought he was, and (*b*) those asked their opinion of my act all judge that what I ought to have done was to answer 'No' and spare him any possible pain. Nevertheless, I think most of them would agree with Price that 'an agent, who does what is *objectively wrong*, may often be entitled to commendation' (p. 184) and that, if I sincerely believed the man to be dying and honestly thought it my duty to tell him, then I cannot be blamed for doing so, and may even merit some praise for having gone through with what must have been a difficult and distressing duty.

But I think some might not feel too happy about approving my action here, even though I did 'follow conscience steadily and faithfully'. In what respect can the agent in such cases be said to have failed in his duty and merited blame? I do not think that we need here abandon our view that it is one's duty to do acts of kind PV-2 for the view that the agent ought to have done the objectively right action in such cases.[13] If he is culpable, it is because he has failed to fulfil the second part of Price's rule. When deciding what we ought to do, we always have a secondary duty (which is also of type PV-2) to inform our consciences as fully as possible. We cannot, says Price, 'be too diligent in labouring rightly to inform our consciences' (p. 198). One thing this means is gaining as accurate information as possible about the *facts* of the case; for instance, I should have been culpable, in the above illustration, if I had told the man he was dying on the strength of some rumour to that effect which I had heard or on the strength of the doctor's opinion that there was merely a chance that he might do so. But this duty applies to more than the facts. I must always be mindful of my own *moral* fallibility and check my own judgements of obligation against those of other men. This, of course, is only possible where there are clearly defined judgements of other men as to the kind of act which ought to be done in situations such as that in which I find myself; and this is not always the case. But where I have reason to believe that what I think I ought to do in a given situation conflicts with what most other men, or at least most wise and good men, think ought to be done in such a situation, I must recognise that it is more than likely that I am mistaken. The general opinion of humane men, for instance, seems to be that it is usually better to spare dying men the painful truth. Who am I to contravene this judgement? If I find that my confidence in a particular judgement of my own is unshaken by reflexion on the fact that all or most of the wise and good men I know, or have heard of, would judge otherwise in such a case, then I am either a heaven-sent prophet or a psychopath.

II. THE ESSENTIALS OF PRACTICAL VIRTUE

Having differentiated absolute and practical virtue, Price proceeds to discuss the nature and essentials of the latter (pp. 181 ff.).

II.i LIBERTY

Practical virtue, says Price, presupposes liberty (p. 181). We shall consider his treatment of this subject under four heads.

(a) The Alleged Self-evidence of Liberty
Price alleges that liberty is self-evident. He seems to argue this on two levels. He thinks that the notion of liberty is implicit in moral talk: we cannot say what we mean by virtue, vice, etc., 'if they do not suppose *agency*, free choice' (p. 182). To this line of thought we return below. But Price also seems to be saying here that liberty can be seen to be self-evident from a consideration of the ordinary language we use to describe actions: 'Let anyone try to put a sense on the expressions: *I will*; *I act*; which is consistent with supposing that the volition or action does not proceed from myself' (p. 181). Now, of course, if we say that by 'I act' we mean 'not–I acts', this is, as Price says, 'a palpable contradiction'. But the point is analytic and trivial. Price says again: 'In short: who must not *feel* the absurdity of saying, *my* volitions are produced by a *foreign* cause, that is, are not *mine*; I determine *voluntarily*, and yet *necessarily*?' (p. 182). This is absurd on the purely formal ground that if I say 'X are my volitions', it is then logically impossible for me to say 'X are not mine.' Or, if I define 'voluntarily' as 'not necessarily', then it is a contradiction to say 'I determine voluntarily and yet necessarily.' Again, these points are linguistic; in themselves they do not answer what I think Price would have regarded as the questions of fact: are any acts free? what acts are free? etc.

It may be, of course, that the only way of solving the freewill versus determinism issue is by linguistic analysis. It can be shown, I think, that the language of agency, if we may so speak, is logically irreducible to the language of event or bodily movement. An agent as such is always logically distinct from his situation. It makes perfectly good sense always to ask what the agent is going to do about his situation. This is obvious where the situation is clearly external to him – e.g. 'What are you going to do about the fact that your house has been burnt down?' – but it is equally true where the situation is, in some sense, internal to him – e.g.

'What are you going to do about the fact that you are suffering from
a cold?' (or, 'you are suffering from kleptomania', or, 'you have an
I.Q. of only 100', or, 'you are an inveterate liar', etc.).

Again, it makes perfectly good sense when an account of what has
happened in terms of bodily movement has been offered, to ask 'But
what was the agent doing?' Suppose White's boot comes forcefully
into contact with Black's posterior. What was White doing? The same
account of these events in terms of bodily movement would be com-
patible with any of the following answers: 'He was dancing a jig', 'He
was playfully accosting Black', 'He was trying to lame Black', etc.

The question of agency is endlessly elusive to an answer in terms of
bodily movement. The latter must always refer to the agent's situation.
As we saw a moment ago, an agent's intelligence or character may be
conceived as part of his situation. Whether the same is true of his
motives or volitions, and whether the 'systematic elusiveness of "I"'
provides any ground for indeterminism, are questions to which we
must turn.[14]

(b) Motives and the Self

Price is intent upon refuting what he considers the absurd view that
action is determined by motives, i.e. by motives apart from the self. He
concedes that our desires or fears 'may be the *occasions* of our putting
ourselves into motion' (p. 183 n.), but he points out that this is quite
different from the notion that they can be the efficient causes of action:
'What sense would there be in saying, that the *situation* of a body,
which may properly be the occasion or account of its being struck by
another body, is the *efficient* of its motion or its impeller?' This comparison with the occasions of physical motion is not very helpful. If we
accepted it, we should have to think of human action as determined in
accordance with a kind of parallelogram of forces, i.e. as always the
attempt of the agent to get, each in the degree to which he desires it,
all the things which he does desire at the time of action; just as all the
physical forces acting upon a body have their degree of influence on its
movement.[15] Now, this seems quite clearly not to be the case, at least
with people of settled character. They sometimes attempt, and to all
appearance often manage, to suppress altogether the strongest single
desire which they feel at a given time. It may remain in some form, as
a temptation perhaps, but they do not consciously act upon it.

Our very reasons for feeling unhappy about his reference to occa-
sionalism, however, strengthen the case for Price's main point: that the

self is the efficient cause of action. Where two desires conflict, it is not simply that which is stronger at the time on which I act, nor a combination of both of them, but that which I think is more consistent with my universe of desire or system of interests. This applies equally where the conflict is between a desire (or desires) and my sense of duty; and, of course, the fact that the sense of duty influences action only in the degree that there is a desire to do one's duty, or a specific emotion of reverence (Kant's *Achtung*), does not affect this issue. The point is that the desire which emerges as the motive of action is not simply the strongest single desire nor a combination of all the desires one feels, but that which most harmonises with one's whole character. This presupposes deliberation before action and, between libertarians and determinists, the nature of that deliberation is a point of controversy; but this need not concern us here because, on either view, it seems clear that, between desires and action, what we may legitimately call a determining self intervenes. Price professed that he wished to prove no more: 'Determination requires an efficient cause. If this cause is the being himself, I plead for no more' (p. 181).

(c) *Responsibility and Freedom*

Price wrote: 'it is hard to say what virtue and vice, commendation and blame, mean, if they do not suppose *agency*, free choice, and an absolute dominion over our resolutions' (p. 182). In other words, 'ought' implies 'can'.[16] Like Kant, he thinks that this general implication of the 'language' men use, and the 'sentiments' they feel, about morality is an intellectual intuition of the nature of things, a '*natural* sense'. Without subscribing to this view, we may, none the less, acknowledge the validity of the logical point. It is meaningless (i.e. it is pointless, a sentence for which we have no use, something we should never do) to say 'You ought to do X' if we know that it is empirically impossible for you to do X because of your limited control over the natural world. Where the empirical impossibility is not due to limited control over the natural world, there is some difference of opinion as to whether moral judgements are meaningless. The impossibility may consist in a defect of character or a pathological condition of the mind: is it then equally meaningless to pass moral judgement? This raises a problem to which we shall return in a moment.

Whatever doubts there may be as to the view which Price held concerning free will, there is no doubt at all about the view which he rejected. This was:

... that nothing is made to depend on ourselves, or that our purposes and determinations are not subjected to our own command, but the result of physical laws, not possible to be resisted. (pp. 182–3)

It was the view which denied the part played by the self in acting and determining: that I never could have done other than I did in the sense that I never would have done other than I did, *even if I had willed differently*. Price was certainly right to reject this view: it is neither (i) necessitated by the idea of causation, nor (ii) consistent with the implications of ethical language. If 'I could' is analysed into 'I would, if I had willed', which seems to be its sense in most contexts, then it does not violate the principle of causality.[17] Moral talk implies an agent from whom acts proceed; moral judgement is judgement of this agent. We judge actions, not events; and the *differentia* of actions is that they do not merely happen, but are done, i.e. they imply agents. No moral issues arise if a stone falls, apart from all human agency, and kills a man: this is a regrettable event, no more. But if human agency comes in, if, for instance, the stone was pushed (or even if it falls from a building and may have become loose because carelessly laid), moral issues at once arise. There is a self to whom the act is attributable and so it can be the subject of moral talk, i.e. praise, blame, imputation of obligation or responsibility, etc. Having thus rejected physical or extrinsic determinism, two possible views remained for Price, libertarianism and self-determinism. Which did he hold?

(i) *Libertarianism or Indeterminism.* According to this theory, 'can' and 'could' must be taken in an absolute or categorical sense; analysed or interpreted *as implying no condition whatever.* This theory has often been held and still finds its champions.[18] It is the passionate concern of in-determinists to establish the moral responsibility of the self as the source of actions against the theory that actions are determined by motives or the result of physical laws, etc. Unfortunately, their interpretation of 'can', 'could', etc., implies the surrender of the very thing which they are endeavouring to safeguard.

There is a distinction which the moral consciousness of most men deems all-important: it is between (a) acts which the agent could have refrained from doing, if he had willed, and (b) acts which the agent could *not* have refrained from doing, if he had willed. If, because I am in a hurry or a bad temper, I drive furiously and cause a fatal accident, I may justly be blamed for my action; but if I cause a fatal accident as a result of a 'blackout' while driving, this is not my fault (assuming that there are no special circumstances which render it my fault, e.g. not having taken proper care of my health, driving even though I know that I am subject to blackouts, etc.). The first is a case of crime; the second of illness. Now, the tough-minded physical or extrinsic determinist classes these two kinds of action together as both equally unavoidable and sees no reason to distinguish one as a fit subject for moral judgement from the other as not: to him crime is a form of disease, neither more nor less. But this is not the view which is implied in the moral judgements of most men; and it is certainly not the view to which indeterminists subscribe. It is just such abrogation of moral responsibility against which they protest. But, on their categorical interpretation of 'can', 'could', etc., it is difficult to see what ground there is for the distinction between crime and disease, since this distinction turns upon the condition 'If he had willed'. Crimes (sins, and whatever else morally reprehensible acts may be called) are actions which the agent could have refrained from doing, *if he had willed*; acts due to disease he could *not* have refrained from doing, *if he had willed*. Leave out the condition, and what becomes of the criterion by which to distinguish the one sort of act from the other?[19] The categorical analysis will not do: 'could have' is meaningless, *except on a condition which must be stateable.* As Mr R. E. Hobart showed in a memorable article,[20] the libertarian theory purports to affirm the freedom of the self but, in fact, it denies both freedom and the moral self. If an act of volition is entirely undetermined, than it is just as if the agent had been pushed, or as if his legs had suddenly sprung up and carried him off where he did not wish to go. The libertarian theory, like its arch-enemy, extrinsic determinism, reduces actions to the status of events. It affirms that the self acts freely, but if the source of actions really is a self, then they are determined in that they flow from this self and not another. In denying all determinism, the libertarian denies the very thing he intended to affirm.

Can the libertarian escape from this dilemma – either some form of determinism or self-stultification by appeal to what Professor G. Ryle called 'the systematic elusiveness of the notion of "I"'? Ryle says that we begin to understand this notion when we see that 'in such a statement as "I caught myself beginning to dream", the two pronouns are not names of different persons, since they are not names at all, but that they are index words being used in different senses in different sorts of context . . .'. He points out that in specifically human behaviour (as distinct from that of animals, infants or idiots) some sorts of actions are concerned with, or are operations upon, other actions. He calls these 'higher order actions'; and he writes: 'To concern oneself about one-self in any way, theoretical or practical, is to perform a higher order act, just as it is to concern oneself about anybody else . . . my commentary on my performances must always be silent about one performance, namely itself, and this performance can be the target only of another commentary. Self-commentary, self-ridicule and self-admonition are logically condemned to eternal penultimacy.'[21] The picture of an 'inner self' has affected our language, particularly our use of the pro-nouns 'I', 'you', 'he', and the possessive adjectives 'my', 'yours', 'his'. We differentiate factors of the mind such as desire, reason, determina-tion, sense of duty, from one another; and then we talk about 'his desire', 'his sense of duty', etc. This use of 'his' seems to imply an 'inner self' which controls, or may be controlled by, these various 'parts' of the mind. As Mr John Wilson has argued, 'By this usage, it is always possible for us to regard any cause as "outside", by the simple expedient of using "he" or "his" in a way that seems logically to ex-clude the cause mentioned.'[22] Ryle indicates the bearing of all this on the problem of free will: 'A prediction of a deed or a thought is a higher order operation, the performance of which cannot be among the things considered in making the prediction. Yet as the state of mind in which I am just before I do something may make some difference to what I do, it follows that I must overlook at least one of the data relevant to my prediction. . . . There is therefore no paradox in saying that while normally I am not at all surprised to find myself doing or thinking what I do, yet when I try most carefully to anticipate what I shall do or think, then the outcome is likely to falsify my expectation. My process of pre-envisaging may divert the course of my ensuing behaviour in a direction and degree of which my prognosis cannot take account. One thing that I cannot prepare myself for is the next thought that I am going to think.' But, as he says: 'The fact that my immediate future is in this way systematically elusive to me has, of course, no tendency to prove that my career is in principle unpredictable to prophets other than myself, or even that it is inexplicable to myself after the heat of action. I can point to any other thing with my index-finger, and other people can point at this finger. But it cannot be the object at which it itself is pointing. Nor can a missile be its own target, though anything else may be thrown at it.'[23] Although he may seem to be helped by this systematic elusiveness of the self, however, the indeter-minist cannot really escape from determinism. He says that an agent's choice is not determined by his character, etc., that he can at a given moment choose between his several desires, whatever these may be. But what, or rather who, performs this choice? Answer: *he* does. In so far as it is his choice, it is determined. The point has been pushed a little further back, but it remains.

Did Price hold the libertarian position? There are some considerations which suggest an affirmative answer. His argument at certain points seems to be very similar to arguments put forward by the libertarians. C. A. Campbell, in his latest discussion of free will, says that the libertarian thesis is established in two ways: (i) by a consideration of the evidence of the moral agent's own inner experience, and (ii) by showing that extraneous considerations, supposed to be fatal to it, are in fact not so. On (i) Campbell says: 'The appeal is throughout to one's own experience in the actual taking of the moral decision in the situation of moral temptation. "Is it possible", we must ask, "for anyone so circumstanced to *dis*believe that he could be deciding otherwise?" The answer is surely not in doubt.'[24] Now, this reads very like Price's words: 'We have, in truth, the same constant and necessary consciousness of liberty, that we have that we think, choose, will, or even exist; and whatever to the contrary any person may say, it is impossible for them in earnest to think they have no active, self-moving powers, and are not the causes of *their own* volitions, or not to ascribe to *themselves*, what they must be conscious *they* think and do' (p. 182). If Price went so far with the view Campbell represents, it may be that he would have been willing to assent when the latter goes on to say: 'the very essence of the moral decision as it is experienced is that it is a decision whether or not to *combat* our strongest desire, and our strongest desire *is* the expression in the situation of our character as so far formed. Now clearly our character cannot be a factor in determining the decision whether or not to *oppose* our character. I think we are entitled to say, therefore, that the act of moral decision is one in which the self is for itself not merely "author" but "sole author"'.

On the second foundation of his libertarian thesis Campbell says that his theory offers no more barriers to successful prediction on the basis of character than any other. Given knowledge of a man's character, it is possible on the libertarian view 'to predict within certain limits how he will respond'. 'I claim, therefore,' says Campbell, 'that the view of free will I have been putting forward is consistent with predictability of conduct on the basis of character over a very wide field indeed. And I make the further claim that that field will cover all the situations in life concerning which there is any empirical evidence that successful prediction is possible.'[25] This too can be paralleled from Price: 'If, upon examination, any of the advocates of the doctrine of necessity should find, that what they mean by necessity is not inconsistent with the ideas of *agency* and *self-determination*, there will be little room for farther disputes; and that liberty which I insist upon as essential to morality, will be acknowledged . . .' (p. 183). And again: 'All voluntary action is, *by the terms*, free and implies the *physical possibility* of forebearing it. What is meant by this *possibility* is not in the least inconsistent with the utmost *certainty of event*, or with the *impossibility*, IN ANOTHER SENSE, that the action should be omitted' (pp. 244–5; cf. pp. 210–11). In the first of these quotations, Price may have been thinking of Hume's account of causation and making the point (which Campbell also makes) that no such idea of causation as Hume's constitutes a valid objection to his theory. In the second, he was quite explicitly dealing with dependability of character and affirming that conduct may be predicted with a high degree of probability in the case of some characters, and with what amounts to utmost certainty in the case of God, without denying free will. Price certainly does appear sometimes to think of the self as distinct from motives (i.e. character) in a way similar to that in which libertarians like Campbell do. He writes in a footnote, ' 1hough, at the same time it be very plain that motives can have no concern in *effecting* his [the agent's] determination, or that there is no *physical connexion* between his judgment and views, and the actions consequent upon them. What would be more absurd than to say, that our inclinations act upon us, or compel us; that our desires and fears *put* us into motion, or *produce* our volitions; that is, are agents?' (p. 183).

But there are considerations which are consistent with a negative answer to our question: did Price hold a libertarian position? For instance, he writes: 'Virtue supposes determination, and determination supposes a determiner; and a determiner that determines not himself, is a palpable contradiction. Determination requires an efficient cause. If this cause is the being himself, I plead for no more' (p. 181). Hobart might easily have written that. Again, Price explicitly refers to his view as that of '*agency* and *self-determination*' (p. 183). Furthermore, the opening sentence of the footnote immediately preceding those quoted above might well be taken to imply that Price did not think of the self as distinct from motives: 'With respect to this, however, one may observe, that there seems to be very little mysterious in a man's choosing to follow his judgment and desires, or his actually doing what he is *inclined* to do: which is what we mean when we say, motives determine him.' It is impossible to say precisely what Price would have written on this issue if he had been confronted by contemporary arguments. It may well be that he would have subscribed to a limited libertarianism like that of Campbell rather than to self-determinism as propounded by Hobart. Whatever Price's choice between such alternatives would have been, nothing he says entirely excludes the self-determinism which we shall now consider.[26]

(ii) *Self-determinism.* The correct interpretation or analysis of 'can', 'could', etc., on this view is hypothetical; a fact which, from what has already been said, seems to indicate at once that it is more consistent with the deliverances of the developed moral consciousness and the ordinary use of moral terms. On this interpretation, 'can' equals 'will, if . . .' and the conditions are of three kinds:

Type 1: if external conditions allow.
Type 2: if the agent possesses certain qualities of mind and character.
Type 3: if the agent chooses.[27]

To illustrate, let us suppose that I have taken £10 belonging to a friend without his knowledge. I ought to return this money. I can, i.e. I will, if conditions of the following kind are fulfilled:

Type 1. Conditions such as: if I still have it and have not lost or spent it, if there is a means of returning it, if my friend has not gone to a country beyond the Iron Curtain where I cannot reach him, if he has not disappeared altogether, etc. It seems natural to group with conditions of this first type (i.e. freedom from external hindrances) conditions such as: if I *know* where he is, if I *know* how to reach him; and there is much to be said for taking them together, although conditions of knowledge are placed in our classification under the second type. It should be noted that we can never enumerate *all* the conditions of Type 1 which have to be fulfilled for an action to take place: however fully I specify the external hindrances which would curtail my freedom, there *may* be circumstances which I overlook when I say that I can return it.

Type 2. I will return the £10 to my friend if I possess certain qualities of, and am free from certain defects of, mind and character. It is necessary to introduce some sub-classes within this type of condition, three at least:

(i) *Knowledge.* My returning the £10 depends upon my knowing where my friend is and how to reach him, as we have already noticed. If I have no idea where he is (ignorance) or believe him to be where he is not (error), then I cannot return the money. Aristotle defined voluntary action as that unhindered by compulsion or ignorance, putting this type of condition alongside our Type 1.[28]

(ii) *Freedom from pathological defects of character.* There are cases where much moral exhortation, and much remorse and resolution to do better on the part of the agent himself, have resulted in no improvement of behaviour; whereas psychiatrical or psycho-therapeutical treatment has done so. In the case of the £10, it is conceivable that, having got it, I find myself incapable of returning it. Every time I take it out to the post, I come back having forgotten why I went out; or every time I reach for it to send it back my hand is paralysed and I cannot pick it up. Compulsive psychological mechanisms of this kind do arise and have an effect upon conduct. Such defects as, for instance, kleptomania and sex-mania are compulsive.

(iii) *Ordinary qualities of character.* Our ordinary language seems to imply that there is a third condition of this kind. 'I can return the £10' may be analysed 'I will, if I am honest.' This condition appears to be analogous to those of the two preceding types (i.e. Type 2 (i) and (ii)). But there are objections to so regarding it. We could conceivably devise empirical tests for the existence or non-existence of the two previous types of condition. If, for instance (see Type 2 (i)), I claim that I am ignorant of my friend's whereabouts, this claim could (in some cases at any rate) be tested and the fact of my ignorance verified or otherwise, quite apart from my action (or lack of action) in not returning the £10. Similarly, if I claim (see Type 2 (ii)) that I cannot remember to take the letter to the post, or that my arm becomes paralysed every time I try to reach for it, the genuineness of these claims could (in some cases at any rate) be established. But if I say that I have not returned the £10 because I am dishonest, what empirical tests are there for proving the existence or non-existence of this dishonesty, apart from my not returning the money? Is to say 'I didn't do X because I was too dishonest' to say any more than 'I didn't do X'?

I think we must recognise that nouns (and the corresponding adjectives) which describe dispositions or traits of character (courage, courageous; honesty, honest; sense of duty, dutiful; etc.) are, so to speak, really adverbs. To say '*A* has a lot of courage' or 'is courageous' tells us how he behaves, or rather how he has been observed to behave on a number of past occasions. Where a person has been observed to act in a specific and consistent (e.g. courageous) way on many past occasions, this leads us to expect that he will act in a similar way on the next occasion. It is this expectation which we express when we say that he 'has courage' or 'is courageous'. And so the question arises as to whether, when our ordinary ways of speaking seem to imply an analysis of 'can' in terms of 'will if he has courage' etc., this analysis amounts to anything more than 'will if he does'. I think we must say that there *is* more to it than that. Do we not believe that a man who is courageous (and this may be taken to mean simply that he has fairly consistently done a certain kind of action in the past) can, in some more complete sense of 'can' than would be the case with a man who is not courageous, do a certain act, or acts, in the present? There is empirical evidence that he finds it easier, in some cases at least. Suppose two men, one whom we call courageous and the other whom we call timid, face an ordeal together. There may well be signs of strain on the face or in the behaviour of the timid man which indicate that he is finding it harder to go through with the ordeal than the other man. And there may come a point where the courageous man goes on with the ordeal and the timid man runs away from it. In that case we may well say 'He just couldn't take any more.' Do we mean simply 'He just *didn't* take any more'? This disposition, courage, whatever we mean by it (and certainly character, the system of such dispositions), is thought and spoken of as a factor in conduct like external conditions, knowledge and freedom from kleptomania, etc.

Now consider the analogous case of a judge estimating A's responsibility for a crime and considering how far the latter's dishonesty is his own fault. When he speaks of A's dishonesty, may he not be thinking of this disposition apart from any particular actions of A? May he not think of it as, in some degree, the product of early influence or training? A has a character which is in part the product of such factors, and the kind of character he has is a condition of which we take account in estimating what he can or cannot do. Ordinary people speak and think of character as a condition determining possibilities of action. A psychologist has said that the two questions they most commonly ask him are, How is character to be judged? and, How is it to be improved?[29] I think that 'if I am honest' is a stateable condition in the analysis of 'I can', etc., just as are the other conditions given here. But it certainly cannot be separated from action in the way that the conditions of freedom from compulsion, ignorance or pathological defects can. This will be apparent when we ask how far not being honest, etc., seems to us to cancel obligation or absolve from responsibility.

Type 3. I will return the £10, if I choose to do so. The evidence for attributing to me the power to do what I choose is empirical. There is a regular sequence which holds good where nothing interferes with it. Suppose *A* has open to him certain courses of action, *a*, *b*, *c*, etc. If asked to tell us which of these he prefers to the rest, he will name a group; of these, his preferences, he will choose one as that which he prefers most; this, he will say, is what I want or will to do. This will be followed by the appropriate action unless something prevents it. We have preferences; we make choices; we perform actions. Our preferences are determined by being ours, not someone else's. Our choices are determined by following upon our preferences. Our actions are determined by following on our choices. This is determinism, but it is also freedom: my freedom to do what I prefer, what I choose, what I will, which is surely the only kind of freedom that is intelligible.

The question which now arises is: of which of these conditions may we say that, if they are unfulfilled, that fact cancels obligation and absolves from responsibility? Certainly we can say this of Type 1 conditions; and equally certainly of Type 2 (i).[30]

The greatest difficulties arise with regard to conditions of Type 2 (ii). It is difficult, for one thing, to define the limits of this sub-class precisely. There are some types of action which all would agree are not culpable because the agent is quite clearly under a pathological compulsion to behave as he does: a man who suffers acutely from claustrophobia, for instance, can scarcely be blamed, if, trapped suddenly in a confined space with others, he fights to get out. But if a person who was just 'nervy' behaved like this, his failure of nerve would by most people be considered reprehensible, though kinder, more sympathetic people might hesitate to condemn him. Even within the same condition, distinctions which are very difficult to draw nevertheless seem to be called for – for instance, between those in whose case homosexuality should be regarded as a disease and those in whose case it should be regarded as a vice. For another thing, it is difficult to decide whether moral terms are appropriate in the case of agents whose acts quite clearly spring from character defects for which they are not responsible. Hare points out that we say, and he thinks rightly, of the kleptomaniac, 'He ought not to have stolen', even though we think psychological treatment, not moral censure or punishment, is appropriate in his case.[31] Hare thinks this is perplexing and perhaps calls for some modification of our terminology. Here, it seems, we have an 'ought' which does not imply 'can'. It is certainly very odd, if 'ought' here is to be given its full moral significance in a context which excludes praise, blame, all imputation of responsibility, as inapplicable. This is a use to which 'ought' is admittedly put, but it fails to satisfy the tests for the appropriateness of 'ought' which are normally applied in moral contexts; and so we can only conclude that it is a loose use of the word expressing disapproval of a type of activity, but not implying what is normally implied by 'ought'.

Do unfulfilled conditions of Type 2 (iii) and Type 3 cancel obligation? Is it any excuse for failing to return the £10, if I say 'I am not honest enough' or 'I do not choose to'? I think the exponents of both self-determinism and indeterminism would agree that the answer is in the negative at least in some cases. But the interesting point is this: the assumption which would have to be made, if these excuses were *accepted*, is the very one which indeterminists make. It is the assumption that there is, so to speak, a self within the self distinct from character and preferences. The indeterminists believe that there is indeed such a self; but they believe it just because they *reject* the view that my character or preferences excuse my failures of duty.[32] If, however, there were a self which chose between, say, the motive of conscientiousness, which would lead me to return the £10, the motive of benevolence, which would lead me to give it to an orphanage, and the motive of lust, which would lead me to spend it on pornography, and so on, this self's choice would be determined by its character or preferences, unless there were another self 'inside' it, choosing between its motives, and so on *ad infinitum*. In this infinite regress we pursue the self, but it always disappears again the moment we seem to have caught it. With it go freedom and responsibility. Such an indeterminate self's choice, if we could ever get to it, must be undetermined by character or desires; as such it would not be, in any intelligible sense, the choice *of this self*, for there would be nothing in the self giving rise to one choice rather than another, nor anything in the choice associating it with this self rather than another. And so, neither would it be a choice for which *this self* could be, in any intelligible sense, held responsible. It would be a spontaneous occurrence; an event attributable to chance.

In reply to all this, the indeterminist contends that if an action is determined even by the self, i.e. by character, there is no point in moral judgement, praise, blame, etc. But this assumes that the constitution of the self is static, whereas it seems to be ever changing under certain 'pressures'. Training, example, exhortation, reward and punishment are instances of such pressures. Through them moral judgements are expressed and under such influence characteristics and desires within the self grow stronger or weaker, the constitution of the self is changed, and consequently the actions determined by it improve or deteriorate in moral quality.

Here the question may be put:[33] why do we call such pressures moral and other pressures (e.g. brain surgery, psychiatry), which also alter character, non-moral, when the point of all of them is simply utilitarian? I think the answer is: because there is a real distinction here and this is the way we mark it. Some characteristics are strengthened or weakened by praise, blame, reward, punishment, etc., and others are not. We call the former characteristics moral qualities and the latter non-moral. We differentiate these by learning from experience to which of these classes characteristics or situations belong.[34] Experience has taught us that certain types of character or action which would once have been called wicked are pathological rather than immoral; that is to say, they are not altered by moral judgements being passed on them. And so we have ceased to think or talk of them in terms of right and wrong, or at least to do so when we are using ethical terms to imply merit or demerit. This alterability by praise, blame, etc., does seem to be the criterion by which we differentiate between 'moral' and 'non-moral' in practice; and it seems to explain the changes which take place in our views as to what falls under each term. We cease to talk or think in moral terms of that which is unalterable in these ways. We call the one class moral and the other non-moral, when the difference is simply between types of alterability, because marking this distinction is the job which the words 'moral' and 'non-moral' do in contexts where changes in character or desire are under discussion; they indicate what can and what cannot be altered by praise, blame, etc.

It is, therefore, not true that ' "self-determinism" would make merit and remorse depend upon illusion'[35] (the illusion being that there is a distinction between, for instance, remorse, i.e. regret about something which I could have helped, and regret about a bad memory, which I could not). This is not illusion: we have already shown that there is a real and important distinction here. We have also shown that some difficulties arise if 'I could have' is analysed in terms other than 'I would have, if I had chosen (or willed)' which is deterministic. The reference to remorse, however, raises an interesting point: can one feel remorse for that which one could not have helped? I think one can, i.e. one will, if one is of a certain character. The consciences of saints have sometimes been burdened with the sins of mankind, for which they themselves were not responsible in the narrow sense of having committed them; with the guilt of these sins they have identified themselves, however, confessing them as their own. This may, of course, be dismissed by some as no more than a psychological abnormality, but it does raise the question whether we do not frequently conceive of the self in terms which are too insular. I think the critics of self-determinism sometimes assume that the self which is postulated by that theory is an isolated, eternally and absolutely determinate, moral individual. But the moral self, or at least most moral selves, are certainly indeterminate in the sense that their moral conduct lacks absolute consistency. This may not be true of the best or the worst of men, but it is of most men. Sometimes I lie; sometimes I tell the truth. After a tiring day, dealing with difficult people, I am bad-tempered with my children; on holiday, in the company of people I like, I am more kind to them. In some company 'I find myself' doing what in other company I should not. The moral self is neither changeless nor isolated. It is continually in the making. It would not be possible, in the logic of self-determinism, to conceive of a self improving itself spontaneously; but it is perfectly possible to conceive of self-improvement as promoted or hindered, and desires for it as strengthened or weakened, by social influences from innumerable sources: teaching, example, encouragement, companionship, etc. Moral judgements are one such influence. They have part in that process whereby any given self is continually being made. Certain settled moral principles, good or evil, are laid down in most of us; very firmly laid down in the best and the worst of us. But, however dependable, the self is never determinate in the sense that it is beyond the influence of society. 'No man is the whole of himself; his friends are the rest of him.'

(d) Necessity and Freedom

As we have seen, Price says that, if advocates of necessity would consider what they mean by necessity, they might find that it is not inconsistent with his doctrine of agency or self-determination (p. 183). It is very plain that 'motives can have no concern in *effecting* his [the agent's] determination', he says and that 'there is no *physical connexion* between his judgment and views, and the actions consequent upon them'. Price elsewhere uses the expression 'physical possibility' in the sense of logical possibility (p. 244); and, if we take the word 'physical' in the same sense here, the point he is making would seem to be that the connexion is not a logically necessary one. The connexion between

the judgements and views, motives or desires of the agent, on the one
hand, and his actions, on the other, is one which might not have been
and is, therefore, Price thinks, quite consistent with the notion of
liberty. Price differentiates two necessities in the divine nature: the
moral impossibility that God should deviate from rectitude, and the
'natural' or 'physical' impossibility that he should not exist (pp. 244–5).
Price compares the first kind of necessity, whether in God or man, to
the impossibility that a million, or indeed an infinite number of, dice,
each having a million, or even an infinite number of, faces, should be
thrown a million, or even an infinite number of, times, and invariably
all come up the same – 'which though infallibly true that it will not
happen, yet *may* happen' (p. 247). There is 'the same *natural* possibility
of this, as of any other event'. The second kind of necessity, which he
calls 'natural' or 'physical', Price compares to 'the impossibility of
throwing any faces which there are not upon a die' (p. 246); that is, of
saying 'This face is on the die and came up' and also 'This face is not
on the die.'

This distinction is valid enough, but what is its bearing upon the free
will versus determinism controversy? Price writes:

> Now, he that should in such cases [of the dice], confound these
> different kinds of impossibility (or necessity) would be much more
> excusable than he that confounds them, when considering the events
> depending on the determinations of free beings, and comparing them
> with those arising from the operation of blind and unintelligent
> causes. The one admits of endlessly various degrees; the other of
> none. That necessity by which twice two is not twenty, or a mass of
> matter does not continue at rest when impelled by another, is,
> wherever found, always the same, and incapable of the least increase
> or diminution. (pp. 246–7)

According to Price, then, the necessity by which actions follow from
volitions is the first kind of necessity, i.e. a high degree of probability;
the necessity by which events follow upon events is the second kind,
i.e. natural or logical necessity. On this three comments may be made:
(i) I think *some* such distinction certainly is suggested by some at least
of our ordinary ways of thinking and speaking. We do differentiate
actions from events. For instance, we pass moral judgements upon the
former, but not the latter. If asked to say how a death due to the accidental fall of a rock differs from an act of murder, I think the plain man
would very probably reply, 'Well, it couldn't be helped' – i.e. there
was a necessity about it which would not have applied to an act of

murder. (ii) The whole point of the free will versus determinism controversy, however, is whether this distinction which seems to be implied by our ways of speaking and thinking is a valid distinction. Price simply begs the question: he starts from the fact that actions and events are different and explains the difference as being (or as being like) that between probability and logical necessity. But the undoubted fact that there is a difference between a high degree of improbability and logical impossibility does not provide any grounds for differentiating the occurrences we call actions, as occurrences which may not have occurred, from all other occurrences, as being bound within the causal nexus and therefore bound to occur. (iii) Price, of course, believed that logical necessity is the necessity of the nature of things (this is why he speaks of it as 'natural' or 'physical') and so it was open to him, on his own theory, to regard events as logically necessary. But if this is rejected, then the distinction between logical necessity and probability becomes completely irrelevant to the present issue. The 'necessity' whereby events follow from other events belongs to the realm of probability just as much as that whereby actions follow from volitions.

Price's hope that the free will versus determinism controversy could be resolved and the two viewpoints reconciled was, no doubt, inspired by reading David Hume; and we will conclude our discussion of liberty by considering some of the points made by Hume. He said[36] that he hoped to show that all men have always really believed in both necessity and liberty, according to any reasonable meaning which can be put on these terms, and that the whole controversy has been merely verbal. He argued that all we ever really know about causation is that particular objects are constantly conjoined in our experience and that the mind is carried by custom from the appearance of certain objects (causes) to expect the appearance of certain others (effects). We believe, however, that we perceive more than this: that we perceive a necessary connexion between cause and effect. When we reflect upon the operations of our own minds though, we '*feel* no such connexion of the motive and the action' and therefore 'suppose that there is a difference between the effects which result from material force, and those which arise from thought and intelligence'. Of course, there is no such necessary connexion between motive, or character, and action but there is regular conjunction between them and we can, and do, in practice, draw inferences from one to the other just as in the case of other events. All this is clearly consistent with a deterministic account of morals, but the interesting question is: what place did Hume allow to liberty? We will consider the answer to this question under three divisions:

(i)

He acknowledges that men often do unusual and surprising things, for which they may even be unable to account themselyes. But this is no concession to indeterminism since he compares it to unexpected changes in the weather, the causes of which are simply not easily discoverable; he says that the conjunction of motives and actions is 'as regular and uniform as that between the cause and effect in any part of nature'.

(ii)

Hume defines liberty, in a footnote, as 'a certain looseness or indifference which we feel in passing, or not passing, from the idea of one object to that of any succeeding one'. He says that as *agents*, at the time of performing an action, we feel this looseness of conjunction between motive, or character, and action; and we interpret it to mean that we have free will, or even take it as demonstrative or intuitive proof of such freedom. As *spectators*, reflecting on our own actions or those of others, we 'seldom feel such looseness or indifference, but are commonly able to infer them with considerable certainty from their motives, and from the dispositions of the agent'. Even when, as spectators, we cannot do this, we assume that we could, if we were more perfectly acquainted with the agent's motives and character. Our belief in free will is strengthened by the fact that if, when we have done a certain action from among conceivable alternatives, it is denied that we could have done any but the act we did, we find that, if we put ourselves in the same position again, we can act in one of these alternative ways. But Hume will not accept this as a refutation of his theory: what we fail to take account of in such a case, he says, is 'that the fantastical desire of showing liberty is here the motive of our actions'.

Indeterminists accuse determinists of dismissing far too lightly this feeling of 'looseness', or free will, which the agent has at the time of acting. Campbell thinks that they ought to be a good deal more worried about it than they usually are. He says that they seem to imagine that a strong case on general theoretical grounds is enough to prove that belief in free will is mere illusion; but he sees no reason why a practical belief, as universal and unavoidable as that which the agent has in his own freedom to do otherwise at the time of moral action, should give way before a theoretical belief, like that which we may feel compelled to hold, as theoretical beings, in determinism. There is just as much obligation, he thinks, upon the determinist to show that 'the assurance of free will is not really an inexpugnable element in man's practical consciousness' as there is upon the libertarian to show that 'the extraneous considerations so often supposed to be fatal to the belief in moral freedom are in fact innocuous to it'.[37]

At this point two comments suggest themselves: (i) The way in which determinists sometimes deal with this feeling of freedom is certainly open to serious criticism. (*a*) For instance, they say that it is just an illusion.[38] But an illusion of what? The answer can only be: of genuine freedom. It has been pointed out that if there is something which is my *illusion* of freedom, then there must also be something else which is my *genuine* freedom. This is implied in the meaning of the word 'illusion'.[39] (*b*) Determinists may not deny that we have the feeling of freedom (Hume certainly did not), but they might allege that, in calling it a 'feeling of freedom', we are not reporting, but interpreting, experience. If, however, this is interpretation in the sense in which we interpret sense-data, the determinist gives his case away again. The interpretation of clouds as meaning rain, for instance, is 'established by *association* between units of *experience*'.[40] Similarly, when we interpret a sense-datum, or group of sense-data, by saying 'It is the top of a table', the content of 'table' is drawn from experience. If the interpretation of our feeling of freedom is compared to either of these cases, it implies that we have the experience of freedom as well as the feeling of freedom. But the expression 'a feeling of freedom' is like the expression 'a feeling of awe'. It denotes a certain type of experience. Now, just as to say 'Because he feels this feeling which we call a feeling of awe man is a spiritual being' is not interpretation in the sense in which it would be interpretation if we were to say 'Because man feels this feeling there must be a God' – and this because part of the meaning of 'man is a spiritual being' is 'man feels this feeling of awe'; so to say 'Because man feels this feeling which we call a feeling of freedom he is free' is not interpretation, if part of the meaning of 'man is free' is 'man feels this feeling'. Or so the indeterminists contend. Their point is that the definition of freedom must include some reference to this feeling and that, in denying freedom, the determinist is denying the existence of this feeling; and so he cannot say that he does *not* deny it. More is said on the attempt to give the term 'free' positive content from the feeling of freedom towards the close of the present subsection. (ii) The psychological point here needs to be considered a little more closely. Is the assurance of free will really an 'inexpugnable element' in man's practical consciousness, in the way that indeterminists believe it to be? Campbell means by this 'inexpugnable element' that 'when actually confronted with a personal situation of conflict between duty and desire, he [the moral agent] is quite certain that it lies with him here and now whether or not he will rise to duty'.[41] Now, if 'he is quite clear that it lies with him' is taken in the sense that he feels responsible for what he does, none will dispute the point. But the indeterminist means that the moral agent is clear that it lies with him in the sense that he feels he can at the moment of action make a free choice independently of his character; and, furthermore, that *if he did not believe this*, he would not feel his action to be morally culpable. Is this so? A homosexual, for instance, may feel quite unable to act otherwise (and in fact be unable) and yet feel intense shame and remorse. Priests and other advisers are frequently consulted by persons who do not feel that they could have done other than they did, and yet are ashamed *of themselves*. Is not this to some extent true of most people? There have been occasions when it would have been right for me to do something which I lacked the physical courage to do. I may accept that, being who I am, I could not have done it, but I still feel ashamed. If I am told that this element in my character is due, in part at least, to heredity (e.g. to my having inherited a certain nervous system) or environment (e.g. to my having been pampered when young), I feel no less ashamed *of myself*. I think this distinction, between what I feel that I could not have done and what I feel I could not *not* have done, does not have the definitive importance in our practical consciousness which indeterminists deem it to have. When Christians, for instance, speak of man's 'sinful state' or in worship confess that they are 'miserable offenders', they refer not to actions so much as to a condition which they take to be theirs; and they do not differentiate those elements in this condition which are due, for instance, to heredity and environment, factors they cannot control, from the expression of this condition in actions due to their own free choice, feeling guilty about the latter but not about the former. They feel guilty about what they *are* and seek forgiveness for that.

Hume's distinction between the 'agent' and the 'spectator' is one which many writers on this problem have drawn in some form or other. Among contemporary philosophers, for example, Raphael develops a view which he directly attributes to Hume.[42] He writes: 'From the outlook of scientific observation (Hume's spectator), a man's act is "explained" by bringing it under a regular law through comparison with similar acts in similar circumstances; it is dealt with as a "thing" or event observed, and as liable to be correlated with similar observed events ("things happening"). From the outlook of agents (which may be taken not only by the actual agent, as Hume suggests, but also by spectators thinking of themselves as potential agents, imagining themselves in the actual agent's shoes, instead of thinking of the situation detachedly as an external object of their observation), the act is considered not in relation to similar past acts, but as issuing from a freely choosing and responsible "person"'. He says that the problem of free will versus determinism arose because natural science began before our primitive conception of material change had been purified of animism; and so the language of science, which really describes the uniformity, or regular sequences, of nature, became infected with purposive terms drawn from everyday language about human actions. 'The two languages are quite different, expressing two different points of view, and there is no conflict between them,' says Raphael. He does not believe, however, that we could go on talking about actions in both scientific and 'plain man' terms, whatever happened. If the laws of human action were laws of 100 per cent regularity, then, he says, he would cease to maintain a case for free will. He is surely correct in this. Suppose a man is undecided as to what he will do. Some degree of certainty as to what he will do based on empirical evidence (i.e. prediction) may conflict with some degree of certainty about it based on reasons (i.e. decision). A man may, for instance, say 'I have not yet decided whether to do or not to do X', even though, knowing how he has invariably acted in this kind of situation before, he is fairly certain that he will do the same this time. But if from empirical evidence he predicts with absolute certainty 'I will do X', then he cannot at the same time think that whether he does or does not do X is still a question the answer to which depends upon his decision.[43] Raphael thinks, however, that, though not logically impossible, the fulfilment of the condition of universal regularity is factually impossible.

Other writers have been more thorough-going in their separation of the 'spectator' and 'agent' roles, and have suggested that, however complete the scientific or deterministic way of talking about actions becomes, the indeterministic or 'plain man' way may remain valid. Spinoza represents one line of thought on this. For all his determinism, he would appear to admit that the indeterministic way of speaking about actions must, in its own dimension, always be logically valid:

'Now all these things clearly show that the decision of the mind and the desire and determination of the body are simultaneous in nature, or rather one and the same thing, which when considered under the attribute of thought and explained through the same we call decision (*decretum*), and when considered under the attribute of extension and deduced from the laws of motion and rest we call determination (*determinatio*) . . .'[44] Another line, this time dynamic not static, is that which Leibniz,[45] Bergson and the existentialists develop in their several ways. According to this, the moral agent lives in a creative present (*natura naturans*) of which nature, as science describes it, is the *depositum*, and as such is phenomenal to our senses. Only when the present has thus become the past (*natura naturata*) can it be described in terms of the structural patterns and causal connexions of science. The fact that it can be so described after it has happened is no indication that it could have been foretold with absolute certainty before it happened.[46] In the existentialists' terminology, man's existence comes before his essence. As J.-P. Sartre puts it, he 'first of all exists, encounters himself, surges up in the world – and defines himself afterwards'. To begin with he is nothing; he becomes what he makes himself; 'he is what he wills'.[47] Or, as N. Berdyaev put it, the freedom of the spirit is the primary sphere, and 'the determined world of physical and psychical causality is a secondary sphere and is the product of freedom, for freedom is not the result of necessity, as many thinkers assert, but rather it is necessity which results from freedom as a consequence of its own peculiar orientation. The natural, psychical, and physical world is the result of events and actions in the spiritual world.'[48]

These, of course, are highly metaphysical solutions of our problem. Is there any solution on the linguistic plane?

(iii)

This brings us to the solution which Hume himself offered: 'And if the definition above mentioned be admitted, liberty, when opposed to necessity, not to constraint, is the same thing with chance, which is universally allowed to have no existence.'[49] The 'definition' referred to was that of 'cause' in terms of constant conjunction (not of some necessary connexion underlying this). Hume's point is that, if this definition of causation ('necessity' as used in this quotation) is adopted, then 'free', if opposed to 'caused' (and not to 'constrained' or 'compelled', which is something quite different) is a term empty of all positive content. It is, like 'chance', 'a mere negative word'.

The distinction between being caused, in the sense of compelled, and being caused, in a sense which does not imply compulsion, has been taken by some writers to solve the whole problem.[50] They suggest that it satisfies our common use of 'free', if we restrict the application of the word to cases where action, though caused, is not compelled. There is undoubtedly something to be said for this. Obviously, we would never use the word 'free' of acts which were clearly done under compulsion; but do we conceive of any acts as caused, but not compelled? Yes: we speak of moral acts as free, even though our common notions of moral responsibility imply that there is a self which caused them. And the fact that in all our ways of talking about moral actions some personal noun or pronoun has to be used for the subject of action also implies a self which causes the action. So this notion of an act which is caused but not compelled certainly seems to be in accordance with some of the things which we think and say about free acts.[51] Nevertheless, we do speak and think about voluntary actions differently from the way in which we speak and think about other events; and this difference seems to consist in the belief that the volitions from which voluntary actions spring are mental events to which no other events, mental or physical, stand in precisely the relation we call cause.[52] But when we try to analyse the expression 'free acts', we find that the word 'free' seems to admit only of definition in *negative* terms. All attempts at positive definition break down. Suppose that the definition suggested is that a free act is one regarding which the agent has the feeling of freedom: a mad or drunken person may have this feeling even though he is in fact unable to stop doing what he is doing.[53] If the feeling may deceive us in one case, how are we to know that it does not deceive us in others? Only if we have some other empirical evidence besides this feeling by which to differentiate actions really free and those not so. The same would apply if it were suggested that the criterion for the use of 'free' is that such acts are ones on which we are prepared to pass a moral judgement or for which we will accept responsibility. What is deemed to be a morally culpable act by one man or age is sometimes not so regarded by another. If moral judgements are perceptions of objective truth, it then appears that we are sometimes deceived. How are we to tell cases where we are from those where we are not? Only if we have some other empirical evidence; but we have none. And if we do not accept the objective theory of moral judgements, we should still have the odd position that an act in one age is free, but not in another, or for one man and not another. We can say what a free act is *not*; but not what it *is*. The fact that the plain man has such a firm belief that free acts are different from those determined may be explained by the linguistic fact that the rule for the use of 'free' is that it applies in cases where the rules for the use of 'determined' do not.[54]

The generally accepted criterion for the use of 'free' and 'determined' is that the former describes action from an internal (i.e. within the agent) cause, and the latter action from an external (i.e. outside the agent) cause. The important question is, What counts as an internal, and what as an external, cause? The answer will depend upon our conception of the self. If we identify the true self with reason, as Price would, then irrational desires are 'outside' it and action due to them may be considered compulsive. As a result of psychological investigations, many acts which would once have been thought free are now thought of as determined (e.g. those due to pathological defects of character). Psychology investigates the empirical causes of actions, and we must face the possibility that it will eventually be able to explain all action in terms of such causes. We do differentiate between 'caused' and 'compelled'. We may speak of a man's action as caused by his choice; but we should not say that his own choice compelled him. What is taken to be a compulsive cause and what is not will depend upon where we draw the limits of the self and what, in consequence, we regard as external or internal. Our notions of responsibility will, similarly, be formed in the light of our conception of the self.

All this does not settle the free will versus determinism controversy, as traditionally understood. The metaphysician will still claim that he has the right to fill the term 'free' with his own meaning; whereas the anti-metaphysical philosopher will rest content in that he has shown that the metaphysician can do this only because 'free' is a term which has no positive, empirical content.

II.ii INTELLIGENCE

Price's second essential of practical virtue is intelligence (pp. 183-4). His view of practical virtue, if we are correct in interpreting it as what we have called kind PV-2, certainly presupposes both intuitive and discursive intelligence in the agent. A benevolent action, for example, if it were a case of practical virtue, would be the act which the agent thought right in a particular situation; to think it right at all he would have to intuit the general moral principle of beneficence; and to understand whether, in a given situation, he ought to do a benevolent action rather than, for example, keep a promise, he would have to think out the relations and effects of alternative possible actions.

Price remarks that, whereas intelligence is not essential to liberty, liberty is essential to intelligence. 'A thinking, designing, reasoning being', he writes, 'without liberty, without any inward, spontaneous, active, self-directing principle, is what no one can frame any idea of.' But why not? The adjective 'designing' is difficult; it may necessitate liberty: if 'designing' is defined to mean 'exercising a power to act and determine freely', then, of course, it implies liberty. But if we leave out 'designing' and consider simply Price's point that intelligence presupposes liberty, I think it possible to conceive of a being who experienced those modifications of consciousness which we refer to when we speak of self-consciousness, and who was able to understand the working of his own nature and of the world, but who was nevertheless determined, not free.[55]

II.iii REGARD FOR RECTITUDE

Price writes thus of the third and 'main' essential of practical virtue:

> . . . that an agent cannot be justly denominated *virtuous*, except he acts from a consciousness of rectitude, and with a regard to it as his *rule* and *end*. (p. 184)

And he proceeds to discuss in this connexion whether the perception of right and wrong 'excites' to action, and whether it is the 'only spring' of virtuous action; but before considering these points, he makes certain preliminary observations. Liberty and intelligence are the '*capacity*' of virtue, he says, but intention gives it '*actual being*' in a character. He distinguishes '*the virtue of the action*' from '*the virtue of the agent*' and says:

> To the former, no particular intention is requisite; for what is *objectively* right, may be done from any motive good or bad; and, therefore, from hence alone, no merit is communicated to the agent; nay, it is consistent with the greatest guilt. On the contrary, to the other the particular intention is what is most essential. When this is good, there is so far virtue, whatever is true of the *matter* of the action; for an agent, who does what is *objectively wrong*, may often be entitled to commendation. (p. 184)

There are two distinctions which Price fails to draw:

(i)

The first is that which Bentham and others have drawn between motive and intention.[56] Price seems to use these words interchangeably (see the first sentence of the last quotation); and in ordinary speech they often seem to be used interchangeably): 'He intended to get rich quick', 'His motive was to get rich quick.' But this is not always the case. There are differences in the way we use them. For instance, a single woman might say to a psycho-analyst, 'I thought my motive in doing social work among unmarried mothers was concern to promote their welfare, but I see now that my motive was really sexual curiosity.' There is nothing odd about this statement so far as the use of 'motive' is concerned. But now suppose someone alighted at a railway station and asked where he was. Receiving the answer 'Crewe', he then said, 'I thought it was my intention to go to Birmingham. You have convinced me that I was mistaken; my intention was really to go to Crewe.' This would sound very odd. I may perform a conscious, voluntary act without knowing my motive, but should we ever say that I could do so without knowing my intention? So I think that there is something to be said for drawing a distinction between 'motive' and 'intention' in terms of old-fashioned definitions. Though ordinary speech does not rigidly conform to this distinction, the words in many of their uses do.[57] The distinction provides us with useful pegs on which to hang, and keep apart from one another, some of our notions about virtue.

I think the motive of an act is best defined (following Bentham's suggestion) as the 'inducement'; that is, the thought of some end which the agent desires.[58] The intention is, I think, best defined as 'what the agent wills to do';[59] that is, the thought of the action, in all its aspects, which he consciously and deliberately sets himself to do. Obviously, these two do not completely coincide. The scientists who place animals or men in spacecraft consciously and deliberately endanger life, but this is not their motive. What induces them to act is the thought of the extension of knowledge which they hope to achieve by their experiments; but while this may be said to be part of their intention (i.e. what they will to do) it is not the whole of it – other things, including causing danger or pain, are willed as well. It seems, then, that the motive is included in the intention, but is not identical with the whole of it (or not always). Some recent writers would draw the limits of the application of 'intention' more narrowly than we do here. Professors S.

Hampshire and H. L. A. Hart, for instance,[60] consider the case of a man shooting at a bird and in the process making a loud noise as the cartridge explodes. Was it his intention to make a noise? He certainly did not make it unintentionally: he did not make it without knowing that he would do so, i.e. by accident or mistake. But it would be misleading to say that he intended to make the noise. This would suggest that if asked, 'What are you doing?' he would have replied, 'Making a noise.' He would not; he would have replied, 'Shooting a bird.' The latter was what he intended to do in a sense in which making a noise was not. And so, to say of a man 'X was his intention' means that X was what he willed to do in a sense which differentiates it from other actions performed at the same time with the agent's full knowledge. But it is a problem to know just where to draw the limits of indirect intention, so to speak. Miss G. E. M. Anscombe argues[61] that, if a man whose *regular* job it was to pump water to a house pumped it, knowing that it was poisoned, but said sincerely, 'I didn't care about that, I wanted my pay and just did my usual job', then, 'in that case . . . it would be incorrect to say that his act of replenishing the house supply with poisoned water was intentional.' If, however, a man whose regular job it was *not* was hired by the poisoner to pump the poisoned water, knowing it was poisoned, and he said sincerely, 'I didn't care about that, I wanted the money', then, says Miss Anscombe, 'the case is different': in such a case she thinks it would be correct to say that the act was intentional. I find this distinction rather subtle. It seems to me that we should more naturally say that in both cases the fact that the water was poisoned did not enter directly into the intention, though it was accepted, and the consequences of it for the occupants of the house, as part of the indirect intention. I would agree, however, with Miss Anscombe's conclusion at this point: that the man 'cannot profess not to have had the intention of doing the thing that was a means to an end of his'. Surely, in both cases pumping poisoned water was accepted as a means to the end. I find it hard to see that whether the job was *regular* and this an incident in it or *special* and this the whole of it makes much difference.

But what of those instances where two agents will to do identical acts, yet from completely different motives? A and B each give a million pounds to build a hospital; A's inducement is the relief of others' pain which his act will achieve, B's is the enhancement of his own reputation. It is even conceivable that the act in both cases should be an act of kind PV–2: that is, the act which the agent thinks right in the circumstances as he thinks them to be; yet, even so, the two acts may be done from very different motives. Now it is possible to take either of two lines concerning such cases: (*a*) To say, as J. S. Mackenzie would have done, that (since intention includes motive)[62] the acts of *A* and *B* differ in both motive and intention. (*b*) To say, as I think Mill would,[63] that they are identical in intention but differ in motive.

Before saying why the latter seems preferable, it will be as well to notice that in the present passage (pp. 184-5) Price does not differentiate practical from absolute virtue in quite the terms that he did previously. Here he seems to equate absolute virtue with that of the agent. But previously (p. 178) he spoke of *both* absolute and practical virtue as different views of the rightness or wrongness '*of actions*'; and we interpreted him to mean that it is the nature of the act, as being the act which the agent thinks right in what he thinks to be the circumstances, which renders it right in this (subjective) sense of rightness. Now such a definition of right clearly implies an agent; yet 'the virtue of the act' is said to be distinct in meaning from 'the virtue of the agent'. It is, as we have said, possible to say of two acts that they are both right in sense PV-2, and yet at the same time to say that the agent in one case is more virtuous than the agent in the other (i.e. one acts from desire for others' good, the other from desire to gain in reputation). We need terms which imply a reference to the agent in action, and yet preserve the distinction between the virtue of the act and of the agent. There is some advantage therefore in taking 'intention' to refer to the thought of the *act* which the agent sets himself to do, and 'motive' to refer to that desire in the *agent* from which the act springs. 'Intention' always implies reference to an agent who thinks of the act and sets himself to do it but, if clearly differentiated from 'motive', does not imply anything about the virtue of the agent as distinct from that of the act. If the words are taken in the senses suggested, then *both* absolute and practical virtue (objective and subjective rightness) require that the *intention*, i.e. what the agent wills to do, should be right. Price says that objective rightness implies nothing about the 'intention', but as we have remarked, he probably meant by this word what we mean by 'motive'. If objective rightness or wrongness involved no reference to intention in this sense, then they would refer to events, not actions, and could be used of saplings overtopping parent plants, etc.; that is, they would not be ethical expressions at all. But *neither* acts of practical nor of absolute virtue require to be done from any particular *motive*.

(ii)

This brings us to the second distinction which Price overlooks: that between rightness and moral goodness. He says at one point (p. 104) that they mean the same. The distinction between them which later writers have drawn has been useful. We have already considered the case of two men doing the same thing from different motives. It is useful, and indeed essential, to have some way of differentiating those respects in which we approve *equally* of A's and B's action from those in which we approve of A's (his motive was to relieve the pain of others) *more* than B's (his motive was to enhance his own repute). It seems artificial to say that A's action was right but B's was wrong; but not in the least artificial to say that A's was better than B's. If asked to say why it was better, our reply will have something to do with character and motive: 'A wanted to help other people', 'A wasn't so vain, ambitious, calculating . . . as B', etc. One way of drawing this necessary distinction is to say that both acts were *right* but both were not equally (morally) *good*, that is, the moral values realised in the motives were not equal. In terms of this distinction, 'right' refers to acts (in the sense of objective or subjective rightness); 'morally good' refers more directly to the agent, i.e. to his motives or character. A man's acts may be right or wrong, but it is *he* who is morally good or bad. As Mill said: 'the motive has nothing to do with the morality of the action, though much with the worth of the agent'.[64]

If anyone doubts the necessity of this distinction between rightness and moral goodness, let him reflect on the following points. An act cannot be right or wrong until it is done; but moral goodness is thought of as consisting not only in acts done from certain motives but also in desires (e.g. that for another's pleasure), emotions (e.g. that of satisfaction at another's pleasure) and qualities of character, even when these are not issuing in actions but simply exist in the agent.[65] Furthermore, just as an act may be the right act and yet its motive not be morally good, so an agent may be actuated by a good motive and yet not do the right action: because he wishes to spare his friend pain a man may tell a lie, even though he would agree that the right thing would have been to tell him the painful truth. If an act is the completely good act, however, i.e. if it is such as an ideal agent would be motivated to do in such circumstances, then, as Ross says,[66] it will also be the right act; for such an agent would do what he thinks right in the circumstances as he thinks them to be. Moreover, in practice, right acts are only done (except accidentally) by agents in whom good motives arise.[67]

Price goes on to say that an agent can only be held morally responsible for what he *intends* to do; this alone 'we have absolute power over, and are responsible for' (p. 185). He says that there are two senses in which we speak of actions: (i) 'the determinations or volitions themselves of a being', and (ii) 'the real event, or external effect produced'. A being with infinite knowledge and power always does what he intends, neither more nor less; but this is not the case with inferior beings. And so, an agent should *not* be held responsible for 'what arises beyond or contrary to his intention', that is, beyond what he wills to do. Now, 'ought' implies 'can' and so all the agent can be obliged to do is to set himself to do a certain action. If this is all he ought to do, then Price is perfectly correct: it is all for which he can be held responsible. Of course, he must not simply have the intention (i.e. the thought of the right act), but this together with a deliberate setting of himself to do the right act.[68] But moral praise and blame may attach to the agent in two ways and Price did not clearly distinguish these from one another. No doubt this was because he took 'intention' in the sense both of intention and of motive. The agent may be commended, or blamed, for the rightness, or wrongness, of his actions; and also for the moral quality of his motives. He is responsible for his actions, he is also responsible for what he is. We may judge his conduct or his character. Would it be fanciful to suggest that the difference between these two sorts of moral judgement has had something to do with the libertarian versus determinist controversy? So long as we think only in terms of the rightness or wrongness of actions, we can think of them in isolation from the determinate nature of the self, and the libertarian hypothesis seems not unreasonable; but when we take account of moral goodness, the thought of actions as determined by self or character becomes much more congenial to us.

(a) Is Regard for Rectitude a Sufficient Principle of Action?

Price now turns to consider the first main problem under this heading of regard for rectitude, namely, whether 'the perception of right and wrong does *excite* to action, and is alone a sufficient *principle* of action' (p. 185). He believes that 'experience' and 'the reason of the thing' clearly indicate that it does and is. On experience, he points out that 'all men continually feel, that the perception of right and wrong excites to action', and few, if any, would fail to be surprised on first hearing doubts expressed as to whether this is so. He quotes cases where he

thinks no other reason of action can be given except a sense of duty:
e.g. helping a benefactor rather than a stranger, accomplishing ends by
truthful means rather than by deceit, not taking the opportunity to
increase one's own fortune dishonestly – each when considerations of
private or public good, or the strongest natural desires, would incline
us to a different course. There is no denying that men normally think
themselves able to act from a sense of duty and often appear to do so.
As for the reason of the thing, Price writes: 'it seems extremely evident,
that excitement belongs to the very ideas of moral right and wrong,
and is essentially inseparable from the apprehension of them' (p. 186).
When we are conscious that we ought to do a certain act, 'it is not
conceivable that we can remain *uninfluenced*, or want a *motive* to action'.
Price, of course, puts the point in terms of rational intuitionism. If we
were to deny it, he says, it would be like asking whether the reasonableness of an action is a reason for doing it. 'The knowledge of what is
right, without any approbation of it, or concern to practise it, is not
conceivable or possible' (p. 187). Though we have taken exception to
his way of putting it (that rectitude or obligatoriness is a necessary perception of the understanding), we have recognised that there is a valid
logical point underlying his insistence upon the autonomy of ethics.
When I have expressed an ethical judgement of the form 'I ought to do
X' or 'It is right that I should do X', it is logically odd for me to ask
'Why should I do X?' My judgement is a commitment to action. To
ask me, when I have made this judgement, whether I have a motive for
action is like asking a man who has just signed the appropriate
documents whether he has any motive for enlisting in the army.

Aristotle believed that moral actions are – or depend on – the choice
of means to ends.[69] If this is accepted, the question remains: how are
these ends apprehended? The view Price is opposing here is the view
that they are apprehended only by the instinctive or appetitive elements
in human nature. Hobbes had said that a man is moved to action only
by desire for his own preservation, pleasure or power;[70] and Hume had
said that reason (either as judgement of relations or matters of fact) is,
and can never pretend to be anything but, the 'slave of the passions'.[71]
Against such opinions Price propounds a view which is reminiscent of
Samuel Clarke and anticipates Kant. The former had written: ' 'tis as
natural and (morally speaking) necessary, that the will should be
determined in every action by the reason of the thing, and the right of
the case, as 'tis natural and (absolutely speaking) necessary, that the
understanding should submit to a demonstrated truth';[72] and Kant was

to say that the categorical imperative was that which 'represented an action as necessary of itself without reference to another end'.[73] Price holds the view that there are certain objects which, from their very nature, must necessarily be desired by a rational being. He calls such rational desires 'affections'; and the desires for private and public happiness, for fame and honour, and for knowledge are examples which he gives (pp. 69 ff.). As he says in the passage under consideration here: 'Instincts, therefore, as before observed in other instances, are not necessary to the choice of ends.' He thinks of virtue or rectitude as the object of an affection like those already mentioned. He goes on: 'The intellectual nature is its own law. It has, within itself, a spring and guide of action which it cannot suppress or reject. Rectitude is itself an end, an ultimate end, an end superior to all other ends. . . .' To behold virtue, he has already said, 'is to possess supreme affection for it' (p. 59). He has admitted, of course, that certain conditions of the percipient (e.g. pain or sickness, biases, etc.) 'may lessen or prevent the effects that would otherwise follow the perception of moral good and evil' (p. 60). The influence of such perceptions is proportionate to the rational faculties of the percipient (p. 61). Urgent passions may interfere with our affection for rectitude, but to compensate for this God has wisely annexed some instincts to our intellectual perceptions (e.g. instinctive self-love and benevolence) (p. 62). In short, according to Price, 'in contemplating the actions of moral agents, we have both a *perception of the understanding*, and a *feeling of the heart*; and . . . the latter, or the effects in us accompanying our moral perceptions, depend on two causes. Partly, on the positive constitution of our natures: But principally on the essential congruity or incongruity between moral ideas and our intellectual faculties' (p. 62).

We have already taken exception to his view that there are ends which rational beings, from their own nature and that of the objects, *must necessarily* desire. It could be argued with some force that there are desires which only arise in us because we are rational beings, e.g. the desire for knowledge. But even in the case of knowledge it can be doubted whether reason ever supplies the ultimate end. Knowledge is usually desired as a means to something else; and even when it is desired without some obviously ulterior end directly in view the desire for it may be the expression of the will to power. The important point is that all the desires of a human being are not so many isolated units, but parts within a whole or self. The desire, when there is a conflict, which prevails depends, not upon the strength of that single

desire in isolation, but upon its consistency with all the other desires of
the being who feels it. This is why, for instance, urgent desires of the
moment are resisted for the sake of long-term ends which the individual
desires. If, perceiving a course of action to be right, a person chooses to
follow it, he acts from a desire to do his duty. There is no reason to say
that this desire to do his duty proves that he has perceived a necessary
implication of a non-natural quality of the act, comparable to the
necessary implications of mathematics or logic; but there is every
reason to say that it proves him to be a certain sort of person, i.e. a person to whom the doing of his duty is a more desirable end than any
other of which he is aware at the time. But this need not imply that
reason chooses ends. Hume recognised the facts. But he said that there
are 'certain calm desires', more known by their effects than their immediate sensation; these are of two kinds: (i) implanted instincts such
as benevolence, resentment, love of life, kindness to children; and (ii)
'the general appetite to good, and aversion to evil, considered merely
as such'.[74] Where such calm passions come into conflict with more
violent ones, which of them prevails, he said, depends upon 'the *general*
character or *present* disposition of the person'. It is certain that the
motives or desires form a system and that this system may be reformed
– and is constantly being reformed – by the influence of one self upon
another.

It has recently been pointed out that the dichotomy between reason
and desire in the moral psychology of some rationalists has not been
so complete as has often been supposed.[75] I think this might be said of
Price also. He does not separate reason and desire absolutely. On the
one hand, he has the idea of reason as a sort of love, its ends being the
objects of affections or rational desires. And, on the other, at one point
(pp. 191–2) I think he could be taken to suggest that some reflexion
upon reasonableness and fitness has contributed to the production even
of acts of instinctive benevolence, e.g. of mother love or good temper:
speaking of instinctive benevolence, he says that the actions of a good-
natured man or of a fond mother, being 'less attended with reflexion
on their reasonableness and fitness' seem to have 'less moral value'. He
adds, however: 'But it must not be forgot, that such reflexion will, in
general, accompany friendly and benevolent actions, and cannot but
have some concern in producing them . . . some ideas of right and
wrong are present always with all men, and must more or less influence
almost all they do.' It is doubtful whether Price (any more than some
other rationalists) subscribed so completely to the faculty psychology

of reason, will, desire, each sharply divided from the others, as eighteenth-century rationalists are supposed to have done.

(b) Is Regard for Rectitude the Only Principle of Actions which Engage our Esteem of the Agents?

Price now considers whether regard for rectitude is 'the *only* principle from which all actions flow which engage our esteem of the agents' (p. 188). He says that if we consider an act as only done by the agent when he intended to do it, then a virtuous act is an act of the agent if he does it intentionally, i.e. with rectitude 'in his view'. Furthermore, Price argues, an act which is not directed by a moral judgement cannot be moral: 'when virtue is not pursued or intended, there is no virtue in the agent. Morally good intention, without any idea of moral good, is a contradiction. To act virtuously is to obey or follow reason: But can this be done without knowing and designing it?' If, by saying that A's act is moral, I mean that it is right in sense PV–2, then this obviously implies a moral judgement on A's part; it is, by definition, the act which he thinks right. Now Price, as we have seen, did not distinguish between rightness and moral goodness. If he had done so, he might have modified what he says here. Whereas to be right in sense PV–2 an act must have been the act which was thought right, it is highly debatable whether an act is only morally good if it is done *from* a sense of duty. Suppose A and B are sons of C. A promised years ago, at a time when various financial responsibilities were being undertaken by members of the family, that he would provide for C's old age. B undertook some other responsibility at the time and is now under no obligation to contribute to his father's keep. A is prepared to keep his promise because he believes it his duty to do so. He asks nothing of B. B, however, says, 'I want to make a contribution to my father's keep. I shall enjoy doing so.' This is quite conceivable; there are people of such large generosity that they would get positive satisfaction from such a course. Would anyone say in this case that A's action (contributing to his father's keep from a sense of duty) had moral value, but B's (contributing from a desire to be benevolent) had none? Most contemporary philosophers would recognise that acts in so far as they are done from such motives as benevolence have a positive moral value thereby, and those done from such a motive as cruelty have a negative moral value thereby, quite apart from sense of duty. Some would say that sense of duty is a more excellent motive than any other; but others would even question this.[76]

I think, however, that the sharp and complete distinction which is now commonly drawn, no doubt under the influence of Kant or his interpreters, and which is drawn in the above illustration, between actions from a sense of duty and actions from such motives as benevolence or cruelty, would not have been drawn by Price, or at least not in quite the same way. There is, of course, much in chapters VIII and IX of the *Review* which is Kantian in tone, as readers have pointed out;[77] but I think it is important to notice how Price's rationalism differs from that of Kant, or at any rate from that of his interpreters. True, Price differentiates rational and instinctive benevolence (and also rational and instinctive self-love). He identifies the former with regard for rectitude: '*Rational benevolence* entirely coincides with rectitude, and the actions proceeding from it with the actions proceeding from a regard to rectitude' (p. 191). This, of course, can be paralleled from Kant: 'benevolence from principle (not from instinct)' has 'intrinsic worth'.[78] But Price thought of rational benevolence as 'part of the idea of virtue' (p. 193): this is the idea which reason necessarily discerns, approves and desires (p. 191). In discussing action from a sense of duty, it is customary, no doubt from Kantian influences, to distinguish between (*a*) doing what is benevolent *for the sake of duty* and (*b*) doing what is benevolent *for its own sake*.[79] But I do not think Price would have considered this distinction a valid one. I think he would have said that, in the above illustration, *A* was acting from regard to the principle of promise-keeping and *B* from regard to the principle of benevolence, or beneficence, and this was all the difference. True, on rational and instinctive benevolence (or self-love), he does say that the difference between them lies in 'rational reflexion on what is right to be done' (p. 195), which accompanies the former but not the latter. But note two things here: (i) Is it right? would not have been interpreted by Price as equivalent to the purely formal Kantian question, Is it universalisable? Rectitude, he believed, has a content. It *is* benevolence, among other things (p. 193). Benevolent action for the sake of duty is not something different from benevolent action for the sake of benevolence, to Price. He says, even of benevolent actions which can be classed as instinctive, that 'approbation is inseparable from the view of them' (p. 192). Consciousness of benevolence *is* consciousness of rectitude. Acts of humanity and kindness, in so far as they are intentional acts, are instances of virtue. (ii) The rigid separation of action-from-sense-of-duty and action-from-desire, which Kant drew,[80] or which some of his interpreters take him to have drawn, is not suggested by Price's

language. True, he differentiates action from mere instinct, with all
rational reflexion lacking, from action in which such reflexion plays a
part. But he believes that the heads of virtue, when contemplated,
arouse, of necessity, desire, indeed 'love' (p. 191), in a rational agent.
Such affection always accompanies our perceptions of rectitude. The
question for reflexion, Price would have said, is not: is this my duty or
is it what I want? but: is this my duty, that is, is it what I, as a rational
being, find that I must desire?

Sense of duty, then, in Price, does not consist simply in an awareness
of the formal principle of law as such, but in obeying and following
reason and this means (i) perceiving by rational intuition those ultimate
principles (duty to God, etc.) called heads of virtue, and (ii) experiencing
the affection for these which necessarily arises in a rational being who is
aware of them.

II.iv ESSENTIALS OF GOOD CHARACTER

Price gives in his own terms an account of the essentials of good
character which is, for the most part, unexceptionable. He considers
first whether temptations to be overcome are essential to virtue
(pp. 200–8). He thinks not. They are often the cause not of virtue but
vice. Men sometimes attain a degree of virtue in which temptations
lose all their force, and this must certainly be the state of angels and of
God. The number and strength of temptations which a person feels
'may argue nothing more' than his moral weakness. Price does not
deny, of course, that temptations 'have a tendency, by obliging us to
a more anxious, attentive, and constant exercise of virtue, in a peculiar
manner, to accelerate our progress in it and establish our regard to it';
but he expressly repudiates the idea that duty is necessarily opposed to
desire. He certainly did not hold the view, sometimes attributed to
Kant,[81] that to be virtuous an act must be done *against* inclination, or at
least in the complete *absence* of it. After pointing out that there are
certainly different degrees of practical, if not of absolute, virtue, and that
benevolence is not the whole of it, Price considers whether acts are
more virtuous as they are more free (pp. 209–11). It is, he says, 'very
improper to speak of degrees of *natural* liberty and necessity . . . between *agency* and its contrary, there seems no conceivable medium.
Every act of volition I am conscious of, if *my* act, must be entirely *mine*
and cannot be more or less *mine* . . . it being a contradiction to suppose,
that the determination of a being may be partly *his*, and partly

another's'. If an act is mine, that is to say, it is logically impossible to say that it is *not* mine. There is no disputing this, but it is about words. Price goes on to consider the contention that 'a *moral* necessity, or such as arises from the influence of motives and affections on the mind' can 'diminish the merit of good actions'. Of this he says: 'it is undeniable, that the very greatest necessity of this sort is consistent with, nay, is implied in, the idea of the most perfect and meritorious virtue; and, consequently, can by no means lessen it'. But in a footnote here he carefully distinguishes such compulsion from that of 'instinctive desires' and is prepared to concede that if, when we say that an action is more virtuous the less necessary it is, we mean 'that it will be more amiable the less the agent is urged to it by instinctive desires', this is 'very true'. But, he says, what increases its virtue in this case is not 'the mere circumstance of its being less necessary', but 'its proceeding more from the influence of love to virtue'. A man of good character, he continues (pp. 211–13), will be impartial in his moral judgements, e.g. will not judge acts affecting strangers differently from those affecting friends, nor approve a deed just because it happens to have good results, nor regard one branch of rectitude but not another.

Price quotes Butler and Hutcheson to the effect that the moral faculty is a directing and controlling principle in human nature. He charges Hutcheson with inconsistency in claiming this for it. The latter had written of the moral sense as a determination in our natures to be pleased or displeased with acts proceeding from certain motives (Price says this is the view in the *Illustrations*): Price argues that it therefore always presupposes some distinct motives, and so cannot be itself a motive or spring of action. Yet Hutcheson writes of it also (Price says this is the view in the *System of Moral Philosophy*) as a distinct spring of conduct in the mind, superior to all other affections and actions and commanding them. Price's point is that, if the moral faculty is sense, not reason, then it cannot be a directing principle. But the mere fact that Hutcheson's moral faculty experiences pleasure and pain, whereas Price's perceives truth, does not imply that Price's reason is a directing principle, whereas Hutcheson's sense is not. If the moral faculty discerns the real characters of actions, as Price here claims, how does that make it more likely to be a directing principle than if it simply feels pleasure or pain? It is just as conceivable that a regulating principle should regulate in accordance with its own feelings as in accordance with its perceptions of objective reality. Hutcheson was certainly inconsistent if he thought of it in one place as merely a capacity for sensation and in another as a directing principle, since these are different (though not mutually exclusive); but there seems no inherent reason why a faculty which experiences pleasure and pain should not be a directing principle while one which perceives truth should. Price, of course, believes that, in so far as it is a regulating principle, it must be reason because there can be no 'higher power' in a rational being than reason. But, though there is an indisputable verbal point here (if man can be said to be in the class denoted by 'rational', then the highest in man must be in that class also), there is nothing beyond that. It is not at all inconceivable that man should exercise those powers which we call reason or reasoning and, at the same time, possess and exercise a separate faculty which provides him with authoritative information concerning right and wrong. Price, however, thinks of the moral faculty as a power of reflexion, a power, that is, which puts and answers the question: what do reason and right require of you? (p. 219). On his view, as that which answers this question, it must be reason. Price sums up (pp. 217 ff.) goodness of character thus: 'It is the power of reflexion raised to its due seat of direction and sovereignty in the mind; conscience fixed and kept in the throne, and holding under its sway all our passions.' The marks of this supremacy of conscience are: (a) One's *chief* concern when deliberating about any undertaking is: what do reason and right require? (b) One tries to act in accordance with rectitude, as one perceives it, as consistently as is humanly possible. (c) One *delights* in so acting. Like Aristotle,[82] Price believes that happiness goes with virtue; indeed, that a man is not really good unless he is happy, i.e. unless he takes pleasure in virtuous activity. He dismisses the view that if we delight in virtue, our virtue is less disinterested and therefore less virtuous. This delight arises from acting from the motive of regard for rectitude. It is 'scarcely in our power', says Price, to act from one motive (desire for this delight) in order to have the pleasure of reflecting that we acted from another (regard for rectitude). (d) One constantly tries to *improve* one's character. 'A person who thinks himself *good enough*, may be sure that he is not *good at all*. When the *love of virtue* becomes the *reigning affection*, it will not be possible for us to satisfy ourselves with any degree of it we can acquire.' (e) In one's character there is a *due order* and equilibrium among the passions, achieved by reason. Virtue consists in this 'just regulation of the passions'.

6

Morality and the Divine Nature

In this chapter I shall consider some of the questions which confronted Price when he came to relate his moral philosophy to theism.

I. THE RELATION OF MORALITY TO THE DIVINE NATURE

Price recognises more clearly than any of his fellow-rationalists had done that 'something distinct from God, which is independent of him, and equally eternal and necessary' appears to have been set up by his kind of theory (p. 85). He points out, in his own defence, that this objection would apply to all necessary truth. His main concern has been to show that morality is a branch of the latter, and he declares that he would be 'very willing that truth and morality should stand and fall together'. However, he does not deny the importance of the objection and proceeds to give it some consideration. He affirms that 'we must allow' that there is *something* independent of the will of God and supports this contention with the following arguments.

(i) The will, existence, eternity and immensity of God himself; the difference between power and impotence, wisdom and folly, truth and falsehood – these must all be 'creatures' of God's will, if all truth is so; but this would be such an 'extravagant' notion that no one could hold it (p. 86). To assert that any of these is dependent on his will 'would imply, that he is a changeable and precarious being, and render it impossible for us to form any consistent ideas of his existence and attributes'. But surely Price's point here is by no means self-evident. Provided God willed consistently, then (a) there would be no grounds for pronouncing him 'a changeable and precarious being', and (b) it would be perfectly possible for us to have ideas of his existence and attributes which were consistent (with the additional proviso, of course, that we could apprehend them correctly).

(ii) Closely allied to the last point, and open to much the same objection, is Price's contention that, if the difference between benevolence and cruelty is not grounded in the nature of things, then God 'if benevolent, must be so *contrary* to his understanding' (p. 238). His understanding would inform him that benevolence is morally indifferent, and so, if he decided to act upon it, this would be due to 'unintelligent inclination'. This, says Price, would lead to the conclusion that 'the Deity can be of no character' (p. 239); a conclusion which is contradicted 'by certain fact', for God's having created at all, the evidence of final causes, and the uniformity and wisdom manifest in creation, all 'imply . . . some character' in the creator. A determinate character must be determinate as a result of some determining cause, says Price (p. 237) and he believes that such a cause can only be something in the nature of things, knowledge of which determines God's character. But we must reject completely this notion of his that, unless a being's moral ideas are perceptions of non-natural properties belonging to the nature of things, his conduct must be motivated by mere 'unintelligent inclination' and there is no sense in which he can be said to have a character. Against 'unintelligent inclination', as we have seen, it makes perfectly good sense to talk of 'reasons why' in morals, even when Price's intuitionism is rejected. And as for character, the analysis of this concept must surely be in terms of principles of action and these do not need to be, and indeed cannot validly be, interpreted as perceptions of non-natural reality.

(iii) To speak of God as mind presupposes independent truth, according to Price. 'Intelligence', 'wisdom', 'knowledge' are words he uses (p. 86) of mind's activity, and he contends that each presupposes objects. 'Infinite, independent, necessary *mind*' presupposes 'eternal, necessary, independent' objective truth. Now, it is a perfectly valid argument to maintain that 'knowledge', as we commonly use this word, implies a difference between what *is* the case and what *is thought* to be the case. If we drew no such distinction, then we should have no way of differentiating the application of 'knowledge' from that of 'ignorance'. But the question which arises concerns Price's assumption that the activity of the divine mind can only be knowledge in our sense of the word. It is conceivable that it should not be. There are other mental activities besides cognition – imagination, for example. Price, of course, took a very poor view of imagination (pp. 21, 32). It is interesting to note, however, that other theists have protested against the tendency to conceive of the activity of the divine mind in terms solely of cognition; and have suggested that to conceive of it in terms of artistic or creative imagination will take us further into the mystery than any other guide.[1] Of course, in the case of man, the raw materials of imagination are supplied from previous experience of objects of cognition; but the products of human imagination do not, at least on the higher levels of art, seem to be simply rearrangements of previous experience. They are genuinely new. A character created by a great playwright or novelist is a new creation, grounded no doubt in the author's observation of others and his own inner experiences, but not identifiable with any of them nor with the mere sum of some of them. If such invention is within the power of mind, as we know it, there is nothing logically inconceivable in the idea of a mind existing independently and inventing an imaginary universe of its own.

(iv) Price's next point is one to which the answer has already been given in preceding pages. He writes: 'If there were nothing eternally and unalterably right and wrong, there could be nothing meant by his eternal, and unalterable rectitude or holiness' (p. 86). The point is that the statement 'God is righteous' has no *meaning* unless 'righteous' has a referent; but this view fails to recognise that there is, as we have argued, more than one sense of 'meaning'. Moral statements could make perfectly good sense, even if moral terms had no referents.[2] If this is so of statements concerning men, there is no reason why it should not also be true of those concerning God.

(v) Price thinks it absurd to suppose that God's intelligence and knowledge depend upon his will, but much more reasonable to conceive of his will as dependent upon, and regulated by, his understanding of objective truths (pp. 86–7). The absurdity seemed so patent to Price, presumably, because he believed that the necessity whereby God wills and acts is merely a high degree of probability (pp. 244–7) and this could not serve as a ground for the necessary knowledge which, Price believed, God's knowledge must be. He recognises, however, that the point he is now making, like all the others which he has made so far, only confirms the initial objection to his theory: that it sets up certain objects as necessarily existing independently of God. So he tries to draw the teeth of this objection now. Objective truths exist independently of God's will, he says, but *not* of his *nature*: 'It by no means follows, because they are independent of his *will*, that they are also independent of his *nature*' (p. 87). Now, it is certainly conceivable that something should depend on the nature of being, but not upon his will; it makes sense, for instance, to say that, if I am by nature a disease-carrier, I may infect another person without willing to do so. Price saw in this con-

ceivable distinction between nature and will a way of saving the
necessity of God's knowledge without supposing there to be a reality
independent of him. The necessity whereby God exists, he claimed,
unlike that by which he acts, is logical necessity. But, as we have
already contended[3] the propositional necessity which constitutes
necessary knowledge cannot belong to existence.

(vi) So far Price has been arguing, so to speak, from God to necessary
truth; now he turns about and argues from the latter to the former. He
says (pp. 87–8) that wherever we apprehend necessity in objects of
thought we are apprehending God. He thinks we shall see this, if we
try to draw a limit to truth or possibility. There is an infinite number
of truths possible to be known; and an infinite number of things
possible to exist. He maintains that we cannot in thought destroy this
infinity of truth and possibility: 'the very notion of arriving at a point,
beyond which there is nothing farther, implies a contradiction'. The
argument is valid enough so far as it goes: in order to draw a limit to
thinking we must think both sides of the limit, and this of course would
mean that it was not a limit to thinking.[4] If *X* represents the truths or
existences known to us, then, however comprehensive *X* may be (short
of being equivalent to 'all truths' or 'all existences') there is nothing
self-contradictory in saying 'More than *X* may be true' or 'More than
X may exist.' Price believes that this logical possibility must have a
foundation in the nature of things; and therefore that it is a fair inference to say that there is a 'divine . . . *reason and power*, from whence
all other reason and power are derived . . . *necessarily existing* which
contain in themselves all things, from which all things sprung, and
upon which all things depend'. God is all truth and all existence; and
the logical possibility, implicit in all our thinking about particular
truths or existences, that there is more truth and more existence, points
to him as its foundation. Once again, Price's error is the assumption
that necessary truth implies (p. 88) necessary (and note that Price quite
definitely means *logically* necessary (pp. 244–5)) existence.

II. THE TELEOLOGICAL ARGUMENT

Price thinks the argument from design very convincing. He writes:

It is impossible to survey the world without being assured, that the
contrivance in it has proceeded from some contriver, the design in it
from some *designing* cause, and the art it displays from some artist. To
say the contrary, or to assert that it was produced by the accidental

falling together of its component parts, must appear to every man whose understanding is not perverted, a folly as gross as it would be to assert the same of any other work of art that could be presented to him; of a commodious house, of a fine picture, or an exquisite machine. (p. 285)

The order, regularity and immensity of the universe, he says in one place, '*demonstrate*' (p. 239) that the first cause is intelligent and powerful to an infinite degree. The question which he feels it necessary to clear up, however, is whether this divine designer is also good. In support of an affirmative answer, he takes two lines. First, he argues from empirical observation: 'we are to judge of what we do *not* see by what we *do* see, and not the contrary; and . . . the whole of what lies before us of God's works . . . is clearly as if happiness was their end' (p. 241). He is rejecting the kind of objection which Hume makes, that God is 'so remote and incomprehensible'[5] that we can form no hypotheses concerning him. It is, however, surprising that Price should have allowed himself to say that the 'whole' of creation evidences benevolence. He could not, of course, close his eyes to all 'appearances of evil', but he claims that 'all the corruptions and disorders we observe are plainly *unnatural deviations and excesses*; and . . . no instance can be produced wherein *ill* as such is the genuine tendency and result of the original constitution of things' (p. 241). He does not, however, give us a criterion with which to distinguish conformity from deviation, original from non-original, beyond the contention that, in each case, the former is evident in what is good. In other words, he places his theory beyond refutation by any empirical evidence. Whatever seems to refute the benevolence of God will be dismissed as deviation or non-original. To Professor A. Flew's question: What would have to occur or to have occurred to constitute for you a disproof of the love of, or the existence of, God? the answer is 'Nothing.'[6]

Though he has claimed that the argument from design 'demonstrates' the existence of God, Price later notes the objection which Hume levelled against it and admits its force. Hume said: 'It is only when two *species* of objects are found to be constantly conjoined that we can infer the one from the other; and were an effect presented, which was entirely singular, and could not be comprehended under any known *species*, I do not see, that we could form any conjecture or inference at all concerning its cause.'[7] Price concedes: 'it might be said (and much the same [he refers to Hume] has been said) that [the universe] being an object *wholly singular* to us, we cannot draw any conclusions from it . . . concerning the nature, designs and properties of its *cause*, or even know that it has a cause' (pp. 264–5). But Price claims that, though this objection has force against an argument grounded only on empirical evidence, his own belief in the goodness of God has another foundation.

This is his rational intuitionism, of which he writes: 'Our approbation of goodness, if derived from intellectual perception, infers *demonstrably* the goodness of God' (p. 242). Benevolence and every other aspect of rectitude is 'a part of the idea of reason, and therefore, in the *self-existent infinite reason*, must be of absolute and sovereign influence' (p. 243). 'But to go on; the independency and self-sufficiency of God raise him above the possibility of being tempted to what is wrong. . . . His nature admits of nothing arbitrary or instinctive; of no determinations that are independent of reason. . . . The same necessity and reasons of things cannot be the ground of the approbation and love of rectitude, and of biases contradictory to it' (p. 244). These points are perfectly consistent with Price's account of the relation of morality to the divine nature; but, if we have been right in our criticisms of the latter, then these points must be rejected also as groundless.

III. THE COSMOLOGICAL ARGUMENT

Price thinks the argument from design 'sufficient for all practical purposes' (p. 286), but he adds to it an argument which he found in S. Clarke's *Evidences of Natural and Revealed Religion* and, he thinks, in Newton too (pp. 290–1 n.). This argument rests on the putative self-evidence of the claim that 'were there no existence which required no reason to be given for it, that is, were there no being whose non-existence can no more be conceived than contradictions can be conceived to be true; it would follow, that nothing could ever have existed' (p. 292). This claim that there must be necessary existence has, of course, been contested ever since Hume, and Price's presentation of the cosmological argument does not deliver it from his criticisms.[8] But he shows exceptional ingenuity in identifying the First Cause with the God of theism. He corrects Clarke's unfortunate terminology in speaking of 'necessity' as 'the *cause* of God's existence' (p. 292), saying that Clarke only meant that 'the *account* of the existence of the first cause must be, that it is *necessary*' (p. 292). He follows Clarke in claiming that this necessary existence must be (*a*) that the existence of which is necessary 'to the very *conception* of all other existence', and (*b*) that which may without contradiction be conceived to exist independently of anything else (p. 288). From (*a*) it seems to Price, as it did to Clarke, to follow that space and time are part of necessary existence. 'We can, for instance, very well conceive of *space* and *time* without presupposing, in that conception, the existence of a *material world*; and this is conceiving it not to exist; and therefore, proves it to be contingent. And could we, in the same manner, conceive of the *material world* without *space* and *time*, these themselves would likewise appear to be contingent' (p. 288). From (*b*) it seems to Price to follow – and this is where he fulfils his declared intention of pursuing further (p. 286) Clarke's line of thought – that, not only space and time, but the divine intelligence, power, benevolence, rectitude, etc. must also be included within necessary existence. If this were not the case, then 'God is benevolent' would imply something independent of God and we should either have to refrain from saying this or surrender the claim that God is necessary being. But why should we not refrain from saying that God is benevolent? Price's answer would appear to be that we have two intuitions of necessary truth, namely (i) that there is a first cause and (ii) that certain acts are benevolent. Now, Price claims, these belong together because necessary truth is 'essentially one' (p. 88). 'Simplicity and unity are included in the idea of necessity' (p. 294). Every necessary truth is shown to be one and indivisible from the fact that any attempt to divide it into two truths is self-contradictory; it is either (*a*) the division of it into itself and another truth, i.e. no division, or (*b*) the division of it into two other truths 'and consequently its annihilation', i.e. the original truth was falsely called necessary. Price claims that what is true of each necessary truth is true of the whole of necessary truth. He would have been entitled to claim that any part of any system of necessary truth hangs together with the rest: given the axioms and rules of inference on which it is founded, then the whole system follows. But the trouble is that this is patently not the case with what he took to be necessary truth. If necessary truth is both space and time *and* moral truth, then how do these imply one another? It is logically possible to assert the existence of space and time, while denying that of moral truth, and vice versa; so how can they be aspects of one necessary truth?[9]

IV. BENEVOLENCE AND VIRTUE IN GOD

Price has argued that benevolence is not the whole of virtue in men, but what of God? Butler, for example, seems to think that in the case of God it is the whole of virtue.[10] Rightness is prior to goodness in Price's moral theory, and he says that it 'stands first in the divine mind' (p. 248). It is because it is right to do so that God promotes the happiness of his creatures. The character of God, however, is 'much more nearly reducible' to goodness or benevolence than a virtuous man's would be. Price borrows the arguments of a dissenting minister, Bayes, to support this. A solitary being (having no connexion with any other reasonable being) who was not perfectly happy would have no obligation but to pursue his own interest. But a similar being who is perfectly happy will have no end to engage his attention and effort except the good of his creatures (p. 249). It is 'inconceivable' what else could lead him at first to produce any creatures, and afterwards to preserve them. Price believed happiness to be an object of far more worth than order or beauty; unlike some philosophers, G. E. Moore for example,[11] he thinks a world of order and beauty, with no beings in it to enjoy them, would be 'just nothing' so far as value is concerned. The idea that God created such a world for his own enjoyment is, one supposes, excluded by the premise that God is perfectly happy.

God's benevolence is not, however, a mere physical propensity of the divine nature, but is grounded in and guided by reason. It is therefore free; and deserving of gratitude and praise (p. 250). It follows also that God pursues the happiness of men, but in subordination to rectitude, i.e. to justice and veracity. He distributes happiness in proportion to virtue; this is the law of creation and the principle of all divine government. Again, we cannot suppose his benevolence to be exercised in deceiving men. We must not think of justice and veracity, however, as limiting God's goodness, but rather directing it: they are consistent with unlimited communications of happiness; though they would not, in themselves, have led him to create. Goodness comprehends the whole of the divine character, if by it we mean 'a reasonable, sincere, holy, and just goodness' (p. 252). Goodness, justice and veracity are all different manifestations of one supreme principle: everlasting rectitude or reason.

V. REWARDS AND PUNISHMENTS

The question of the relation between virtue and happiness, vice and misery, has exercised many moral philosophers. Price rejected the view put forward by Shaftesbury and Butler[12] that duty and interest perfectly coincide in this world. This, he claims, is patently not the case (pp. 255–60). And so he looks to a future life in which virtue will find its due reward and vice its due punishment. Price, however, did not simply claim that, if there is a God such as theists believe in, then they can reconcile their belief in the justice of this God with the injustices of the world only on the supposition of a future life: he claimed to 'prove' this future state (p. 260). His argument goes as follows: We know by rational intuition that there is a God who is eternal reason; we know by rational intuition that 'virtue ought to be happier than vice'; God, who is eternal reason, will necessarily do what it is reasonable to do; and so it follows that 'we may be very confident that what *ought to be*, the universal governing mind will take care *shall be*' (p. 253). The argument is consistent with Price's views concerning morality and the divine nature but, of course, wholly unconvincing to anyone who rejects these. But, even for Price, there are problems. First, why should this perfect distribution have to wait for a future state? He suggests the following solution. If every virtuous act were rewarded, or vicious act punished, *immediately*, then 'the characters of men could not be formed; virtue would be rendered interested and mercenary; some of the most important branches of it could not be practised; adversity, frequently its best friend, could never find access to it; and all those trials would be removed which are requisite to train up to maturity and perfection' (p. 261). Apart from the obvious rejoinder to all this, that the prospect of future rewards may also render virtue interested and mercenary, this passage raises all the thorny problems of divine omnipotence. Price seems to have been quite insensitive to the difficulty, with which theists have to wrestle, of reconciling the belief that God is omnipotent with the belief that he can create moral beings only under certain conditions.[13]

The second problem which Price, as a Christian apologist, has to face is that although, on his view, reason demonstrates that there is a future state, it can give us no proof that repentance, 'the return of every man to his duty', will secure everlasting glory and bliss. The sinner cannot be sure that, if he changes his ways, the consequences in this world, or the next, will be an ultimate balance of happiness over misery. The Christian revelation claims this, but what reason has one for accepting it? Price has two answers to this. On the one hand, with due acknowledgement to Butler (pp. 273–4), he takes probability as his guide and claims that his arguments from natural religion for a future state constitute '*some degree* of *real* evidence', even 'a *great probability*' for the truth of the Christian revelation. What Price is arguing for now is not a future state in which virtue is rewarded and vice punished, but that inequitable dispensation of divine grace whereby even the eleventh-hour penitent inherits eternal bliss. Proofs of the former would really provide no ground at all for a belief in the latter. And Price seems actually to be aware of this, as his second answer shows. This turns on the infinite good of that which the Christian revelation promises. If there is any possibility, however slender, of this revelation being true, then, since the good which it holds out is infinite, 'the value of any chance of it must be likewise infinite'. We cannot be certain that there is *no* chance, and so 'it will be the most foolish conduct not to practise virtue, and even to sacrifice to it all present advantages and gratifications' (p. 270). So, if the Christian revelation is the longest of shots, we should back it none the less because the winnings would be so great if it were true. It is perhaps to Price's credit, as a Christian, that his last argument for religion, though it purports to be a piece of cautious calculation, is really an appeal to the instincts of the gambler, who will stake all upon a throw.

Notes

CHAPTER 1

1. In this book references to Price's *Review* (3rd ed. 1787, ed. D. D. Raphael, Oxford, 1948) are contained in brackets throughout the text. At certain points I have modernised the spelling and punctuation.
2. *An Inquiry concerning the Original of our Ideas of Virtue and Moral Good* 1. i: L. A. Selby-Bigge, *British Moralists* (Oxford, 1897) p. 74. In quotations from other classical writers besides Price I have occasionally modernised the spelling and punctuation.
3. *The Moral Sense* (1947) p. 19.
4. *Essay on the Nature and Conduct of the Passions and Affections* (third ed.) 1.i: Selby-Bigge, op. cit. 433.
5. See his attacks on rationalism in *Inquiry* and *Illustrations on the Moral Sense*.
6. *Inquiry* iii.iii: Selby-Bigge, op. cit. 130.
7. In a footnote Price refers to his fuller discussion of the phrase 'foundation of virtue' at the beginning of chapter x. He says there that his expression admits of various meanings, namely (i) 'the *true account or reason* that such and such actions are *right*' (p. 233). Only two accounts are possible: (*a*) '*right is a species of sensation*', or (*b*) it denotes '*a real character of actions*', discerned by rational intuition of the nature of things. (ii) 'the *primary principles and heads* of virtue' (p. 234), e.g. private happiness, the will of God, etc. Such principles, says Price, are taken to be 'the *subject-matter* of virtue'. (iii) 'the *motives* and *reasons*, which lead us to it' (p. 235). As Raphael says (op. cit. p. 109), this is excellent analysis and carries a stage further Hutcheson's distinction between the faculty of approbation (Price's (i) above) and that of election (Price's (iii)). (*Illustrations:* Selby-Bigge, op. cit. 448).
8. *Foundations of Ethics* (Oxford, 1939) p. 259; cf. J. S. Mill, *System of Logic* 1. ii.5.
9. These questions had no doubt been raised in his mind by reading R. Cudworth (cf. the latter's *Concerning Eternal an Immutable Morality* 1.ii.1) and possibly also Shaftesbury (cf. the latter's *An Inquiry concerning Virtue* 1.iii.ii) and Hutcheson (cf. the latter's *Inquiry* vii.v).On the history of the refutation of the naturalistic fallacy cf. A. N. Prior, *Logic and the Basis of Ethics* (Oxford, 1949).
10. Raphael adds here the footnote: 'Price uses the word "sentiment" to mean opinion, not feeling.'
11. Price's first edition reads 'most triflingly identical' for 'most trifling'.
12. '. . . the definist fallacy is the process of confusing or identifying two properties, of defining one property by another, or of substituting one property for another' (Frankena, 'The Naturalistic Fallacy', *Mind* 1939, p. 471).

13. Cf. D. D. Raphael, *Moral Judgement* (1955) pp. 38–9 and C. H. Langford, 'The Notion of Analysis in Moore's Philosophy', *The Philosophy of G. E. Moore* (Evanston, 1942) ed. P. A. Schilpp, pp. 321 ff.

14. Cf. Frankena, op. cit. p. 471.

15. This is a rather special use of the word 'fallacy'. ' . . . the error of confusing two characters, or . . . the error of defining an indefinable one . . . might, since the term is somewhat loose in its habits, be called "fallacies", though they are not logical fallacies in the sense in which an invalid argument is' (Ibid. p. 476).

16. See L. Abraham, 'The Logic of Ethical Intuitionism', *International Journal of Ethics* 1933–4. G. E. Moore in *Pricipia Ethica* (Cambridge, 1903) often speaks as though this is what he meant by the naturalistic fallacy (see op. cit. pp. 10, 16 and 38).

17. See my *Modern Moral Philosophy* (1970) chap. 3.

18. See below pp. 45–64 where I recognise that there is more to Price's argument against naturalists than simply that they are sometimes inconsistent.

19. Cf. Raphael, *The Moral Sense*, pp. 132–3.

20. Cf. Cudworth, op. cit. 1.ii.3 : Selby-Bigge, op. cit. 816.

21. Cf. P. H. Nowell-Smith, *Ethics* (1954) pp. 112–21.

22. Cf. the works of Moore or Ross.

CHAPTER 2

1. *Examination of Malebranche* 10 and *Essay* intro. 2.

2. *Essay* II.1.2.

3. *Essay* II.2.2.

4. See *Essay* (fourth ed.) II.12.1.

5. (i) Reason superior to sense: *Review* pp. 29–31, cf. Cudworth, *Eternal and Immutable Morality* II.vi.3. (ii) The understanding a source of new ideas, moral, physical, mathematical: *Review* chap. I, sect. II, cf. Cudworth, op. cit. IV.ii.I. (iii) Without these intuitions of the understanding nothing can be known: *Review* p. 39, cf. Cudworth, op. cit. IV.iii.I. (iv) The agreement and disagreement between ideas are new, simple ideas, acquired by the understanding: *Review* p. 36, cf Cudworth, op. cit. IV.ii.I. (v) Clearness and distinctness of apprehension a guarantee of truth: *Review* pp. 95–6, cf. Cudworth, op. cit. IV.v.5. (vi) Abstractionist and nominalist theories of general ideas beg the question: *Review* pp. 29–30, cf. Cudworth, op. cit. IV.iii.14.

6. (i) 'other words': *Review* p. 16, cf. Cudworth, op. cit. 1.ii.3. (ii) antecedent right: *Review* pp. 17, 105–6, cf. Cudworth op. cit. 1.ii.3. (iii) heads of virtue: *Review* chap. VII, cf. Cudworth, op. cit. 1.ii.4.

7. Price acknowledges his debt to Cudworth: *Review* pp. 20 n., 31, 54–5, 88 n., 90, 91 n.

8. J. A. Passmore, *Ralph Cudworth* (Cambridge, 1951) p. 105.

9. This is perhaps a rather odd use of the word. Induction usually leads to generalised conclusions based on a number of particular instances (e.g. natural

laws like 'water boils at 100 °C'), not to particular judgements like this one. The case here is like the reasoning by which a detective infers from a number of clues who did the crime.

10. See *Essay* II.12. Complex ideas, he says, are of three kinds, namely, (i) *substances*, 'such combinations of simple ideas as are taken to represent distinct particular things, subsisting by themselves' (12.6); (ii) *modes*, 'complex ideas which, however, compounded, contain not in them the supposition of subsisting by themselves, but are considered as dependencies on, or affections of, substances; such are the ideas signified by the words, "triangle, gratitude, murder", &c.' (12.4). (Modes may be 'simple', i.e. compounded from the same simple idea, or 'mixed', i.e. compounded from simple ideas of several kinds (12.5).); (iii) *relations*, which consist 'in the consideration and comparing one idea with another' (12.7). In the fourth edition, Locke also said that complex ideas are formed by (*a*) *comparing* ideas, simple or complex, which gives rise to ideas of relation, and (*b*) *abstraction*, which gives rise to general ideas; as well as by combination (II.12.1).

11. *Essay* II.12.5.

12. Cf. *Treatise* I.I.iv: 'As all simple ideas may be separated by the imagination, and may be united again in what form it pleases, nothing would be more unaccountable than the operation of that faculty, were it not guided by some universal principles, which render it, in some measure, uniform with itself in all times and places. . . . The qualities from which this association arises, and by which the mind is after this manner conveyed from one idea to another, are three, namely *resemblance*, *contiguity* in time or place, and *cause* and *effect*.'

13. See M. Lazerowitz, 'Substratum' in *Philosophical Analysis* (1950) ed. M. Black.

14. *Essay* I.4.19.

15. *Essay* II.23.24, cf. pp. 34 ff. below.

16. See his *First Letter to Stillingfleet* and below 2.II.iii.

17. D. J. O'Connor, *John Locke* (Pelican) p. 79.

18. *Essay* III.3.6.

19. *Essay* III.3.15.

20. See *Essay* II.21.4.

21. Op. cit. p. 94.

22. Locke, *First Letter to Stillingfleet*.

23. Cf. O'Connor, op. cit. p. 91; and 2.II.iii below.

24. *Essay* II.1.4.

25. *The Moral Sense* pp. 121–2.

26. Locke defined knowledge as 'nothing but the perception of the connection and agreement, or disagreement and repugnancy, of any of our ideas' (*Essay* IV.1.2). He distinguished four kinds of agreement and disagreement: (i) identity and diversity, (ii) relation, (iii) necessary connexion or coexistence, (iv) real existence (*Essay* IV.1.3). The case Price takes here is of the second kind.

27. See *Essay* II.2.1 and IV.4.4.

28. See *The Right and the Good* (Oxford, 1930) pp. 121–2. Like Price, Ross believes that this distinction applies to both mathematical and moral ideas: to be equiangular is a consequential attribute of equilateral triangles, to be right is a consequential attribute of keeping promises. But Ross points out certain obvious differences: (i) in the mathematical illustration, we select arbitrarily

which of the attributes (equiangularity or equilaterality) to regard as consequential, but in morality consequential and constitutive characteristics are *not* interchangeable. (ii) The rightness of an action is a 'toti-resultant' property, consequential upon its whole nature, whereas mathematical properties (spatial, temporal, numerical) are 'parti-resultant', consequential on part of the nature of their possessors.

29. Cf. Raphael, op. cit. p. 127.
30. *Essay* II.8.9.
31. The representative theory of perception and knowledge has a long history. It dates from Democritus, who said that objects project into space images of themselves compounded of atoms, and these strike the senses, like atoms perceiving like. It is found in Plotinus, St Augustine of Hippo, Galileo, Descartes and Locke. Philosophers had come to take it for granted and to regard it as so obviously true as to need no defence.
32. There are three elements in the traditional theory of substance: (i) as *ens per se stans* – that which can exist independently, (ii) as *quod substa accidentibus* – the substratum in which properties inhere, (iii) as that which could be subject, but not predicate, of a proposition in logical form. Cf. O'Connor, op. cit. 74–5.
33. See above, 2.II.i.
34. *Treatise* I.I.i.
35. Ibid. I.I.vi.
36. Op. cit. p. 186.
37. Cf. B. Russell and A. N. Whitehead, *Principia Mathematica* (1910–13) intro. iii; Russell, *Introduction to Mathematical Philosophy* (1919) chap. XVI; also A. J. Ayer, *Language, Truth and Logic* (second ed. 1946) pp. 63–4.
38. 'Verifiability' in *Logic and Language*, first series (Oxford, 1951) ed. A. Flew, p. 119 and *passim*.
39. Ibid. p. 122.
40. Ibid.
41. Cf. Ayer, op. cit. intro. p. 24; also *Foundations of Empirical Knowledge* (1947) pp. 239–43 and *The Problem of Knowledge* (1956) chap. 3.
42. Cf. Ayer, 'Phenomenalism', *Proceedings of the Aristotelian Society* 1947–8, pp. 171–6.
43. Cf. Ayer, *The Problem of Knowledge* pp. 124–9.
44. *The Concept of Mind* (1949) p. 213.
45. *The Problem of Knowledge* p. 107.
46. *Dilemmas* (Cambridge, 1960) chap. VII.
47. *The Problem of Knowledge* p. 100.
48. See R. J. Hirst, 'The Difference Between Sensing and Observing' in *Belief and Will, Proceedings of the Aristotelian Society*, Supplementary Volume XXVIII (1954).
49. See R. Wollheim, ibid. pp. 218 ff.
50. *Treatise* I. 3. iii.
51. Cf. D. J. O'Connor, 'Causal Statements', *Philosophical Quarterly* 1956, pp. 18–19.
52. Cf. R. G. Collingwood, 'On the So-called Idea of Causation', *Proceedings of the Aristotelian Society* 1937–8, pp. 85–112.

53. G. J. Warnock points out that, if the causal principle is taken to mean that every event has not only a sufficient, but also a necessary, cause, then it appears to be 'synthetic and false'. The same event frequently seems to be related causally to more than one condition or set of conditions. See 'Every Event has a Cause' in *Logic and Languages*, second series (Oxford, 1953), ed. A. Flew, pp. 103–4. The scientist, *qua* scientist, never considers *all* the conditions of an event, but only some of them. For instance, if asked to investigate the activities of a kleptomaniac, a psychologist might say that these are caused by a desire to compensate for some emotional insecurity. But among the sufficient conditions of any particular kleptomaniac's activities would be such facts as that he lived in a particular town, went to certain shops, had an opportunity to steal, etc. All these the psychologist would disregard as irrelevant so far as he was concerned.

54. See *Problems of Philosophy* (1912) chap. VI; 'The Limits of Empiricism', *Proceedings of the Aristotelian Society* 1935–6, p. 148; *History of Western Philosophy* (1946) p. 700; cf. Mill, *System of Logic* III.v.2.

55. 'Bertrand Russell's Doubts about Induction', *Logic and Language*, first series, ed. Flew, pp. 67 and 75.

56. W. H. Walsh, *Reason and Experience* (Oxford, 1947) p. 151; cf. O'Connor, 'Causal Statements', *Philosophical Quarterly* 1956.

57. Cf. Warnock, op. cit. pp. 102 ff.

58. *Critique of Pure Reason* A 498 (B 526); earlier he wrote of it as a synthetic *a priori* truth.

59. B. Russell, 'On the Notion of Cause', in *Mysticism and Logic* (1953) pp. 183–4.

60. Cf. Ayer, *The Problem of Knowledge* pp. 71–5.

61. Cf. H. H. Price, *Thinking and Experience* (1953) p. 43.

62. *Essay* III.3.11.

63. Ibid. III.3.6.

64. Berkeley quotes Locke's description of the general idea of a triangle and then asks the reader 'to look a little into his own thoughts, and there try whether he has, or can attain to have, an idea that shall correspond with the description that is here given' (*Principles of Human Knowledge* intro. XIII). Hume even more explicitly denies any possibility of such a general image: 'the mind cannot form any notion of quantity or quality without forming a precise notion of degrees of each' (*Treatise* I.I.vii) Price agrees with this contention that every image must be particular (p. 30). Titchener (quoted by C. A. Mace, *Berkeley and Modern Problems, Proceedings of the Aristotelian Society*, Supplementary Volume XXVII (1953) p. 145) thought he could imagine Locke's general idea of a triangle.

65. *Principles of Human Knowledge* intro. XI.

66. Ibid. XII.

67. See Russell, *Problems of Philosophy* pp. 150–1 (original ed.); cf. H. H. Price, *Thinking and Representation* (Annual Philosophical Lecture, Hertz Trust, British Academy, 1946) and *Thinking and Experience* chap. I.

68. Cf. S. Hampshire, 'Ideas, Propositions and Signs', *Proceedings of the Aristotelian Society* 1939–40, p. 15.

69. *Treatise* I.I.vii.

70. Cf. J. Holloway, *Language and Intelligence* (1951) p. 8.

71. For this use of *a priori* cf. A. C. Ewing, *A Short Commentary on Kant's Critique of Pure Reason* (1938) p. 29.
72. Op. cit. XVIII.
73. *Essay* III.3.13; cf. R. I. Aaron, *The Theory of Universals* (Oxford, 1952) pp. 241–2.
74. See below, 2.II.iv. (*b*) *Intuition and Valid Reasoning*.
75. D. R. Pears, 'Universals' in *Logic and Language* second series, ed. Flew, pp. 54–5.
76. Passmore, op. cit. p. 7.
77. Cudworth, op. cit. IV.v.5.
78. Cf. Ayer, *The Problem of Knowledge* p. 38.
79. This account of the knowing process needs qualifying. We sometimes recognise an object when we have no word or sign for that type of thing; cf. Price, *Thinking and Experience* pp. 34 ff. However, our point against Price remains, since recognition is always the experience of the same again and so depends on something already learnt; cf. ibid. p. 41.
80. Cf. W. B. Gallie, *Peirce and Pragmatism* (1952) pp. 72–3: 'Common sense has no difficult about accepting the suggestion that in all these cases capacity to think, to speak, to understand or what not, depends, at any mentionable stage, on the exercise of a previously formed capacity. It is only the necessary conclusion from this suggestion – namely that, in a sense which does no violence to the known facts, our thinking life has no definitely assignable beginning in time – that common sense finds unpalatable.'
81. Ibid. p. 71.
82. R. Robinson, *Definition* (Oxford, 1950) p. 155.
83. See E. R. Stabler, *Introduction to Mathematical Thought* (Cambridge, Mass., 1953) pp. 16–17 and 229–31; and D. Gasking, 'Mathematics and the World', *Logic and Language*, second series, ed. Flew.
84. *The Problem of Knowledge* p. 3.
85. Cf. my *Ethical Intuitionism* (1967) pp. 57–60, and my *Modern Moral Philosophy* (1970) chap. 3.

CHAPTER 3

1. Cf. P. Edwards, *The Logic of Moral Discourse* (Glencoe, Ill., 1955) p. 100.
2. See J. Mackie, 'A Refutation of Morals', *Australasian Journal of Psychology and Philosophy* 1946, p. 77 ff.
3. *Principia Ethica* pp. 7–10. There is an important difference between Price and Moore. It is what the latter said about good, not what he said about right, which resembles what Price said about right. In *Principa Ethica* Moore defined right as 'cause of a good result' (p. 147) and duty as expediency (p. 169). In his later work *Ethics* (1912) he modifies this view (pp. 8 and 107, 1947 pagination); he seems to regard being the cause of a good result as the ground of rightness, but no more. Cf. Ross, *The Right and the Good* pp. 10–11 and *Foundations of Ethics* p. 42.
4 J. Bentham said that, when interpreted to mean conformable to the principle

of utility, 'the words *ought* and *right* . . . and others of that stamp have a meaning; when otherwise, they have none' (*Introduction to the Principles of Morals and Legislation* 1.10: Selby-Bigge, op cit. 363). He talked as if moral words could be abolished from the language and moral problems approached like technical problems of any other applied science and settled by quantitative experiments. See W. H. Walsh, 'The Autonomy of Ethics', *Philosophical Quarterly* 1957, pp. 3 and 5.

5. Ross, *Foundations of Ethics*, p. 54 n.; cf. Raphael's introduction to his edition of Price's *Review* pp. xxxii–iv.

6. *The Moral Sense* p. 41.

7. *Essay* II.28.5.

8. Ibid. I. 3.18.

9. Ibid. II.28.8.

10. 'A Reply to My Critics', *The Philosophy of Bertrand Russell* (Evanston, 1946) ed. P. A. Schilpp, p. 724. Cf. my 'On the Alleged Objectivity of Moral Judgments', *Mind* 1962.

11. Hutcheson, *Illustrations* I: Selby-Bigge, op. cit. 456; Hume, *Treatise* III.2.vii. It is worthy of note that at one point, Hutcheson also differentiated our feelings of approval from our perception of moral good: 'The word "moral goodness", in this treatise, denotes our idea of some quality apprehended in actions, which procures approbation and love toward the actor. . . .' (*Inquiry* intro.: Selby-Bigge, op. cit. 68.)

12. Cf. Hume, *Treatise* III.1.i.

13. *Essay* II.8.9.

14. See Raphael, *The Moral Sense* p. 139.

15. Ibid. p. 138.

16. *The Right and the Good* p. 31.

17. *Treatise* III.3.i.

18. *An Enquiry concerning the Principles of Morals*, second ed., ed. Selby-Bigge, p. 217.

19. *The Moral Sense*, p. 91.

20. *Illustrations* I.

21. In a letter to Hutcheson in 1740: see *Letters of David Hume* (Oxford, 1932) ed. Greig, vol. I, p. 40.

22. See *Review* chap. x and appendix, 'A Dissertation on the Being and Attributes of the Deity'.

23. Raphael, *The Moral Sense*, p. 143. For a fuller discussion of the eighteenth-century debate concerning reason and sense in morals, see my *Ethical Institutionism passim*.

24. As, e.g., in Aristotle, *Ethica Nichomachea*, trans. W. D. Ross, 1147a.

25. G. E. M. Anscombe in *Intention* (Oxford, 1957) p. 60 points out that 'Aristotle never states the conclusion of a practical syllogism, and sometimes speaks of it as an action.'

26. Op. cit. VI.

27. See Ross, *The Right and the Good* p. 28 and *Foundations of Ethics* p. 86; also C. D. Broad, 'Some Main Problems of Ethics' in *Philosophy* 1946, p. 117.

28. *The Right and the Good* p. 41 and *Foundations of Ethics* p. 85.

29. 'Ethical Intuitionism', *Philosophy* 1949.

30. The important distinction is of 'fit' in the moral sense from 'fit' in the non-moral. This corresponds to Kant's distinction between categorical and hypothetical imperatives. H. A. Prichard believed that the non-moral 'ought' can be defined (see his *Moral Obligation* (Oxford, 1949) p. 91): 'You ought to give a second dose' means 'If you do not give a second dose, your purpose will not be realised.' On the other hand, 'You ought to tell the truth' cannot be defined – if you ask what we mean, we can only answer with a verbal equivalent, e.g. 'It is your duty to do so', 'You should do so', etc. Price, however, thought that both the moral and the non-moral 'fit' are indefinable. In this he was nearer to Hare than to Prichard. Hare suggests that, in both Prichard's illustrations, the function of 'ought' is the same (if it is used in a primary sense), namely to refer to principles (though, of course, different ones in each case). (See Hare, *The Language of Morals* (Oxford, 1952) p. 161.)
31. *Treatise* III.1.i.
32. *Ethics* pp. 80–7 and 186–90.
33. Ibid. pp. 83–5. This is R. F. Atkinson's 'practical import criterion' (see '"Ought" and "Is"', *Philosophy* 1958, p. 31). He points out that there are sentences which pass the test, but which are not evaluative: e.g. it would be logically odd to say 'I command you to go, but don't!' or 'I intend to go but I shall not.' This criterion, therefore, needs supplementing by the 'ground criterion' (ibid. p. 36). The practical import criterion differentiates value judgements from factual statements; the ground criterion differentiates them from commands, intentions, etc. (ibid. p. 37).
34. Op. cit. pp. 168–9; cf. 'Imperative Sentences', *Mind* 1949, and my *Modern Moral Philosophy*, chap. 5.
35. Nowell-Smith, op. cit. p. 99. It might be better to drop the word 'entail' of this connexion and use some such expression as 'involve as a matter of logic'; cf. Atkinson, op. cit. p. 33.
36. For a discussion of the relationship between theories of meaning and moral discourse, see my *Modern Moral Philosophy* chap. 2.
37. See 47, 7, 421.
38. See my *Ludwig Wittgenstein* (Lutterworth, 1967) and my *Modern Moral Philosophy* chap. 2.
39. *The Language of Morals* p. 85.
40. Ibid. pp. 90–1.
41. For a discussion of Hare's moral philosophy, see my *Modern Moral Philosophy* chap. 5.
42. *Rights and Right Conduct* (Oxford, 1959) pp. 41–2.
43. See his *How to do Things with Words* (Oxford, 1962).
44. Cf. A. Flew, 'On not deriving "ought" from "is"', *Analysis* 1964–5; and my 'The "is–ought" controversy', ibid.
45. First published in *Mind* in 1912, reprinted in his *Moral Obligation* pp. 1–17. Hampshire says that the view taken by Prichard and most latter-day moralists that there is an unbridgeable gap between moral judgements and statements of fact is derived from Kant, not, as is so often said, from Hume. The latter 'never denied that our moral judgments are based on arguments about matters of fact; he only showed that these arguments are not logically conclusive or deductive arguments' ('Fallacies in Moral Philosophy', *Mind* 1949, p. 466 n.).

On the whole is–ought controversy see *The Is–Ought Question: a collection of papers on the central problem in moral philosophy* ed. W. D. Hudson (1969).

46. See II.2.iv.

47. Cf. B. Mayo, 'Mr Hampshire on Fallacies', *Mind* 1950, p. 385: 'it is just here, in the distinction between the problem–situation without argument and the problem–situation involving rational argument and discussion, that we must look for the characteristic difference between the non-moral and the moral problem'. Cf. also Atkinson, op. cit. p. 36: a value-judgement, he says, 'logically commits the speaker (of "I ought to do X") to saying what it is about X or X's situation in virtue of which he judges that he ought to do it'.

48. Nowell-Smith, op. cit. pp. 82–3.

49. Hare, *Freedom and Reason* (Oxford, 1963) pp. 7–50 *et al.*

50. Op. cit. p. 47.

51. *The Moral Point of View* (New York, 1958) pp. 301–3.

52. Cf. 3.III.i. above and 4.VI.v. below.

53. *Contemporary Moral Philosophy* pp. 66–7.

54. Ibid. pp. 60–1.

55. *Philosophical Investigations* 654.

56. Cf. D. Z. Phillips and H. O. Mounce, 'On Morality's Having a Point', *Philosophy* 1965.

57. Ibid.

58. I discuss the issues raised here, in connexion with beliefs and wants, more fully in my *Modern Moral Philosophy* chap. 6.

CHAPTER 4

1. Introduction to *Review* p. x.

2. Hume, *Treatise* III.1.i. Price paid the following tribute to Hume: 'And I cannot help adding, however strange it may seem, that I owe much to the philosophical writings of Mr Hume, which I . . . studied early in life. Though an enemy to his scepticism, I have profited by it. By attacking, with great ability, every principle of truth and reason, he put me upon examining the ground upon which I stood, and taught me not hastily to take anything for granted' (preface to his *Observations on the importance of the American Revolution*, quoted by R. Thomas in his *Richard Price* pp. 31–2). Price's formal education ended in 1744, when he was twenty-one, and 'early in life' does not, presumably, refer beyond this date; this was at least twenty years before Kant was awakened from his dogmatic slumbers. Price and Hume met many times and were on good terms. In William Morgan's *Memoirs of the life of the Rev. Richard Price* we are told that Hume, on one of his visits to Price's home. 'candidly acknowledged that on one point Mr Price had succeeded in convincing him that his arguments were inconclusive'. We are not, unfortunately, told what the point was. (Cf. Thomas, op. cit. p. 30.)

3. Cf. Ross, *Foundations of Ethics* pp. 43–4, 56; also Prichard, *Moral Obligation*, pp. 36–8.

4. Cf. 3. III.i above. Price rejects some naturalistic definitions of obligation

(pp. 113–17) and agrees with Clarke and Butler. He approvingly quotes the former: 'The original obligation of all is the eternal reason of things'; and summarises the latter: 'Every being endowed with reason, and conscious of right and wrong, is, as such, necessarily a *law* to himself' (pp. 118–19). Cf. Prichard, op. cit. pp. 94–5: this notion of moral obligation as a law must not be represented as our being commanded to do something – it is a unique kind of law.

5. 'Modern Moral Philosophy', *Philosophy* 1958, p. 6.

6. Cf. my *Ethical Intuitionism* p. 37.

7. *Sermons* XI.

8. Price out-Butlers Butler in saying of desires that 'their direct tendency is always to some particular object different from private pleasure' (p. 76). Butler never said this (cf. W. R. Matthews' edition of Butler's *Sermons* (1914) p. 168 n.) and it is certainly untrue. We do sometimes desire our own pleasure. But even in such cases we can distinguish, logically at least, between the object of desire and the satisfaction of attaining it.

9. J. S. Mill, *Utilitarianism* (Everyman ed.) pp. 32–3.

10. See 3. II.ii above.

11. Price says that some of these are subordinate to self-love and others to benevolence (p. 76). He follows Butler very closely in his analysis of human nature. He gives, as examples of passions subordinate to self-love, 'hunger, thirst &c.' (p. 74) and, as examples of those subordinate to benevolence, 'parental fondness', 'compassion' and desires for 'esteem' and 'knowledge' (pp. 77 and 73; cf. Butler, *Sermons* I).

12. Cf. St Paul's *Epistle to the Romans*, vii; and on the bias, C. H. Dodd, *Romans* (Moffatt Commentaries (1932)), pp. 112–13. Orthodox Christian theologians have always fully recognised this bias.

13. Cf. *Romans* v. 18–19. It is not, of course, necessary to believe in the historicity of the Fall in order to hold some form of the doctrine of original sin. Dodd suggests that even St Paul may have regarded the Fall as merely a 'symbolic allegory' (op. cit. p. 80).

14. See his *Sermons on Christian Doctrine* (1787) v.

15. Most modern Reformed theologians would not endorse Price's easy solution of the problem of evil. See for instance the works of K. Barth, E. Brunner, H. H. Farmer, R. Niebuhr, P. Tillich. W. R. Matthews writes: 'No candid thinker could dismiss the problem [of evil] as solved and done with. . . . No one, again, can look upon the vacant and terrible face of the idiot or the maniac without being conscious of a mystery in evil which eludes us in the end and covers our "best possible world" with confusion.' (*God* (1930) pp. 244–5.)

16. *The Theory of Moral Sentiments:* Selby-Bigge, 299.

17. *Man, Morals and Society* (1955), pp. 179–80.

18. E. F. Carritt, *Ethical and Political Thinking* (Oxford, 1947) p. 73.

19. A. M. Quinton, 'On Punishment', *Analysis* 1953–4.

20. Cf. Antony Flew, 'The Justification of Punishment', *Philosophy* 1954, p. 306.

21. Cf. J. D. Mabbott, 'Professor Flew on Punishment', *Philosophy* 1955, p. 257; Raphael, *Moral Judgement* pp. 70–1; Carritt, *The Theory of Morals* (1930), p. 113.

22. On such views see J. S. Mackenzie, *A Manual of Ethics* (sixth ed., 1929)

pp. 380–1; F. H. Bradley, *Ethical Studies* (1876) essay I (see especially p. 28 n.). This kind of view has been expressed by an ex-criminal, W. F. R. Macartney, in *Walls Have Mouths* p. 165 (quoted by Mabbott in 'Punishment', *Mind* 1939, p. 158): 'To be punished for an offence against rules is a sane man's right.'

23. e.g. Ross, *The Right and the Good* pp. 57–8.

24. I am thinking, of course, of a case in which I would not be bound by any deontological obligation, as e.g. a judge might be. Cf. 4.vi.v below.

25. Cf. M. R. Glover, 'Mr Mabbott on Punishment', *Mind* 1939, p. 500; Carritt *Ethical and Political Thinking* p. 72.

26. See 3.iii.i above.

27. 'Professor Flew on Punishment', *Philosophy* 1955, p. 265.

28. See Flew, in *Philosophy* 1954, p. 304.

29. Price finds this idea a 'prodigious absurdity', though he admits that 'some writers of great worth' have thought otherwise (p. 139). See 4.v.i.

30. Introduction to *Review*, p. xxxv.

31. Above, 3.iii.iii; 4.vi.v below.

32. e.g. Butler, *Sermons* iii; Carritt, *The Theory of Morals* p. 97; Ross, *The Right and the Good* p. 23.

33. 4.vi.iii.

34. See W. James, *Principles of Psychology* vol. ii, pp. 563–4.

35. G. F. Stout, *A Manual of Psychology* (fifth ed. 1938, ed. C. A. Mace) p. 652.

36. A. N. Whitehead, *The Aims of Education* p. 106, quoted by R. Livingstone, *Education for a World Adrift* (Cambridge, 1943) p. 50.

37. The theory that God can be caused to suffer by men has been a storm centre in the history of Christian doctrine. Patripassianism aroused fierce controversy in the second century and was condemned by Tertullian (see H. R. Mackintosh, *The Person of Jesus Christ* (second ed. Edinburgh, 1913) pp. 149–50). In the fourth century, Apollinarianism was condemned by the councils of Alexandria (362), Rome (377 or 378) and Constantinople (381).

38. Price writes of 'suitable affection' towards a benefactor. Though an emotion may be fitting, it cannot be obligatory. Later intuitionists make it clear that by 'gratitude' they mean acts: e.g. Ross, *The Right and the Good* pp. 22–3.

39. Cf. 1.ii.i; 3 iii i.

40. 4.ii.

41. Cf. 3.ii.ii above.

42. Cf. Mill's essay *On Liberty*.

43. It has sometimes been claimed that there is a 'Christian duty of happiness', but 'happiness' here turns out to be knowledge or virtue under another name.

44. Cf. Ross, *Foundations of Ethics* p. 272; and cf. this with *The Right and the Good* p. 25. Butler, referred to by Price (p. 151), says simply that we do not have 'so sensible a disapprobation of imprudence' as of other vices.

45. P. Inman, *Christ in the Modern Hospital* p. 69.

46. Cf. Carritt, *The Theory of Morals* p. 114.

47. Cf. Raphael, *Moral Judgement* pp. 78–9.

48. It is, of course, possible to perform an action from more than one motive. A man may do *A* a kind act because he desires to do all in his power for *A*'s good, and also because the action gives him pleasure. It seems clear that we

should not judge this second motive to detract from the moral value of the action *provided* that the first motive, namely disinterested charity, would be strong enough to lead him to perform the action apart from the second; cf. Ross, *Foundations of Ethics*, p. 305.

49. He thinks the rational nature of mind evident in its conations and affections as well as in cognition; see p. 73.

50. Carritt, *The Theory of Morals*, p. 102. He points out that perjury, where the promise of veracity has been explicit, is commonly regarded as lying of a particularly bad kind.

51. Cf. Ross, *Foundations of Ethics*, p. 110.

52. Cf. my *Ethical Intuitionism* pp. 48–9.

53. Locke, *Second Treatise of Civil Government* (Everyman ed.) p. 119; T. Paine, *The Rights of Man* part I (Everyman ed.) p. 95.

54. In *Universal Declaration of Human Rights*, adopted and proclaimed by the General Assembly of the United Nations in 1948, Article 3 reads: 'Everyone has a right to life, liberty and security of person.' It is not till Article 17 that we read: 'Everyone has the right to own property alone as well as in association with others. No one shall be arbitrarily deprived of his property.' Note this last sentence: it is significant that there is this supplementary sentence here, but no such sentence as this in Article 3.

55. Bentham, *Introduction to the Principles of Morals and Legislation* chap. IV.

56. *Ethica Nicomachea* 1131a.

57. Locke, *Second Treatise of Civil Government*, p. 189.

58. 2.II.iv.

59. In this analysis of obligation I acknowledge my debt to Raphael's *Moral Judgement* pp. 110 ff.

60. Emotions, like acts, may be 'fitting' or 'unfitting'. Love, for instance, is a fitting emotion between a child and a generous parent (cf. C. D. Broad, *Five Types of Ethical Theory* (1930) pp. 164–5). But obligation is always obligation to perform some action (cf. Prichard, *Moral Obligation* pp. 129–30, Ross, *Foundations of Ethics* p. 158, and above, footnote 38).

61. Locke, *Essay* 1.3.10; Mackie, 'A Refutation of Morals', *Australasian Journal of Psychology and Philosophy* 1946, p. 78.

62. Russell, *A History of Western Philosophy* p. 210, cf. p. 648.

63. Cf. K. Duncker, 'Ethical Relativity?' *Mind* 1939.

64. Butler, *Sermons* XI.

65. F. H. Bradley, *Ethical Studies* pp. 187 and 200.

66. Cf. J.-P. Sartre, *Existentialism and Humanism* (1948, trans. P. Mairet) p. 37.

67. *Utilitarianism* (Everyman ed.) pp. 7–8.

68. H. Sidgwick, *The Methods of Ethics* (sixth ed., 1901) pp. 373–98.

69. H. Rashdall, *The Theory of Good and Evil* (Oxford, 1907) vol. I, pp. 266–9.

70. *Some Problems in Ethics* (Oxford, 1931) pp. 93–8.

71. *Principles of Social and Political Theory* (Oxford, 1951) p. 170.

72. *Existentialism and Humanism* pp. 36–8.

73. Ibid. p. 34.

74. A. MacIntyre questions this (see 'What Morality Is Not', *Philosophy* 1957, p. 325). He argues that this is a moral, not a logical, difficulty. 'To assert that universalisability is of the essence of moral valuation is not to tell us what

"morality" means or how moral words are used. It is to prescribe a meaning for "morality" and other moral words and implicitly it is to prescribe a morality' (p. 333). I agree with MacIntyre that 'What ought I to do?' cannot always be translated easily into 'What ought someone like me to do in this kind of situation?' 'I am the only person sufficiently "like me" to be morally relevant and no situation could be sufficiently like "this kind of situation" without being precisely this situation' (p. 335). None the less, there is a difference between 'What *ought* I to do?' and 'What *shall* I do?' and it seems to me impossible to account for it without supposing the speaker who puts the former question rather than the latter to be looking for a principle which applies, not only to himself, but would apply to other men so placed, if such there were. See my *Modern Moral Philosophy* chap. 5.

75. On such elements in the super-ego, cf. Flugel, *Man, Morals and Society*, chap. 7 ('Nemesism') and 8 ('Aggression and Sado-masochism').

76. So called by Nowell-Smith, *Ethics* pp. 239 ff.

77. 'Purpose and Authority in Morals', *Philosophy* 1956, p. 319–20.

78. *Ethics*, p. 224.

CHAPTER 5

1. *Ethical and Political Thinking* p. 14 n.

2. H. Sidgwick, *Outlines of the History of Ethics* (sixth ed., 1931) p. 203.

3. N. H. G. Robinson, *The Claim of Morality* (1952) p. 47.

4. *Inquiry* III.viii: Selby Bigge 121.

5. A. N. Prior discusses the antecedents of Price's view here in 'The Virtue of the Act and the Virtue of the Agent', *Philosophy* 1951, pp. 121–30.

6. For a careful study of the part played by this notion of an absolutely right action in the thought of the intuitionists and a criticism of it, see D. A. Rees, 'The Idea of Objective Duty', *Proceedings of the Aristotelian Society*, 1951–2.

7. Cf. Prichard, *Moral Obligation* p. 163; also J. M. Hems, 'Reflecting on Morals', *Philosophy* 1956, p. 105. There is, of course, nothing logically impossible about the idea of absolute virtue as a quality of a conceived action.

8. Cf. Prichard, op. cit. pp. 21–3 and Ross, *Foundations of Ethics* pp. 149–50. Ross takes the view in *The Right and the Good* chap. II, that it is our duty to do what is objectively right, but in *Foundations of Ethics* chap. VII, what is subjectively right. He attributes his conversion in the latter work (p. 148) to Prichard's article referred to here. Cf. also Carritt, *The Theory of Morals* p. 16.

9. Prichard, op. cit. p. 24 and Ross, *Foundations of Ethics* p. 150.

10. Cf. Carritt, *The Theory of Morals* p. 18.

11. Ibid. p. 22.

12. e.g. Prichard, op. cit. p. 38 n. 2 and Ross, *Foundations of Ethics* p. 162.

13. As Raphael does. He thinks that the objectively right act in such cases is determined by 'the consensus of public opinion' or by 'some impartial authority' expressing it (e.g. a judge); see his *Moral Judgement* pp. 138–40.

14. On the agent and his situation see: A. I. Melden, *Free Action* (1961), S. Hampshire, *Thought and Action* (1960) and D. F. Pears (ed.) *Freedom and the Will* (1963); and my *Modern Moral Philosophy*, chap. 7.
15. Cf. Ross, *Foundations of Ethics* pp. 229–30.
16. This implication is not the simple and straightforward matter for which it has sometimes been taken; see W. K. Frankena, 'Obligation and Ability' in *Philosophical Analysis*, ed. M. Black.
17. Cf. Moore, *Ethics* (1947 pagination) p. 131, and my *Modern Moral Philosophy*.
18. e.g. C. A. Campbell, 'Is "Free Will" a Pseudo-Problem?', *Mind* 1951 and *On Selfhood and Godhood* (1957) lect. IX and app. B; and Carritt, *The Theory of Morals* chap. XV and *Ethical and Political Thinking* chap. XII.
19. Cf. Nowell-Smith, *Ethics* p. 284.
20. 'Free Will as involving Determinism and Inconceivable without it', *Mind* 1934.
21. *The Concept of Mind* p. 195.
22. 'Freedom and Compulsion', *Mind* 1958, p. 66.
23. Op. cit. p. 174.
24. *On Selfhood and Godhood* p. 169.
25. Ibid. p. 197.
26. Cudworth appears to have adopted self-determinism as his thought matured; see Passmore, *Ralph Cudworth* pp. 64–5.
27. See Moore, *Ethics*, chap. VI. Three conditions similar to those here given are indicated by Ayer in 'Freedom and Necessity', *Philosophical Essays* (1954). I deal in much greater detail with the third of these three conditions in chap. 7. of my *Modern Moral Philosophy*.
28. *Ethica Nicomachea* 1110a–1110b.
29. R. S. Woodworth, *Psychology* (eighteenth ed., 1946) p. 135.
30. The ignorance may be culpable, of course; e.g. a drunken man who does not know what he is doing can be blamed for being in that state, as Price points out (p. 198).
31. Hare, 'Freedom of the Will' in *Freedom, Language and Reality*, Aristotelian Society Supplementary Volume XXV, pp. 215–16.
32. Cf. Carritt, *Ethical and Political Thinking* pp. 135 and 138.
33. As it is, for instance, by Raphael in *Moral Judgement* p. 196.
34. Cf. Nowell-Smith, 'Freewill and Moral Responsibility', *Mind* 1948, p. 59; and Hampshire, 'Freedom of the Will' in *Freedom, Language and Reality*, Aristotelian Society Supplementary Volume XXV, pp. 169–72.
35. Carritt, *The Theory of Morals* p. 130.
36. *An Enquiry concerning Human Understanding* VIII.i.
37. *On Selfhood and Godhood* pp. 169–71.
38. Spinoza, *Ethics* III, prop. II.
39. Cf. D. J. O'Connor, 'Is there a Problem about Free Will?' *Proceedings of the Aristotelian Society* 1948–9, pp. 41 ff.
40. Ibid. p. 42.
41. *On Selfhood and Godhood* p. 170.
42. *Moral Judgement* pp. 207 ff.
43. Cf. S. Hampshire and H. L. A. Hart, 'Decision, Intention and Certainty', *Mind* 1958, pp. 1–12.

44. Op. cit.
45. Russell says that Leibniz held two views: a 'popular' one, that human beings have free will, that the sufficient reasons (motives) for actions 'incline without necessitating'; and a 'private' one, 'that the individual notion of each person involves once for all everything that will ever happen to him', which excludes free will; cf. *A History of Western Philosophy* pp. 607–8 and 616.
46. See H. Bergson, *Creative Evolution* (1911, trans. Mitchell) pp. 49–50.
47. *Existentialism and Humanism* p. 28.
48. *Freedom and Spirit* (third ed., 1944, trans. Clarke) p. 124.
49. *Enquiry concerning Human Understanding* VIII.i.
50. e.g. Hobart, op cit. p. 13; cf. also M. Schlick, *Problems of Ethics* (trans. Rynin) VIII.2 and Ayer, 'Freedom and Necessity', in *Philosophical Essays*.
51. O'Connor, in *Proceedings of the Aristotelian Society* 1948–9, pp. 37–8, points out that the above view (free acts are caused but not compelled) offers an analysis which makes freedom consist in 'unconsciousness of necessity'. But is this what we commonly mean by 'free'? he asks. It is possible to conceive of acts (e.g. those done under hypnosis) which the agent does under compulsion, but is unaware that he so does – would such acts be free in any common sense of the word?
52. Ibid. p. 39.
53. Spinoza, op. cit.
54. Cf. O'Connor, in *Proceedings of the Aristotelian Society* 1948–9, pp. 43–4.
55. Cf. H. J. Paton, *The Categorical Imperative* (1947) p. 82.
56. Bentham, *Introduction to the Principles of Morals and Legislation* VIII–IX: Selby-Bigge 393–7, Mill, *Utilitarianism* chap. II; J. H. Muirhead, *The Elements of Ethics* (rev. ed., 1897) p. 61; Mackenzie, *A Manual of Ethics* book I, chap. II; etc.
57. Cf. Anscombe, *Intention* pp. 19–20.
58. Bentham, op. cit.; cf. Mackenzie, op. cit. pp. 51–2.
59. Mill, *Utilitarianism*, chap. II, p. 27 n.
60. Hampshire and Hart, in *Mind* 1958, pp. 1–12.
61. *Intention* pp. 42 ff.
62. Op. cit. p. 52.
63. Cf. Mill on intention, *Utilitarianism* chap. II p. 27 n.
64. Ibid. (Everyman ed.) p. 17.
65. Cf. Ross, *Foundations of Ethics* pp. 290–2.
66. Ibid. pp. 308–10.
67. Not all contemporary philosophers have agreed with the distinction between rightness and moral goodness which we draw here; cf. Joseph, *Some Problems in Ethics* chap. IV, and Ross's reply to this in *Foundations of Ethics* p. 127.
68. Cf. Prichard, op. cit. pp. 34–5 and Ross, *Foundations of Ethics* pp. 159–60.
69. *Ethica Nicomachea* 1112a–1112b.
70. *Leviathan* I. vi–xi.
71. *Treatise* II.3.iii.
72. *Discourse upon Natural Religion*: Selby-Bigge 490.
73. *Groundwork of the Metaphysics of Morals* p. 38.
74. *Treatise* II.3.iii.
75. See Passmore, op. cit. p. 56 and Paton, op. cit. p. 83.

76. Cf. Nowell-Smith, *Ethics* pp. 251–4.
77. On Price as the 'anticipator of Kant', see Thomas, *Richard Price* pp. 34–7.
78. *Groundwork of the Metaphysics of Morals* p. 65.
79. Cf. Nowell-Smith, *Ethics* p. 256.
80. Paton, op. cit. p. 48, says that Kant believed that action done from rational desire for happiness has no moral worth. This is surely a very different view from Price's. And certainly Paton cannot be accused of interpreting Kant too rigidly in this matter of duty and desire.
81. e.g. by Schiller; but sharply repudiated on Kant's behalf by Paton, op. cit. p. 48.
82. *Ethica Nicomachea* 1177–8.

CHAPTER 6

1. e.g. Matthews, *God* p. 212.
2. 3.III.ii.
3. 2.II.iii. *Cause*.
4. Cf. Wittgenstein, *Tractatus*, preface.
5. *Enquiry concerning Human Understanding* (ed. Selby-Bigge) p. 146.
6. A. Flew, 'Theology and Falsification' in *New Essays in Philosophical Theology*, ed. Flew and MacIntyre, pp. 96–9. For a discussion of this argument, see my *Ludwig Wittgenstein: The Bearing of his Philosophy upon Religious Belief.*
7. *Enquiry concerning Human Understanding* p. 148.
8. *Dialogues concerning Natural Religion* IX.
9. Cf. Raphael's introduction to *Review* p. xlv.
10. See *Sermons* p. 200 n. and *Dissertation upon the Nature of Virtue* (in Matthews' edition of the former) p. 255.
11. *Principia Ethica* pp. 83–4.
12. Shaftesbury *Inquiry* II.ii.1: Selby-Bigge 38; Butler, *Sermons* p. 67.
13. For a discussion of this, see my 'An Attempt to Defend Theism', *Philosophy* 1964.

Index

Aaron, R. I., 192
Abrahams, L., 188
Adams, W., 64
Anscombe, G. E. M., 72, 85, 164, 193, 201
Aristotle, 16, 37, 60, 80, 115, 147, 175
Atkinson, R. F., 194, 195
Augustine, St, 190
Austin, J. L., 71
Ayer, A. J., 25, 26, 44, 190, 191, 192, 201

Baier, K., 78
Barth, K., 196
Bentham, J., 124, 163, 192, 198, 201
Berdyaev, N., 159
Bergson, H., 159, 201
Berkeley, G., 25, 33, 34, 36, 191
Bradley, F. H., 123, 197, 198
Broad, C. D., 193, 198
Brunner, E., 196
Butler, J., 87, 95, 109, 122, 174, 182, 183, 184, 196, 197, 198

Campbell, C. A., 144, 145, 146, 155, 157, 200
Carritt, E. F., 91, 94, 132, 135, 196, 197, 198, 199, 200
Clarke, S., 27, 48, 50, 168, 181, 182, 196
Collingwood, R. G., 190
Cudworth, R., 12, 13, 37, 38, 48, 187, 188, 192, 200

Democritus, 190

Descartes, R., 37, 38, 41, 190
Dodd, C. H., 196
Duncker, K., 198

Edwards, P., 31, 192
Euclid, 42
Ewing, A. C., 192

Farmer, H. H., 196
Flew, A., 97, 180, 190, 191, 192, 194, 196, 197, 202
Flugel, J. C., 90, 91, 199
Foot, P., 78
Frankena, W. K., 187, 188, 200

Galileo, 190
Gallie, W. B., 41, 192
Gandhi, M., 130
Gasking, D., 192
Glover, M. R., 197

Hampshire, S., 163, 164, 191, 195, 200, 201
Hare, R. M., 66, 68, 69, 72, 194, 195, 200
Hart, H. L. A., 164, 200, 201
Heath, E., 69
Hegel, G. W. F., 123
Hems, J. M., 199
Hirst, R. J., 190
Hobart, R. E., 142, 145, 146, 201
Hobbes, T., 168
Holloway, J., 191
Horsburgh, H. J. N., 128, 130
Hudson, W. D., 195

Hume, D., 14, 17, 21, 23, 24, 27, 33, 35, 52, 56, 57, 58, 63, 84, 145, 154, 155, 156, 157, 158, 159, 168, 170, 180, 181, 191, 193, 194, 195
Hutcheson, F., 2, 3, 8, 50, 52, 58, 86, 95, 132, 174, 187, 193

Inman, P., 107, 197

James, W., 197
Joseph, H. W. B., 125

Kant, I., 31, 85, 93, 123, 140, 168, 172, 173, 194

Langford, C. H., 188
Lazerowitz, M., 24, 198
Leibniz, G. W., 159
Livingstone, R., 197
Locke, J., 11, 12, 14, 15, 16, 17, 18, 19, 20, 21, 23, 25, 26, 27, 33, 36, 51, 86, 114, 120, 189, 190, 191, 198

Mabbott, J. D., 97, 196
Macartney, W. F. R., 197
Mace, C. A., 191
Macintosh, H. R., 197
MacIntyre, A. C., 198, 202
Mackenzie, J. S., 165, 196, 201
Mackie, J., 120, 192, 198
Matthews, W. R., 196, 202
Mayo, B., 195
Melden, A. I., 69, 70, 72, 200
Mill, J. S., 31, 80, 87, 125, 165, 166, 187, 191, 196, 197, 201
Moore, G. E., 1, 5, 8, 46, 47, 48, 183, 188, 192, 200
Morgan, W., 195
Mounce, H. O., 195
Muirhead, J. H., 201

Neitzche, F., 81

Newton, I., 30, 181
Niebuhr, R., 196
Nowell-Smith, P. H., 64, 66, 130, 188, 194, 195, 199, 200, 202

O'Connor, D. J., 15, 16, 189, 190, 191, 200, 201

Paine, T., 114
Passmore, J. A., 188, 192, 201
Paton, H. J., 201, 202
Paul, St, 196
Pears, D. F., 192, 200
Peirce, C. S., 41
Phillips, D. Z., 195
Plato, 13, 18
Plotinus, 190
Price, H. H., 191
Prichard, H. A., 73, 74, 194, 198, 199, 201
Prior, A. N., 187, 199

Quinton, A. M., 92, 196

Raphael, D. D., 1, 2, 17, 49, 50, 55, 57, 84, 99, 157, 158, 187, 188, 190, 193, 197, 198, 199, 202
Rashdall, H., 125, 198
Rees, D. A., 199
Reid, T., 22
Robinson, N. H. G., 199
Robinson, R., 192
Ross, W. D., 4, 19, 49, 50, 55, 94, 166, 188, 189, 192, 193, 197, 198, 200, 201
Russell, B., 31, 51, 52, 120, 190, 191, 198, 201
Ryle, G., 25, 142, 143

Sartre, J.-P., 126, 159, 198
Schiller, F. C., 202
Schilpp, P. A., 188, 193

Searle, J. R., 72
Selby-Bigge, L. A., 187
Shaftesbury, Earl of, 86, 132, 183, 187
Sidgwick, H., 125, 132, 198, 199
Smith, A., 90, 91
Spinoza, 200, 201
Stabler, E. R., 192
Stout, G. F., 197
Strawson, P. F., 62

Tertullian, 197
Thomas, R., 195, 202

Tichener, E. B., 191
Tillich, P., 196

Waismann, F., 24, 25
Walsh, W. H., 191, 193
Warnock, G. J., 77, 80, 81, 82, 191
Whitehead, A. N., 190, 197
Wilson, H., 69
Wilson, J., 143
Wittgenstein, L., 68, 82, 202
Wollaston, W., 63
Wollheim, R., 190
Woodworth, R. S., 200

WESTMAR COLLEGE LIBRARY